Richard Lewis  Nettleship

**Philosophical Lectures and Remains**

Edited, with a Biographical Sketch

Richard Lewis  Nettleship

**Philosophical Lectures and Remains**
*Edited, with a Biographical Sketch*

ISBN/EAN: 9783337009601

Printed in Europe, USA, Canada, Australia, Japan

Cover: Foto ©Thomas Meinert / pixelio.de

More available books at **www.hansebooks.com**

*1871.*

# PHILOSOPHICAL
# LECTURES AND REMAINS

OF

## RICHARD LEWIS NETTLESHIP

FELLOW AND TUTOR OF BALLIOL COLLEGE, OXFORD

*EDITED, WITH A BIOGRAPHICAL SKETCH*

BY

## A. C. BRADLEY

PROFESSOR OF ENGLISH LITERATURE IN THE UNIVERSITY OF GLASGOW
FORMERLY FELLOW AND LECTURER OF BALLIOL COLLEGE, OXFORD

AND

## G. R. BENSON

OF BALLIOL COLLEGE, OXFORD

IN TWO VOLUMES : VOL. II

## London
## MACMILLAN AND CO., Ltd.
### NEW YORK: THE MACMILLAN CO.
### 1897

# NOTE

A LARGE part of the subject-matter of the lectures which form the contents of the present volume was also treated by Nettleship in his essay in *Hellenica*, entitled 'The Theory of Education in the *Republic* of Plato,' and again in an essay on 'Plato's Conception of Goodness and the Good,' which will be found in vol. i. of these *Lectures and Remains*. Students of the *Republic* who make use of this volume may be recommended also to read the two essays above mentioned.

In reproducing Nettleship's lectures on the *Republic*, I have followed in the main the very full notes taken by several pupils in the year 1887 and the beginning of 1888. I have, however, made much use of my own and other notes of the lectures as given in 1885, adopting from them, besides single sentences and phrases, many whole passages in which some subject happened to have been more fully treated than in the later year. In every case where there was a substantial discrepancy between the lectures given in the two years I have followed the later version.

In the actual lectures Nettleship used Greek terms and English equivalents for them almost indifferently. As the lectures may be read by some who do not read the original Greek, I have throughout adopted English words, except where no English equivalent for the Greek seems possible, or where the meaning of the Greek word is itself the subject referred to.

While remaining solely responsible in every point for the form in which these lectures finally appear, I have to thank Mr. Bradley, the editor of the preceding volume, for most valuable advice and assistance which I have received from him at several stages in my task.

GODFREY R. BENSON.

# CONTENTS OF VOL. II

## LECTURES ON THE 'REPUBLIC' OF PLATO

# LECTURES

## ON

# PLATO'S 'REPUBLIC'

VOL. II.                    B

# LECTURES ON PLATO'S 'REPUBLIC'

## I. INTRODUCTION

THE *Republic*, though it has something of the nature both of poetry and of preaching, is primarily a book of philosophy.   In studying it, therefore, we have to pay attention above all to the reasoning, the order and connexion of thought.   A philosopher is a man with a greater power of thinking than other people, one who has thought more than others on subjects of common interest.   All philosophy must be critical ; and in thinking facts out to their consequences the philosopher necessarily arrives at conclusions different from and often contradictory to the ideas current around him.   Often indeed the conclusions he arrives at *seem* no different from those of plain people, and yet the difference between the philosopher and the mass of mankind remains a great one, for, though starting from the same facts and arriving at similar conclusions, he has in the interval gone through a process of thinking, and the truth he holds is reasoned truth.   What seems at first sight the same truth, and may be put in the same words that anybody else would use, is yet a very different truth to the philosopher, containing a great deal that is not present to the minds of most men.   In either case, whether the results, at which the philosopher arrives, are what we believe or what we do not believe, the first thing we have to do is to follow his *enquiries*.  We should see how he arrives at his conclusions before we begin to criticize them.

To study the *Republic* in this way is difficult.   Plato's ideas are often expressed in a manner very different from any that we are accustomed to.   This is, in part, a difficulty common to all reading in philosophy.   In arriving at ideas unlike those of most people philosophy does not differ at all from the special sciences ; but while the elementary conceptions of the sciences are approximately fixed, and the meaning of the terms used can be seen at once or quickly learnt, it is otherwise with philosophy ; for the subject-matter of philosophy is of a comparatively general character, being chiefly the main facts about human knowledge and human morality, and in such subjects there can be no absolutely fixed terminology. Sometimes also, in Plato and other Greek philosophers, the significance of what is said escapes us just because it is expressed in a very simple way.   The *Republic*, moreover, has special difficulties arising from the peculiarities of its form and method ;—every great book has characteristics of its own, which have to be studied like the characteristics of a person.

What, in the first place, is the subject of the book ? Its name might suggest that it was a book of political philosophy, but we very soon find that it is rather a book of moral philosophy.   (It starts from the question, ' What is justice (δικαιοσύνη) ? ' that being the most comprehensive of the Greek names for virtues, and in its widest sense, as Aristotle tells us, equivalent to 'the whole of virtue as shown in our dealings with others[1].') It is a book about human life and the human soul or human nature, and the real question in it is, as Plato says, how to live best[2]. What then is implied in calling it the *Republic* (πολιτεία)? To Plato one of the leading facts about human life is that it can only be lived well in some form of organized community, of which the Greeks considered the civic community to be the best form. Therefore the question, What is the best life? is to him inseparable from the question, What is the best order or organization of human society? The subject of the *Republic* is thus a very wide one; and a modern critic, finding such a variety of matter in it, is inclined to think that Plato has confused quite distinct questions. This is not so; he gives us in the *Republic* an ideal picture of the rise and fall of the human soul, its rise to its highest stage of development and its fall to its lowest depth; and in doing so he has tried to take account of everything in the human soul, of its whole nature. Modern associations lead us to expect that the book should be either distinctly ethical or distinctly political, that it should either consider man in his relations as a citizen or consider him simply as a moral agent. Because the Greek philosophers did not separate these two questions it is frequently said that they confused them; whereas it would be truer to say that they looked at human life more simply and more completely than we are apt to do. But of course there are questions which we have to differentiate as ethical or political, and which the Greeks did not thus differentiate. The reason is that their actual life was

---

[1] *Eth. Nic.* V. i. 15 and 20.     [2] 344 E.

less differentiated than ours ; that law, custom, and religion were not in practice the distinct things that they are now.

Along with the main subject there are many incidental and subordinate subjects in the *Republic* ; there is a great deal of criticism of existing institutions, practices, and opinions. The book may be regarded not only as a philosophical work, but as a treatise on social and political reform. It is written in the spirit of a man not merely reflecting on human life, but intensely anxious to reform and revolutionize it. This fact, while giving a peculiar interest to Plato's writing, prejudices the calmness and impartiality of his philosophy. He is always writing with crying evils in his eye—a characteristic in which he differs widely from Aristotle.

We must next consider the form of the book. It was not peculiar to Plato to throw his speculations into the form of dialogues. Several of the pupils of Socrates wrote dialogues, and the fashion lasted to the time of Aristotle. The fact that this form came naturally to a Greek philosopher is part of a more general literary phenomenon. Greek literature is certainly less personal than modern literature (the Greek drama, for instance, is less subjective than ours), but on the other hand Greek literature is more concrete. Thucydides' history differs from modern books of history both in the absence of personal detail and in the absence of general reflexions. The place of general reflexions is taken in Thucydides by fictitious speeches put into the mouths of actual persons ; and in this we see that the distinction now observed in literature between the exposition of ideas and principles and the representation of persons and character had not then become prominent. So Plato takes a number of actual personages, some contemporary, some belonging to the last generation, some of them public men, others friends of his own, and makes them the exponents of the philosophical opinions and ideas that he wishes to set before us. These persons are not used as mere lay figures ; they are chosen because they actually had in them something of what the dialogues attribute to them, and they are often represented with dramatic propriety and vivacity. Nevertheless they are handled without the slightest scruple as to historical truth ;—(the sense of historical truth is a feature of modern times, its absence a feature of ancient, and we see this in Plato, just as we see it in Aristophanes). So the personages of the dialogue are on the one hand simply ideal expressions of certain principles ; on the other hand they carry with them much of their real character. The Platonic dialogue is a form of writing which would be impossible now. We require a writer to keep the exposition of principles distinct from the representation of persons, and to treat characters primarily with an historical interest if they are actual people, primarily with a dramatic interest if they are fictitious. As a rule, when the form of dialogue has been used by modern philosophers, as it was by Berkeley, the personages are not characters at all; the dialogue of Bunyan is the best analogy in English literature to that of Plato. In Plato the dramatic element is present in different degrees in different dialogues. The *Protagoras* is the most finished philosophical drama, and in the *Euthydemus* we have a philosophical burlesque. In the later dialogues the dramatic element is smaller, but all of them are real dialogues, except the *Laws*, in which the conversation is very slight, and the *Timaeus*, in which even the form of conversation is dropped for that of exposition. In the

*Republic* itself the dramatic element diminishes as the book proceeds, but is occasionally resuscitated.

While however Plato's adoption of this form is in agreement with other tendencies in Greek literature generally, there is also a special reason to be found for it in the history of philosophy; the dialogue form has a serious import. Philosophic dialogue had its origin in Socrates himself, with whom Greek philosophy, as distinct from the investigation of nature, practically begins. He passed his life in talking. It was the impulse given by his life that produced Plato's dialogues. Socrates is unique among philosophers because he lived his philosophy; he put out what he had to put out, not in books, but in his life, and he developed his ideas by constant contact with other men. That he was able to do this was his great power; he was a man who, wherever he was and whomsoever he met, showed himself master of the situation. In his case, then, it was apparent that philosophy is a living thing developed by the contact of living minds. We are apt to think of it as something very impersonal and abstract, but, emphatically, all philosophy deals with something in human nature, and differences in philosophy are differences at the bottom of human nature. When, however, philosophy is concentrated and embodied in a book, it speaks a language not understood by most people, and the author, when once he has published his book, cannot help it if his readers misunderstand what he says, for he is not in immediate contact with them. Plato stands between Socrates and a modern writer on philosophy. He has endeavoured to preserve the living philosophy in the written words; he takes types of human nature more or less familiar to his readers, and he makes them develop his ideas by the natural process of question and answer. The literary function of the Platonic dialogue is in modern literature distributed between different kinds of books, chiefly between books of philosophy, and novels, in which ideas grow, embodied in the lives of the characters.

Further, the form of question and answer seems to Plato the natural form for the search after truth to take. He constantly opposes this to the mode, which the sophists adopted, of haranguing or preaching—producing effect by piling up words[1]. Why does he thus insist on question and answer? Because the discovery of truth must be a gradual process, and at every step we should make ourselves realize exactly at what point we have arrived. In Plato this is effected by the dialogue form, each step being made with the agreement of two or more persons. Now, though philosophy need not proceed by discussion between two people, its method must always be in principle the same ; a person who really thinks elicits ideas from himself by questioning himself, and tests those ideas by questioning ; he does, in fact, the same sort of thing with himself that Socrates did with other people. In dialogue two or more minds are represented as combining in the search for truth, and the truth is elicited by the contact of view with view ; in this respect it is replaced in a modern philosophy book by a criticism which endeavours to elicit the truth from opposing views.

In addition to Plato's use of dialogue we have to reckon with his habit of stating ideas in a picturesque manner. Thus in Book II of the *Republic*, when he is analyzing principles which are at work in existing society,

---

[1] See, for example, *Rep.* I. 348 A and B, and 350 D and E, and for a favourable representation of the manner of the sophists see the *Protagoras*.

he exhibits them in what appears to be an historical sketch. He describes first a state organized solely for the production of the necessaries of life, and afterwards makes it grow into a luxurious state; but he knows all the time that the features he ascribes to each are simply taken from the Athens of his own day. This is more noticeable still in Books VIII and IX, where he wishes to exhibit various developments of evil in a logical order of progress, and to do so takes five characters and five states in succession, describing them as historically growing one out of the other. The result of this tendency is to make his writing more vivid, but it is misleading and gives unnecessary occasions for retort. The order in which Plato's thoughts follow upon one another in the *Republic* is logical, but the dramatic or the picturesque medium through which he is constantly presenting his ideas disguises the logical structure of the work.

The logical method of the *Republic* is in accordance with the form of conversational discussion. Plato does not start by collecting all the facts he can, trying afterwards to infer a principle from them; the book is full of facts, but they are all arranged to illustrate principles which he has in mind from the beginning. Nor does he set out by stating a principle and then asking what consequences follow from it. Starting with a certain conception of what man is, he builds up a picture of what human life might be, and in this he is guided throughout by principles which he does not enunciate till he has gone on some way[1]. He begins the con-

---

[1] We may say that the ultimate principle of the *Republic* is that the universe is the manifestation of a single pervading law, and that human life is good so far as it obeys that law; but of this principle Plato does not speak till the end of Book VI.

struction of his picture with admitted facts about human life, and he gradually adds further elements in human life; he at once appeals to and criticizes popular ideas, as he goes on, extracting the truth and rejecting the falsehood in them. Thus neither 'induction' nor 'deduction' is a term that applies to his method; it is a 'genetic' or 'constructive' method; the formation of his principle and the application of it are going on side by side.

Before beginning to follow the argument in detail, we must notice the main divisions into which it falls. They are the following:—

1. Books I and II, to 367 E. This forms an introduction; in it several representative views about human life are examined, and the problem to which the *Republic* offers a solution is put before us. That problem arises in the following manner: we believe that there are moral principles to be observed in life; but this belief is in apparent contradiction to the fact, which meets the eye, that what we should commonly call success in life does not depend upon morality. The sense of this contradiction leads to the demand, with which the Introduction culminates: 'Show us what morality really is, by explaining (without any regard to its external and accidental results) how it operates in the soul of him who possesses it. What does morality mean in a man's innermost life?' This question indicates the central idea of the *Republic*.

2. From Book II, 367 E, to the end of Book IV. In this section Plato describes in outline what, as he conceives, would be the best form of human society; 'justice' is to be traced first in the institutions of this society. These are based, as he considers, upon the requirements of human nature. The society is a community in the life of which every element in human

nature has its proper scope given to it; and in this its justice consists. The external organization, of which this section treats, is only of importance because the inner life of man finds its expression in it. Beginning therefore with the organization of life in the state, and discovering in every part of it a principle upon which the welfare of the community depends, Plato endeavours to trace this principle to its roots in the constitution of human nature, showing how whatever is good or evil in the external order of society depends upon the inner nature of the soul.

3. Books V to VII. Beginning with a further discussion of some points in the institutions of the ideal society, Plato, in the main part of this section, starts from the question by what means this ideal could be realized. The answer is that human life would be as perfect as it is capable of being, if it were governed throughout by knowledge; while the cause of all present evils is that men are blinded, by their own passions and prejudices, to the laws of their own life. Plato expresses this by saying that, if the ideal is to be reached and if present evils are to be brought to an end, philosophy must rule the state ;—(by philosophy he means the best knowledge and the fullest understanding of the most important subjects). In these Books he is occupied on the one hand with the evils that result from the waste and perversion of what he feels to be the most precious thing in human nature, the capacity for attaining truth, and on the other hand with the means by which this capacity might be so trained and so turned to account as to bring the greatest benefit to mankind.

4. Books VIII and IX. As the earlier Books put before us a picture of what human life might be at its

best, so these put before us an ideal picture of human evil, tracing the fall of society and of human nature to the lowest depths they can reach. Plato here tests and develops further his idea of the principle upon which human good depends, by undertaking to show that all existing evil is due to the neglect of that principle.

5. Book X. This is the most detached part of the *Republic*, and consists of two disconnected sections. The first half of it treats over again the subject of art, and especially of poetry, which has already been considered in Book III. The last half continues the consideration of the main subject, the capabilities and destinies of the human soul, by following the soul into the life after death.

# II. EXAMINATION OF SOME REPRE-SENTATIVE OPINIONS ABOUT JUSTICE

[*Republic*, Book I.]

THE First Book of the *Republic*, and the First Book only, is in construction and method closely similar to the earlier dialogues of Plato, the 'Socratic' dialogues. It serves as a prelude to the rest of the work, as we are told at the beginning of Book II. In it certain accepted ideas of morality, which in a modern work would have been formulated as abstract ideas, are embodied before us by various persons. We must first try to see what different kinds of characters Plato has intended to represent to us in these persons.

Socrates is always in the dialogues of Plato the representative of the true philosophic spirit, but this reveals itself in different dialogues in different ways. In this Book it shows itself as a critical spirit which arrives at no apparent positive result whatever. Socrates is the representative of an element always present in philosophy, the sceptical or enquiring spirit which never takes things on trust, but requires that everything shall approve itself to reason. What makes a philosopher is the presence of this spirit, balanced by the conviction that, though everybody must find the truth for himself, the truth is to be found. Socrates then in the First Book comes before us as Philosophy, putting certain questions to certain typical characters and examining certain accepted principles.

In Cephalus we have the gathered experience of a good man of the generation which was just passing away when Socrates was beginning his philosophical work. Philosophy comes to learn from this experience, not to criticize it. Cicero remarks that it would have been inappropriate for Socrates to question Cephalus. What he does is an instance of what Aristotle tells the student of philosophy to do ; we should, he says, attend to the undemonstrated experience of old men, because experience has given them the eye to see rightly[1]. The sort of experience expressed in simple terms, of which Cephalus is made the exponent, is not what we can call a reasoned experience, but the outcome of a life ; the person who has it has not reflected upon it, and is not in a position to answer the questions which the philosopher has to ask. Accordingly, when the criticism begins and the experience is to be analyzed, Cephalus gives way to his son.

In Cephalus' simple utterances some of the philosophical results of the body of the *Republic* are anticipated. In him the delight of philosophical discourse has taken the place of the pleasures of the flesh[2]; he has thereby got rid of 'a raging and cruel master' like the 'tyrant love' of Book IX[3]. In the course of a long life he

327 A to 331 D.

---

[1] *Eth. Nic.* VI. xi. 6.    [2] 328 D, cf. 485 D–E.
[3] 572 E sqq.

has come to see that, though poverty can mar happiness, no material prosperity can command it, and that character is the arbiter of happiness[1]. He retains with a sort of apology his old-fashioned belief in the poet's pictures of a future life, but further he retains the substantial truth of the belief without the accompanying perversions.  Thus his religious belief in its simple and yet pure form contrasts with the corruption of popular religion, which as described in Book II is a gross form of the theory of rewards and punishments.  So the *Republic* begins, as it ends, with the thought of a future life. With Cephalus morality is summed up in the formula, 'to have been true in word and deed, and to have paid one's debts to gods and men,' which, if taken widely and deeply enough, says all that one need wish to say.

331 D to 336 A.    When we come to Polemarchus we pass from the old generation of which Plato knew by report, to a new generation which has inherited the experience of the old, but in a partial way.  Polemarchus, son of Cephalus and brother of Lysias the orator, was put to death by the Thirty Tyrants[2]; he is mentioned in the *Phaedrus*[3] as a convert to philosophy.  Of what sort of person does Plato mean him to be a type?  He comes forward in a confident way to answer the question, What is justice or morality? not with the result of his own experience, but with a borrowed principle of which he is not the master.  We have passed from a man whose conception of justice, though it would not stand as a complete philosophical conception, is yet, in what it means to him, substantially the expression of a good life, to one

[1] 330 A–B, cf. 591 E.      [2] Lysias, *In Eratosthenem.*
[3] 257 B.

who only accepts the same conception from tradition. He formulates it in a maxim borrowed from the poets, which he only very partially understands, and which, so far as he does understand it, is a very imperfect definition of virtue. The maxim may or may not be a good one; with that we are not concerned; all depends on how in this case you understand it.

The argument with Polemarchus falls into two sections. In the first he is gradually led to feel that he does not in the least know what he meant by his maxim from Simonides, that he is at the mercy of any one who can manipulate his definition better than himself, and that his words can be made to mean things quite the contrary to what he does mean. The argument ends in a feeling of intellectual helplessness, or consciousness of ignorance (ἀπορία), which it was the first object of the Socratic dialogue to produce. The second part of the argument has a more positive result: it shows Polemarchus that what he really thought to be the meaning of Simonides, his own real moral belief, that it is right to do good to friends and harm to enemies, does not satisfy the elementary requirements of a moral principle. You cannot say morality is to do harm to anybody without contradicting the very notion of morality. A very similar expression to that of Polemarchus, the maxim that we should love our friends and hate our enemies, is criticized in the Sermon on the Mount. The idea was a commonplace of Greek popular morality[1]. Thus in the poems of Solon there is a prayer, 'May I be pleasant to my friends, hateful to my enemies.'

The method employed in the first part of the argument (331 D to 334 B) is a very good instance of one form

---

[1] Cf. *Meno*, 71 E.

of what is called the Socratic method. The actual conclusion arrived at need not be taken to be what Plato
thought the natural consequence of the principle of
Simonides ; that principle might mean many different
things ; the point to which we must attend is how and
why Polemarchus allows himself to be led to the absurd
conclusion to which he is led. His definition of justice is
that it consists in giving to every man what is 'due' to
him (ὀφειλόμενον). Everything depends on the meaning
of ὀφειλόμενον, and the object is to get him to explain
the conception which exists in his mind in a vague
and fluid state. This is done by the Socratic ἐπαγωγή ;
which means bringing forward admitted facts or instances, which resemble in some points those on which
a given idea is based, with the view of modifying,
correcting, or destroying that idea. We first take that
sense of ὀφειλόμενον in which it means 'legally due.'
This is clearly not what Polemarchus means, for an
instance can be found in which legal restitution is not
just. He then substitutes a vaguer word for 'due,'
προσῆκον. Now 'due' implies a something which is
due, and a somebody to whom it is due. To make him
define his conception further, Socrates brings forward
a number of familiar instances of things 'due' to somebody, each of which he is compelled to exclude from
the conception, thereby gradually narrowing it. Thus
the art of medicine renders something which is due to
somebody. On that analogy what does justice render
that is due, and to whom? This puts justice in the
same category as the arts. What is the point of identity? It is not a fanciful analogy. Justice is a thing
which enables a person to do something (a δύναμις which
makes a person δυνατός). That is the point of contact

between justice and the arts. The just man is a man who has a certain gift or power of doing something; the question is, What? Polemarchus takes the most obvious instance that occurs to him in which services are rendered by justice; he says the just man is most able to help his friends and hurt his enemies in war. Then, seeing that the utility of justice must extend to peace, he again takes the most obvious instance, business. This enables Socrates to compel him again to narrow the conception. Business is a transaction in which two or more persons are concerned; what sort of transaction has Polemarchus in mind? Money transactions. Taking then transactions that have to do with money, Socrates shows that there are many of them in which justice does not enable a man to help his friend. Polemarchus admits that, for instance, it is not justice that makes a man useful to his friend in buying a horse, but knowledge of horses; just as he previously admitted that what enables a man to be useful to his friend in sickness is the art of medicine and not of justice.

By this line of argument Polemarchus is led step by step to empty the conception of justice of everything that is of practical value[1]. This happens because, using a formula which he does not understand, he is at the mercy of any superior dialectician. He ought to have said, justice or morality is not a thing enabling a man to do this or that thing demanding specific knowledge, but a principle of universal application enabling a man to do well everything that he does; it is not one among many arts of doing good, it is the one art of doing the

---

[1] Cf. the more elaborate argument on temperance or self-control in the *Charmides*.

one good. The whole setting of the argument is so strange to us that it hardly makes any impression on us ; yet we might easily throw it into a modern form. Take any current saying about morality, like 'honesty is the best policy,' and ask any one taken at random to explain it, and you would probably find him as much confused as Polemarchus.

The second part of the argument (334 B to 336 A) begins with the confession of Polemarchus that he does not know what he meant ; but he still maintains that at any rate justice is to do good to friends and harm to enemies. Is this really consistent with the most elementary conception of morality? The argument by which Socrates shows that it is not, seems purely verbal ; in all moral discussion however we have to examine words. What he does is to show that if the words 'good' and 'evil' mean anything definite, this cannot be an adequate account of morality, because it involves the contradiction that good can be the cause of evil. For what is 'hurting' a man or doing him 'harm'? It is to make him worse in respect of human excellence ; the only way to hurt a man is to make him a worse man [1]. Now whatever else justice is, it is a form of human excellence, and therefore to say it is just to make a man worse is like saying heat can make us cold. So if Simonides meant what Polemarchus thinks he did, it is not true, and probably that is not what he meant.

The appeal to Simonides is an instance of the constant practice in Greece at that time of appealing to the poets as authorities on conduct and morals. It seems strange to us ; but nearly all the reflective literature of Greece was then to be found in the poets. The poets were the

[1] This was later one of the chief maxims of the Stoics.

precursors of Greek philosophy; they first gave expression to the thoughts of man about himself. It was in poetry, not in prophecy as among the Hebrews, that the early ideas of the Greeks found expression. The result was that, when people wanted to find their ideas formulated, they went to the poets. In that sense Homer and some of the other poets were a sort of Greek Bible[1]. They had not indeed distinct and formally recognized authority; they remained literature and poetry on the same footing as other literature and poetry; but so far as anything took the place taken by the Bible in English thought, it was the older poets. In Plato's time the use of the poets in moral discussion had become something more than a sort of instinctive tradition; learning to interpret them formed a recognized branch of culture. In this passage Socrates says 'Simonides spoke in riddles like a poet as he was[2],' and in the *Protagoras* he parodies the practice of interpreting the words of the poets as riddles or allegories. This practice arose from the growing feeling that new ideas about life could not be got from the poets by superficial reading; they had to be read into them or worked out of them. Here Plato makes Socrates' attitude to Simonides one of ironical courtesy, but his treatment of the poets is· different on different occasions.

The analogy between morality and the arts, which is employed in the argument with Polemarchus, appears frequently in Socrates, Plato, and Aristotle. It is important to realize what is the exact point of comparison, and what it was that led Socrates to employ this comparison so frequently. The arts used as illustrations are

[1] Cf. *Rep.* X, especially 606 E.
[2] See also *Lysis*, 214, *Charmides*, 162 A, *Theaet.* 194 C, *Protag.* 339 sq.

not, as a rule, the fine arts; they are either mechanical
or professional arts, medicine, navigation, shoemaking,
cookery, &c.  If the art of the sculptor or painter is
employed in illustration, it is treated in exactly the same
way as these other arts.  The point of analogy is not
a resemblance between the products of morality and of
the arts, but a certain capacity or ability which must
be common to the artist and the good man.  Justice is
a power to do something, and so far it is like any art.
The cook and the shoemaker are those who possess
ability to do certain things better than other people;
and this ability rests on knowledge of their business.
This is the point of analogy with morality.  In order
to live properly we must understand life; according to
a saying attributed to Socrates, 'virtue is knowledge,'
which really means that to understand life is to be
master of it.  In order to be a successful artist at anything you must understand the theory of the thing; and
morality is represented as an art because the good man
may be represented as a master of the art of living, one
who knows the circumstances in which he lives and the
best mode of living.  One must not jump to conclusions
and think this means that morality, or the art of living,
can be learnt like shoemaking.  The Greeks, who saw
a point of contact between morality and the arts which
is a real one, were not generally inclined to push the
analogy too far, and Plato was at great pains to draw
clearly the distinction between the art of living and
other arts [1], the most obvious difference being that the
art of living cannot be mastered in the same way.  The
applications which Greek thinkers did make of the comparison were that morality is nothing at all unless it

[1] See *Meno* and *Protagoras*.

makes a man practically a better liver, and that, to live well, you must study life with as much attention as any sane man would give to learning his trade. It is naturally supposed that, when the Greeks compared morality to the arts, they were thinking of the fine arts and meant that there was a resemblance between a moral life and a work of art. Many people have looked upon a good life as a work of art, and that is a legitimate point of view ; but it was not the characteristic point of view of Plato or Aristotle, though morality is sometimes in their phraseology described as a beautiful thing (καλόν). To express in modern language the analogy which they found between morality and the arts, one might say that morality means a theory or principle carried out in life, and that we must make life a scientific thing, following the example of the applied sciences, in which success is due to understanding, and failure to ignorance. This is really the characteristic Greek way of looking at life, for the Greeks were not only an artistic but an intellectual people, to whom such a point of view was natural.

Thrasymachus, who next enters into the argument, is not to be taken as representing Plato's idea of the sophists generally; for there was no one class of people called sophists, and they could not be typified by one individual, nor does the antagonism between Plato and them appear in one form but in many. The simplest way of describing the sophists is to say that they were persons who in the fourth and fifth centuries B.C. supplied culture to Greece, or, in other words, who made it their profession to diffuse and popularize ideas. To understand the position they filled one should consider what are the agencies which diffuse culture in the nineteenth century. There is no one agency, no class of persons with one

336 B to end of Book I.

name. But there are, first, writers in newspapers and periodicals, by themselves a large and various assortment of people ; there are, further, writers of fiction ; there are preachers who diffuse moral or religious ideas ; and there are men who, without being in all cases exactly savants or philosophers, popularize certain ideas about science or philosophy. For example, Professor Huxley, besides being a man of science, is a popularizer of science ; and again, Mr. Matthew Arnold, though in the first place a poet, has done a very great deal to spread certain ideas about life and about religion. Now the Greek sophists are no more to be thought of as men of a single kind than any one man is to be taken as a type of the spreaders of culture in England. The class comprised the greatest and the meanest men, men actuated by the most various motives. Some were truly interested in the spread of education, others aimed at overthrowing certain beliefs, others had no higher object in view than making a fortune.

The conditions of Greece were different from those of England, and the particular things in which the sophists educated Greece were different from those taught in England by any analogous agency. Nearly all of them taught rhetoric ; that is to say, the power of using language as an instrument in life. A modern analogy to this teaching of rhetoric may be found in the 'higher education' in England. What is the main thing taught in the English Public Schools and Universities? An outside observer might say with a good deal of truth that it was how to use words, that is, how to understand literature and to write. Acquiring the power to express oneself is an indispensable element in education, and in Greece it was absolutely necessary in order to get on in life. The sophists therefore nearly all taught rhetoric. But teaching language is more than teaching the use of words; one learns from it inevitably how to think and speak about subjects of importance. The chief subjects of interest in Greece were subjects bearing on public life or politics, and the sophists practised their pupils in speaking on these. Thus incidentally, and sometimes intentionally, the teaching of the sophists was a moral education, an education in things which have to do with life. It is not true to say of higher education in England that it is 'a mere linguistic training,' for linguistic training means getting hold of and handling many ideas; nor is it true that the sophistic education in Greece was merely rhetorical, for the sophists were, to a great extent, the moral educators of Greece.

The sophists were more or less professional men; they made their living by teaching, and from the necessities of the case they had to address themselves to a certain public and to strive to get influence over it, just as a modern press-writer has to consider for whom he writes, and, to a certain extent, has to adapt his style and matter to his public. This makes a great, perhaps a most vital distinction between a man of science and a man who discharges a function like that of the sophists. A man of science has not, as such, any interest in the spreading of truth; he is one whose function is to find out what is true, whether any one else believes it or not. Many of the greatest men of science have been grossly misunderstood by their contemporaries, and generally their ideas have to filter through others to the world at large: that filtering is the work of the sophists. Any one who does this work stands, as a man with a gospel to propagate stands, in a difficult and dangerous position; he has to compromise between the truest and most effective way of putting things; the adjustment is difficult, and there are sure to be some who err in it through unscrupulousness. The sophists who appear in Plato include people as different from one another as a distinguished *savant* or literary man is from the most unscrupulous newspaper writer. Protagoras and Gorgias are represented as honourable men desirous of doing good, but still as men who, while desiring to be leaders of the people, really only reflect popular ideas. In other cases sophists appear as charlatans, whose sole object is to produce an effect or to make money. Plato's attitude towards the sophists varies from genuine respect, always touched with a little irony, as towards Gorgias and Protagoras, to scathing contempt, as towards Euthydemus.

Thrasymachus[1] belonged to the class of sophists who made their rhetoric the chief subject of their teaching. We learn that his peculiar strength lay in teaching how to appeal to the passions of an audience. He came from Chalcedon. We have no means of knowing whether Plato is just to him, nor does it matter to us. Certain traits in this picture of him are common to most of Plato's representations of sophists. Indifference to truth, love of money, and caring only for verbal victory, these are characteristics common to all the inferior sophists in Plato, while a disinclination to reason and a tendency to harangue are shared by nearly all. But there are special features in Thrasymachus—perhaps exaggerations by Plato of the features of the real man—coarseness, unmannerliness (which is very

---

[1] *Phaedrus*, 267 C; and Arist. *Rhct.* 1404 a. 14.

unusual in Plato's dialogues), shameless audacity and disregard of consequences, and cynicism. In fact, it is not primarily as a teacher of rhetoric that he is represented here. He appears first as a man who takes a cynical view of political morality, and does not really believe that there is such a thing as morality at· all. He is at the same time a man who assumes the garb of science, and will be nothing if not exact (ἀκριβής) ; and he can put his case in a way which, even in this burlesqued form, would be extremely effective with a popular audience inclined to be unscrupulous. The view of which he is the exponent is one which was very much in the air at that time, though not often put in this naked form. We meet with it in the Melian dialogue in Thucydides[1], and in the argument between the δίκαιος and ἄδικος λόγος in the *Clouds* of Aristophanes. We meet with it also in the *Gorgias*, where it is both stated and answered in a more serious and powerful manner ; for Callicles in that dialogue expresses what is essentially the same position in the most effective way in which it has ever been put.

The argument with Thrasymachus falls into two main sections. The result of the first (338 C to 347 E) is gradually to elicit from the ambiguous formula of Thrasymachus what he really means. This is that the real art of living is to know how to aggrandize oneself (πλεονεκτεῖν) with impunity ; successful selfishness is the true end of life; the distinction between the so-called just and unjust · is only a difference in the point of view ; if selfishness is successful it is just, if not it is unjust. The second part of the argument (347 E to end of Book I) aims at showing that, if you take this principle seriously as a principle

---

[1] *Thuc.* V. 89 sqq.

on which to live, it contradicts itself, because it is the negation of all principle. It cannot be made to satisfy any of the requirements of wisdom, goodness, or happiness (σοφία, ἀρετή, εὐδαιμονία). In manner both parts of the argument bear a resemblance to that with Polemarchus. Certain terms are taken and assumed to bear at least a certain definite minimum of meaning, and it is asked what logically follows if they are taken in their strict meaning (τῷ ἀκριβεῖ λόγῳ). It is essentially an argument from the abstract meaning of certain conceptions. It must therefore strike us at first as unsatisfactory and unconvincing. We feel that Thrasymachus is thinking all the time of certain concrete facts, as we call them, while the argument against him is not concerned with the question what the facts of life are. It merely asks whether, assuming the facts of life to be as Thrasymachus states them, they satisfy certain abstract conceptions; whether, for example, if government is universally selfish, it has any right to be called government. This feeling is expressed by Glaucon at the beginning of Book II. Thrasymachus, he says, has been logically silenced, but the hearers have not been convinced that there is nothing in what he says; they want Socrates not only to prove to them in argument that justice is better than injustice, but to show them justice and injustice as operative principles in human life.

1. Thrasymachus begins (338 C) by laying down the proposition that 'Justice is the interest of the stronger' (κρείττων). The first thing to do is to clear away the ambiguity of his terms. The word κρείττων includes the conceptions of stronger and better, and the first question is, In what particular sense does he mean stronger or better? Putting aside the meaning 'physi-

cally stronger,' Thrasymachus says that he means the government or sovereign for the time being, which is a perfectly good meaning, for the government is always as a matter of fact backed by force amongst other things. By his statement that justice is the interest of the stronger Thrasymachus means, then, that the government legislates in its own interest. This however is ambiguous. It is true that, as he says, the laws of democracy or oligarchy serve democratic or oligarchic interests, because a democracy is a community based on the theory that the democratic interest is the true and best interest of the state, and so with an oligarchy. But the statement may mean something else than this, namely that those who govern legislate in their own personal interests; and it soon becomes clear that this is what Thrasymachus really means.

The first step in the examination of the position as it has now been explained (viz. that justice is the interest of the sovereign or government) is to lead Thrasymachus to admit that there is an art, theory, or principle of government. Socrates does this by appealing to the fact that governments make mistakes as to their interests, so that what the government commands may not be its real interest; upon which Thrasymachus asserts (340 C sqq.) that, in speaking of the sovereign or government for the time being, he does not mean anybody who happens to be in power, but the persons who, holding positions of authority, have also the real capacity and knowledge to govern. By government, he says, he only means the government so far as it does not make mistakes. This at once puts us on different ground, and enables Socrates to advance to a new and important point. It puts government in the category of applied principles or arts; so that we may apply to it all that can be said of art in general.

The next step in the argument is accordingly to develop the abstract conception of art. How does the notion of 'interest' (ξυμφέρον) apply in the case of art? In what sense has an art an interest, or in what sense has any artist an interest *quâ* artist? (The form in which the question is put implies the identification of the artist with the art; the artist is regarded as the art embodied. And there is truth in this, for the arts have no existence whatever except in given persons. Art means the living artists and what they make; just as science again means the living states of certain persons and the fruits of those states.) An art may be said to have an interest in two senses. First, there is the interest which would more accurately be called the interest of its subject-matter. The arts come into existence because of certain wants, flaws, or imperfections[1] in certain things. There is an art of medicine because of the imperfection of the human body; there would be no such art if the body could be kept in perfect health without it. The interest of the subject-matter of the art is that these imperfections should be supplemented; and in a loose way we may call this the interest of the art. But, secondly, what is the interest of the art in the strict sense? An art is a certain power to meet certain wants or supplement certain defects; its interest, end, or motive then can be no other than to do this in the best way possible; its interest is its own perfection (ὅτι μάλιστα τελέαν εἶναι, 341 D). Suppose an artist to be doing his work as well as he can; would he feel, *quâ* artist,

---

[1] Expressed by the word πονηρία, which is badness in the sense of having flaws, the Latin *vitium*.

a want of anything further? No; if he is susceptible
to any other interest, it means that he has gone outside
his art and is something else than an artist. The art
in itself has no want or imperfection for other arts to
supplement, it is self-sufficient. The perfection of art
is its own reward. The argument will be clearer to us
if we speak of the artist instead of the art. We should
allow that the doctor or painter, as doctor or painter,
can have no other interest than to treat his patients or
to paint as well as he can, and, so far as he has any
other interest, he is not for the time being strictly doctor
or painter. Of course it is not implied that he is any
the worse because, as a matter of fact, he has other
interests beyond his art.

Now, to apply this to the art of government, the
relation of arts to their subject-matter or material is
the relation of governor to governed; they are masters
of it and deal with it as they like. When we spoke of
the governors who were really governors, and called
them the stronger or better, it was implied that the
superiority which made them real governors was the same
superiority that any artist has over his subject-matter.
This subject-matter is in their case the community over
which they rule; government is called into existence by
certain wants in its subject-matter, society. Then if
there really is such a thing as this art of government,
which, it is implied, exists, and if what we have called
by that name is not to be resolved into some other quite
different thing, the only sense in which you can speak of
an interest of government is that of securing the interest
of the governed. The only interest of the governor, as
a governor, is to govern well; and if we say justice is
the interest of governors, we do not mean it is their

interest as doing anything else but govern. Thrasymachus of course meant it was their interest in quite a different sense.

This is a perfectly abstract argument; the result of it is that Thrasymachus gives up the pretension to be scientific and logical, which he has so far made. In his answer (343, 344) he does not touch this argument but appeals to the facts. He says 'look at what governments do,' and gives a cynical, though no doubt to some extent a true, picture of some Greek governments. They are like shepherds who feed sheep, not in the interest of the sheep, but in their own. As a matter of fact, he proceeds to say, the honest and honourable man comes off worse in life, he makes less and he is disliked more. The real interest of the stronger is injustice; not injustice on the small scale of ordinary crime, but injustice on a grand scale. What is called justice and what is called injustice are in reality the same thing, only described from different points of view. If the doer of unjust things is strong enough, then what he does is called justice by weaker men; if he is weak, then it is called injustice by stronger men and he is punished.

We thus gradually pass to a different and a wider question, What is the real nature of the distinction between justice and injustice? and (ultimately), What is the real aim or good of human life? For Thrasymachus does away with any distinction of right and wrong; the only principle he recognizes is that of self-interest; if self-interest is successful it gets called justice, that is all.

In the first part of his answer (344 D) Socrates, taking up Thrasymachus' illustration of the shepherd and the sheep, appeals to the admitted fact that all arts which are paid, are paid because it is assumed that the artist, as such, does not work for his own profit. He goes on, still in a rather abstract way, to develop his conception of art. He has before considered the nature of single arts; he now takes the concrete case of a paid artist, and shows that in his case two absolutely distinct arts are involved, his own specific art, and the art of wage-earning which is common to him and other artists. Art is the ability ($\delta\acute{v}\nu\alpha\mu\iota\varsigma$) to do a certain thing; its product is specific to it ($\H{\iota}\delta\iota o\nu$). If, then, we take a steersman who gets money by steering, and a doctor who gets money by curing disease, we can distinguish the specific product of the particular art of either of them, and the common product, money. That this analysis is true, and that we not only can but must thus distinguish the two products, is shown by the fact that a doctor may cease to take fees, and none the less continue to heal. The specific product, then, is not convertible with the common product of the arts. Coming to the art of government, Socrates appeals to the fact that rulers are paid for their work. They are paid either in money or position, or else they have their reward in avoiding the evil to themselves and the community of the bad government which would rule if they did not. This shows that the accepted theory of government is that it is not in itself a paying thing; and, further, Socrates adds that the best governors are those who do not do the work for pay at all, or even for reputation, but simply because, if they did not govern, somebody else would do it worse. Advancing upon what he says, we might say that, the better a man governs, the more he finds his reward simply in performing the function of government as well as it can be performed.

Where Plato distinguishes the art of getting paid

($\mu\iota\sigma\theta\omega\tau\iota\kappa\acute{\eta}$) from the other arts, which, in his language, it accompanies, he is making a distinction which, though in different language, we also might really make. We might, for instance, say that a doctor, considered as a person making an income, was a subject for the economist or the statistician. To them the only question about the doctor might be, What is the price of his work? and it might make no difference what was the specific nature of the art by which he got his income. Conversely, it might have no influence on the art whether the artist was making £10,000 a year or £1,000. The essential point for which Socrates is contending may be illustrated by what is now a generally admitted principle as to the payment of public officers. It is that they should be paid to such an extent as will enable them to devote themselves entirely to their work, and will remove, as far as possible, the temptation to make money out of their offices. Thus it is complained that the low pay of judges in many of the United States has a bad effect upon their work as judges. The facts to which Thrasymachus appeals are undoubted facts, but it is equally clear that the ordinary conscience of mankind accepts in substance Socrates' view of the nature of public authority.

2. We come now (347 E) to the second section of the argument with Thrasymachus. Having completed the analysis of the conception of government, Socrates turns to a more important question: Is successful self-aggrandizement the true principle of life; does the life of the unjust man pay better than that of the just man? For it has come out in the course of the argument that this is what Thrasymachus actually meant by saying 'justice is the interest of the stronger.' To make his exact

meaning clearer, he is led to say that what is called
injustice is, in the true sense of the words, virtue (ἀρετή)
and wisdom (σοφία).

What do these words mean in Greek? 'Αρετή is that
quality in an agent in virtue of which it does its particular
work well; there is no other virtue than that. The
corresponding adjective to ἀρετή is ἀγαθός, good. A thing
is good of its kind when it does its work well. Thus,
whatever else 'a good man' may mean, it must mean
a man who does his work well, a man who lives well,
whatever meaning you may attach to that. Unfortunately
our words 'goodness' and 'good,' which are the natural
equivalent for ἀρετή and ἀγαθός, no longer have this
wide signification when they are applied to men, and
'morality' and 'moral' never had it.

Σοφία is a specific form of ἀρετή; Aristotle, describing
the original use of the word, says it is the virtue of
τέχνη (that is, of art in the widest sense¹). 'Wise' and
'cunning' are used in this sense in the Old Testament.
If we look at human life as the subject-matter of a certain
art, then σοφὸς ἀνήρ means a man who is master of the
art of living. What Thrasymachus means, then, is that
the so-called unjust man is the man who understands the
real art of living. In applying these words, ἀρετή and
σοφία, to injustice, he is, of course, putting his disbelief
in justice in the form that would seem most paradoxical
to his hearers; and this is what Plato intends. If, as
Socrates remarks, Thrasymachus had compromised, and
had said that injustice was advantageous though base
(αἰσχρόν), it would have been easier to answer him.

Next we must understand what he means by injustice

¹ *Eth. Nic.* VI. vii. 1. He proceeds immediately to give it a very different
sense.

(ἀδικία)? The essence of injustice was traditionally understood to lie in πλεονεξία, the attempt to get more than anybody else of the good things of life. The unjust man is he who is always trying to get more of something than somebody else. The dominant idea of justice in Greek thought was some sort of equality ; that is, that every one should have, not actually the same amount, but a fair proportion, measured according to his position in life or by some other standard.

Thrasymachus then claims for injustice that it is the true wisdom of life, and, as will be understood from what has been said of the meaning of the words, the claim that it is the true virtue or goodness is taken as standing or falling with this ; he further claims that it is the true strength of life ; and lastly, that it is the true happiness or welfare (εὐδαιμονία) of life. His position is now examined under the head of these three claims.

(a) On the first of these claims the substance of Socrates' argument (349 A to 350 C) may be stated as follows. If we examine the principle upon which the man who is perfectly unjust acts, we find it consists in the denial that there is any principle at all. He says, Let every man get what he can ; because he recognizes no distinction of good and bad, right and wrong, and does not allow that there is any such thing as a limit beyond which he ought to get no more. Thrasymachus is taken as accepting this view, and asserting that the man with no principle is the true artist in life (the σοφός). Now let us compare such a man with a good artist or craftsman in other arts. In all other arts the man who is without the idea of right or wrong (in the wider sense of the words), or the idea of a limit at which he must

stop, is not the man who understands his art; he is the
man who knows nothing about it. For suppose two
musicians meet over the tuning of an instrument; if they
are really musicians, they at once recognize a principle
of right and wrong, which sets a limit beyond which it
would never occur to them to go; in plain English, if
the instrument is rightly tuned, the musician, the man
who knows, would never think of tuning it further. Or,
if two good doctors meet in consultation, when the one
has treated the patient rightly the other would not
depart from the right treatment in order to outdo him.
This idea of a limit, up to which you try to go
and beyond which you do not try to go, is that of
a standard of perfection or of rightness which you try
to hit off exactly. It appears, then, that in all arts the
mark of skill and understanding is that the man who has
them (the σοφός or ἐπιστήμων) knows when that limit is
reached. He does not, Plato says, go beyond another
person who understands his art; or, as we should rather
say, he does not go beyond what he knows to be the
principle of his art. If this then is the case with all
good craftsmen, the unjust man, the man of limitless
acquisition (πλεονεξία), would seem to be the type of the
bad and ignorant craftsman.

Socrates' argument seems unconvincing, not only because of its abstract character but for a further reason.
It goes very much to the root of the whole question,
and people are very seldom able to face the ultimate
issues raised by any question. There are several other
passages in Plato that throw light on the argument
here. In the *Politicus* two kinds of 'measure' (μέτρον)
are distinguished—that by which things are measured
against each other in respect of magnitude, and that by

which things are measured against each other, not in
respect of their mere magnitude, but in respect of some
proportion between them; and Plato goes on to say
that all arts depend for their existence on measure in
the latter sense[1]. A passage in the *Gorgias* expresses
much the same antithesis as we find here. Callicles is
made to maintain, though more forcibly, the same
position as Thrasymachus, and it is shown against him,
more fully than here, that if you are quite logical in
this position you make life strictly impossible, that the
logically non-moral life is logically impossible and self-
destructive; proportion (ἰσότης γεωμετρική) is the great
principle that holds life and the universe together[2]. In
the *Philebus*, Socrates talks of limit (πέρας); this is
essentially what is elsewhere described as measure;
it is what makes things measurable which would be
incomparable and immeasurable without it; and this
principle is declared to be that on which not only arts
but also laws of nature depend[3]. In various other
passages we have the same idea applied equally to
morality and the life of man, to nature and its processes,
and to art and its processes.

There is one total misunderstanding of this idea which
we must avoid. The modern associations of the word
'limit,' and sometimes also those of the word 'measure,'
are the exact opposite of those which these words had for
Plato. The word limit certainly suggests to us something
that stops progress, and prevents us reaching perfection
in anything. The Greek associations of the words, at least
in Plato and Aristotle, are quite different. The idea of

---

[1] *Politicus*, 283 C sqq. It is in this passage that we find the nearest
verbal approach in Plato to Aristotle's doctrine of the 'mean.'
[2] *Gorgias*, 507 E sq.          [3] *Philebus*, 25 E sqq.

limit is that of something on the attainment of which perfection is attained; it is not that which puts a stop to progress, but that without which progress would be a meaningless process *ad infinitum*. Both ways of using the word are justifiable; but it is a difference in the use of language which indicates a fundamental difference between our ways of looking at things. The modern conception, which most answers to the Greek idea of measure, is that of law. In our conceptions of nature and morality the idea of law is becoming more and more dominant. This idea also admits of two different applications. Law may be looked upon as a restraining and repressive force, or it may be looked upon as an undeviating mode of activity; the latter is the true meaning of 'laws of nature,' and it is also the true meaning of 'measure' in Plato. To Plato and Aristotle alike the natural way of expressing the truth that there is some distinction between right and wrong, or that there is such a thing as moral principle, is to say that there is such a thing as limit or measure, without which it is literally true that human life would be impossible. The whole of the Aristotelian doctrine, that virtue is a mean between two extremes, is an expression of the same conception of measure, that the right, or good, or beautiful, always appears as something which is neither too much nor too little. With the Greeks the presence of such a standard is the symbol of the presence of reason in the world, and in morals, and in the whole of human life. It is not a moral conception, but a perfectly universal conception applied to human life. The characteristically Greek way of describing morality is to say, that the moral man is the man who recognizes that there is a principle. That is to the Greeks the point of contact between morality, art, science, and everything in which reason is concerned. Thus the issue involved in this argument with Thrasymachus is the most elementary issue conceivable; that is, it goes very much further back than we are accustomed to go in our discussions of morality. The question is whether there is or is not any principle in human life at all. We, in our discussions about what is 'right' or 'good,' generally move in a much more concrete atmosphere. (The answer that Thrasymachus could at once have made to the argument is, of course, that by the man who takes all he can (the πλεονέκτης) he did not mean the man who takes absolutely and literally all he can without recognizing any principle or any limit at all. But to make this answer would have been to surrender the position he had undertaken to defend.)

(*b*) Injustice, or taking all one can, has further been represented as power or strength. Under this head of the argument (351 A to 352 D) the issue is again between having some principle and having none. Thrasymachus' contention is met by showing that, if we take any instance of the successful exertion of force, we always find present some element of unity, some standard which the people acting together tacitly recognize; and that absolutely taking all one can, absolute absence of principle, means *incapacity to act together*, and consequently disintegration and dissolution. In any society, in the large society of the state, in an army, or in a small body of men such as a band of robbers, success in injustice is always due to some implicit recognition of justice. This leads Socrates to the assertion that justice is not a term describing a mere external form of action, but something with a power or force (δύναμις) of its own, which wherever it exists, either in society or in the individual soul, will always make itself felt; and, passing to the individual soul, he points out that this principle of union is the condition of strength in it as in society. Here we have a transition from the view of justice as a matter of external conduct to the view of it as a living principle in the human soul which works itself out in the conduct of life. This is the first indication of a manner of looking at the subject which dominates the whole of the rest of the *Republic*. The principle of absolute injustice means the impossibility of union with oneself, with other men, and with God; and wherever strength is found, it is in virtue of some admixture of justice or unity.

(*c*) There remains the contention that the unjust man is happier (more εὐδαίμων) or 'lives better' than the just man. In answer to this Plato (352 D to end of Book I) develops very simply a conception which is the funda-mental conception of Aristotle's *Ethics*. In the first Book of the *Ethics*[1], Aristotle asks the question, What is hap-piness (εὐδαιμονία), what is the true thing to live for? And to answer it he asks, What, if any, is the function (ἔργον) of man as man? Virtue (ἀρετή) he defines as strictly correlative to function; it simply means excellence of work, excellence in the performance of function[2]; and to understand what is said of 'virtue' in Greek thought one must realize that this is its meaning. In the present passage the argument of Socrates is as follows :— Everything which has a function—everything, that is to say, which does or produces anything—has a corre-sponding virtue. The function of a thing is that for which it is the sole agent, or the best agent. The

[1] I. vii. 9-15.    [2] II. vi. 1-3.

virtue of a thing is that quality in it which enables it to perform its function; virtue is the quality of the agent when it is working well. For example, the function of the eye is to see, and that of the ear to hear, and their virtues are seeing and hearing well. Now the soul of man is a thing with a function; it may be said to have various functions, but they may be expressed in general terms by saying that its function is to live (the 'soul' meant to the Greeks the principle of life). Its virtue, then, will be that quality which enables it to live well. So, if we have been right in saying that not injustice but justice is the virtue of man, it is the just man and not the unjust who will live well; and to live well is to be happy.

Here again the argument is intensely abstract. We should be inclined to break in on it and say that virtue means something very different in morality from what it means in the case of seeing or hearing, and that by happiness we mean a great many other things besides what seems to be meant here by living well. All depends, in this argument, on the strictness of the terms, upon assuming each of them to have a definite and distinct meaning. The virtues of a man and of a horse are very different, but what is the common element in them which makes us call them both virtue? Can we call anything virtue which does not involve the doing well of the function, never mind what, of the agent that possesses the virtue? Is there any other sense in which we can call a thing good or bad, except that it does or does not do well that which it was made to do? Again, happiness in its largest sense, welfare, well-being, or doing well, is a very complex thing, and one cannot readily describe in detail all that goes to make it up; but does it not necessarily imply that the human soul, man's vital activity as a whole, is in its best state, or is performing well the function it is made to perform? If by virtue and by happiness we mean what it seems we do mean, this consequence follows: when men are agreed that a certain sort of conduct constitutes virtue, if they mean anything at all, they must mean that in that conduct man finds happiness. And if a man says that what he calls virtue has nothing to do with what he calls happiness or well-being, then either in calling the one virtue he does not really mean what he says, or in calling the other happiness he does not really mean what he says. This is substantially the position that Plato takes up in this section.

The last two sections of the argument prepare the way for the first half of Book II. The view of morality is becoming less external, we are invited to regard it now as an inherent activity of the soul. In Book II Glaucon and Adeimantus demand that this idea should be taken up and developed.

Before leaving Book I, we may consider two further incidental points. (1) Thrasymachus is made to refer bitterly to the well-known 'irony' (εἰρωνεία) of Socrates (337 A). In the *Ethics* of Aristotle[1] the 'ironical' man (εἴρων) is a person who in his conversation represents himself at less than his actual worth. In this general sense 'irony' is a social quality which is the extreme opposite of boastfulness or vanity. It becomes affectation or false modesty when a person is always depreciating himself, and we generally think that such a person is in reality anything but modest. But the 'irony' of Socrates was not a mere grace of manner

[1] IV. vii.

in social behaviour; still less was it affectation or mock
humility. It arose in him from a genuine sense of the
inexhaustibility of knowledge. We may compare his
expressions of it with the question in the Gospels, 'Why
callest thou me good?' This is the deeper significance
of the Socratic 'irony'; compared with what is to be
known, neither Socrates nor anybody else knows anything; he was wiser, he said, than those with whom he
conversed only because he knew his own ignorance[1].
But the people with whom he spoke were, no doubt,
generally more ignorant than he, and if one had been
a stranger talking with him, this perpetual assumption
of ignorance would have appeared a sort of humorous
irony, in our sense of the word, designed to make
Socrates appear to advantage[2]. (One may compare
the expression 'irony of fate'; we speak of the irony
of fate when we see a man behaving in a way which
shows that he is quite unconscious of the real circumstances.)

(2) Thrasymachus in the *Republic* (337 D) requires to be
paid for his contribution to the discussion. It is always
represented in Plato as one of the contrasts between
Socrates and the sophists that the latter took pay
and the former did not. We know from Xenophon
that Socrates, like Plato, regarded this practice of
taking pay not indeed as wrong, but as marking
a certain inferiority in the receiver. Xenophon in
saying how little Socrates cared about luxury or
money, mentions that he never demanded pay for
his teaching. 'In this,' he tells us, 'he conceived

---

[1] *Apology*, 21 D.
[2] For the irony of Socrates compare *Symp.* 216 E, *Theaet.* 150 C, *Meno*,
80 A, and Xen. *Mem.* I. ii. 36, and IV. iv. 9.

he was assuring his liberty, for he felt that those who took pay for the advantage of their society made themselves the slaves of those who paid them.' It was not money, but the acquisition of good friends that he regarded as his greatest gain[1]. Xenophon tells us too that Antiphon reproached Socrates with not taking money, because it showed that, though he was an honest man, he did not know his own interests. Socrates answered that he regarded wisdom as beauty, and thought that to sell wisdom for money was to prostitute it; that is to say, that truth is something which cannot be bought or sold, and to put a money value on it is to degrade it.

The notion that there is a degradation in taking pay for anything seems absurd to the modern mind. The whole question is whether, and how far, money taken affects the motive and attitude of the person who takes it. Some persons are not affected by it in the smallest degree; but there is a very real danger in the relation of the receiver of pay to the giver, and with the majority it does diminish independence and clearness of view. It is often felt now, chiefly perhaps about the clergy, but also and with equal justice about barristers, doctors, and men of any profession, that every kind of work *tends* to be lowered by becoming a profession. This is exactly what Socrates and Plato seem to have felt about the sophists, and it is quite a true feeling. No doubt, by being professional men whose business it was to communicate wisdom, the sophists put themselves more under the public that paid them than they would otherwise have been, and exposed themselves more to the danger of confounding what was true with

[1] Xen. *Mem*. I. ii. 6 and 60; v. 6; vi. 13, 14.

what was likely to please the public. At the same
time there is no ground for accusing the greater sophists
of having been avaricious; Protagoras, for example,
is said to have left it to his hearers to pay him what
they thought fit.

# III. STATEMENT OF THE PROBLEM
# OF THE 'REPUBLIC'

[*Republic*, II. to 367 E.]

AT the end of Book I, Plato himself gives us a criticism upon it. He makes Socrates confess that in one way the result of the argument is nothing, because we have not settled what justice is, and cannot therefore determine whether it is a virtue and whether it makes men happy. We have been discussing the concomitant circumstances of the thing without knowing what it is in itself[1].

If we ask what the discussion has done, we may say that it has shown several things which justice cannot be; that various leading conceptions, those, for example, of art, wisdom, function, interest, have been analyzed; and further that it has been shown that the theory of Thrasymachus in its naked form will not account for the facts—that consistent and thorough-going selfishness will not give one a working principle of life at all. But Glaucon and Adeimantus feel that, though Thrasymachus has been silenced, the argument

[1] Cf. *Meno*, 71 B.

is not convincing. They undertake to renew his contention, and they demand an answer quite different
from that which has so far been given. They want,
as Glaucon says, to be shown what justice and injustice are in themselves, as powers in the soul of
man; or, as Adeimantus says, not merely to have
it logically proved that justice is better than injustice,
but to be shown the actual effects of each upon the
possessor. This is the question to which the last
sections of Book I have led.

In passing then from Book I to Book II, we pass
from the region of logic, and from an analysis of terms
in which all depends on their being used precisely and
consistently, to the region of psychology and to the
analysis of concrete human nature (an analysis which
leads Plato to construct an imaginary community upon
the basis of his psychology). We pass at the same
time from the consideration of utterances of individual
experience, borrowed and half-understood maxims, and
paradoxes of cynical rhetoricians, to criticism of the
voice of society and public opinion, as it speaks through
its recognized leaders or in the everyday intercourse
of social and family life. To notice one more feature
of the transition from Book I to Book II, we pass
from a Socrates represented as knowing nothing, but
simply listening, questioning, and refuting, to a Socrates
represented as the exponent of a new and higher
morality.

The two personages through whom this transition
is made, Glaucon and Adeimantus, are of a type
that Plato takes an interest in representing. They
cannot be better described than in the words of
Adeimantus himself, where he speaks of 'young men

of the day, who are gifted (εὐφυεῖς), and able to flit over the surface of public opinion and draw inferences from it' as to the true principle of life (365 A). They are greatly interested in speculation, convinced in their hearts that justice is better than injustice, but unable to defend their conviction against the voice of public opinion in its various manifestations; they are dissatisfied with the modern enlightenment, but cannot see where the real flaw in it lies, and how it should be corrected. They differ from one another in character, as Professor Jowett points out; but one feeling, common to both, is at the root of all they say: both are puzzled by the apparent incongruity between morality itself and the external circumstances amid which it exists, between the being of things and the seeming, the externals of life which all seem to point one way, and the principles which, they are themselves convinced, point the other way. The literature of all peoples shows that this has always been one of the first problems to strike the human mind.

Glaucon begins with a classification of good things, based on the distinction of things good in themselves and things good for their ulterior results. He and Adeimantus are persuaded that justice is good in itself and for its results, but to realize the intrinsic good of justice they wish to have it examined absolutely apart from its results; for until you distinguish morality from the external or tangible results and accompaniments which are always found connected with it, you cannot be sure what it is you are dealing with. Thrasymachus' position had resulted in reducing morality to certain external results of conduct, and had

in fact done away with any real moral distinctions.
The object to aim at was to get as much material
prosperity as one could; success in this was called
justice, and failure was called injustice; there was no
essential morality, but only conventional. Accordingly
Glaucon requires that the distinction between justice
and injustice should be represented in the most naked
way. He will have justice put on one side, and on
the other side he will have put all the material results
of justice that can be separated from it. Strip justice
bare, he says; set against it all the good things that
may often go with it but are not connected with it
really, and may equally result from being thought just
when one really is unjust; and then, convince me that
this bare principle, with nothing to show for itself except
itself, is better worth living for than everything that can
be set against it.

This is the view which both young men wish Socrates
to maintain. They themselves, for the sake of putting
before him something to answer, give expression to views
opposed to it, current views, which are not their own but
which they have a difficulty in withstanding.

First, Glaucon represents the view which troubles him
most. It is that morality is indeed a good thing, but
is only good because it secures certain external results;
it is not the 'natural good' (the best thing), but a compromise between a greater good and a greater evil; the
greater good is to obtain the same external rewards
without justice, the greater evil is to suffer the retribution
of injustice. There are three distinct points in Glaucon's
representation of this view. First (358 E to 359 B), he
gives a theory of the origin of justice, explaining the
nature of justice by showing how it arose. Secondly

(359 B to 360 D), he maintains that justice is only pursued by men as a second-best thing, and not naturally but against their real desire; if we dared, he says, we should all be unjust. Thirdly (360 E to 362 C), he argues that in this the general feeling of mankind is reasonable, because if we look at the facts we see that all the advantages of life are on the side of injustice, or at any rate may be if the unjust man is clever. The conclusion is this: it is at any rate a possibility that you might have to choose between, on the one side, all the powers and all the material advantages of life, and on the other side the naked principle of justice. In that case, can you say that justice is the better of the two? And if you do say so, then what do you understand by 'good'?

Adeimantus gives expression to two different beliefs. The first (362 D to 363 E) is one which externally seems the direct opposite of that described by Glaucon, but which really tends to the same practical results. It says, Be just; for justice pays best in this world and the next; on the whole, the just man prospers. It says, Honesty is the best policy, and it says nothing more. It does not add, If you can be immoral with impunity, so much the better. Thus it is widely different from Glaucon's position; and yet, like Glaucon's, it resolves justice into the seeking of external rewards. And therefore it leads, as Adeimantus points out, to the same conclusion, namely that the really valuable thing is the reputation of justice and not justice itself. This, he says, is the view which is inculcated in ordinary education and in family life. The second view he expresses (363 E to 365 A) is this: Justice is in itself the best thing in the world, but injustice is much pleasanter, and, if proper steps be taken, can be made to secure as satisfactory results; for,

E 2

to go to the root of the matter, the gods are not just themselves, but can be bought over with the fruits of injustice. This is the most thorough-going demolition of justice, for it asserts that the divine nature, its fountain-head, can be corrupted.

The passage in which these various beliefs are expressed has a great incidental interest for us from the light that it throws on certain opinions current at that time about religion, political right, and law. First, as we have seen, 358 E to 359 B. Glaucon gives us a popular theory of the nature of justice, explaining it by its historical origin. This is the earliest written statement that we have of a theory which has ever since played a great part in the world, the theory that moral obligations have their origin (whether wholly or in part) in contract (ξυνθήκη)[1]. This theory can be and has been applied in the most opposite interests and in defence of the most opposite positions. As Glaucon states it, and as we here have to deal with it, it is simply this: In the nature of things to do injustice is best, but men have found by experience that they cannot do it with impunity, and the greatest evil is to suffer injustice without power of retaliation. Men have therefore compromised the matter by making laws and institutions which save them from the worst evil, but do not secure them the greatest good.

The conception of an original contract upon which society is based is, emphatically, unhistorical (in some writers, who have used it, it is avowedly fictitious), but it has not the less been influential. It is one of the most striking examples of the reflexion of an idea into the past to give it apparent solidity and concreteness. In this respect it is like the beliefs about a golden age

[1] See Maine's *Ancient Law*.

which reflect into the past an ideal which men carry about with them for the present. Again, it may be compared with beliefs in a future millennium. It is based upon a very important fact, that every civilized community, perhaps any real community, requires, in order that it may exist at all, a mutual recognition of rights on the part of its members, which is a tacit contract. It becomes unhistorical if one goes on to say that at a certain period in the world's history people met together and said, Let us come to an understanding, and make a society on the basis of contract. This has never taken place, but the potency of the idea lies not in the fictitious historical account it gives of the matter, but in the real present truth which it expresses.

As has been remarked, this idea has been used in the most diverse interests. It was applied by Hobbes to justify absolute monarchy, and by Rousseau to prove the absolute authority of the will of the people. It is easy to see how it lends itself to such opposite applications. On the one hand it may be said, Members of a civilized community have contracted themselves out of certain original rights, and the existence of the community depends on the maintenance of that contract; therefore a strong government, or at any rate the maintenance of some government, is necessary, and nothing can be allowed to violate existing law. On the other hand it may equally well be said, The present government depends only on tacit contract, and the people who entered into this contract are at liberty to dissolve it whenever they think fit. As Glaucon here applies it, the theory is used destructively and in a revolutionary interest, to show that justice is a matter of contract and convention *only*; and there is further a most important implication that all convention, and therefore all law, is a sort of artificial violence done to human nature.

The antithesis of nature (φύσις) and law or convention [1] (νόμος), which thus lies at the root of Glaucon's argument, is one which was widely current in Plato's time [2]. Like many other antitheses, it has different meanings in different people's mouths, and it generally owes its effectiveness to the fact of having no definite meaning but confusing different views. We first hear of it in the history of philosophy as applied to physical nature. Democritus distinguished the real constitution of the physical world from those secondary qualities which plainly are relative to human sensation ('hot' and 'cold,' 'sweet' and 'bitter,' and the like), saying that the former existed φύσει and the latter νόμῳ. And in the various uses of the antithesis we can generally trace a contrast between that which is radical and underived and that which is acquired, or between that which is permanent and universal and that which changes with circumstances. But no word is more ambiguous than nature; and in applying the formula to human action and feeling, some theorists have held that what is 'natural' in man is what he has most in common with the rest of the animal world; some, at the opposite extreme, think (as Plato and Aristotle emphatically did) that human nature is properly that in man which most distinguishes him from the rest of the animal world, the 'differentia' of man, not his 'genus.'

In one sense everything that man does is natural to him, law, morality, science, as much as anything else;

---

[1] The word νόμος combines the senses of 'law' and 'convention.'

[2] Cf. *Gorgias*, 482 E sqq., 492 A–C, *Theaet.* 172 B, *Laws*, X. 888 E to 890 A. Cf. also Aristotle, *Eth. Nic.* I. iii. 2 and V. vii. 2.

his nature is all that he does. When this antithesis between law and nature is made, the antithesis is, so to say, within man. What then, it may be asked, remembering all the time that· we are within human nature, is the ground upon which certain products of human nature are distinguished as natural, and others as conventional? In the antithesis as it is here used 'conventional' appears to stand for that which depends for its existence upon certain mutual understandings which society necessarily employs. Now, to speak of these as conventional is to recognize the truth that the existence of society does in the last resort depend on a mutual understanding ; all the institutions of the state and of society are forms of mutual understanding, and, as they are emphatically creations of man, there is no reason why he should not dispense with them if he wished. If the theory of contract is understood in this sense, it is not profitable to dismiss it by saying it is unhistorical. That does not invalidate the fact, for it is a fact, that society is based upon contract. And we may go on to say with equal truth that the existence of society implies that the individual members of it agree to sacrifice a part of their individuality, or to sacrifice a part of their rights, if we call what a man *can* do his rights. Two people cannot live and work together without surrendering something which they would do if separate, for joint action is not the same as separate action. But is there any point in representing the results of this mutual understanding not only as conventional but as *merely* conventional, contrasting them with something natural which has a deeper authority? What is this something natural ? What would man be naturally, in this sense of the word? The only answer to the question is that he would be himself *minus* everything that he is by convention, and that means *minus* everything in him which the existence of society implies. Such a 'natural' man does not exist, but that is the way in which we should have to think of him.

It appears, then, that while we may, in a true sense, describe laws and institutions as 'conventional,' it does not follow that they are therefore, in any true sense, contrary to 'nature'; and that there is all the difference in the world between saying that the institutions of society are based on compact, and saying that therefore they are unnatural or merely conventional. How is it, then, that the antithesis between natural and conventional is so common and has such a strong hold on us, and what do we mean by 'conventional' when we use the word, as we commonly do, with a bad signification? When we say an institution or custom is merely conventional, what we really mean is that it has no right to exist, because it has ceased to have the use which it once had. A law which has ceased to have any justification for its existence is the best instance of what people have in mind when they employ this antithesis. And the reason why there are endless debates as to what is merely conventional and what is not, is simply that people have very different ideas as to when the real occasion for a law or custom or institution has ceased to exist.

While then Glaucon's theory, by which justice is set down as a something conventional and contrary to nature, contains the great truth that laws and customs would not exist but for a mutual understanding, it ignores the significance of this mutual understanding. For not only is this understanding the work of man, it is what man in society has deliberately judged to be best.

How has this deliberate judgment come to be passed? If it were true that to commit injustice with impunity is the real nature of man, there would have been no force to create society. The strongest motives are those which impel to action; and it would be impossible to account for the existence of society at all, if injustice had a special claim to be called the natural tendency of human action.

Glaucon, in the second place, goes on to contend that, 359 B to as a matter of fact, justice is always observed unwillingly; 360 D. that is to say, that morality, public and private, is only maintained by force. Here again a very real and important fact is made the basis of a very false theory. The existence of society does imply force, which is exercised in various ways. In every civilized community the established order of things is ultimately backed by the force of the police and the army. There are a certain number of people who can only be kept from injuring society by force, and the law of the land can only exist if there is physical force in the background. But it is quite another thing to say that force and the fear of force, in that sense of the word, is what maintains morality in the community; and it would be easy to show that, if the morality of a community really depended on force and on fear in the usual sense, it could not possibly continue to exist. You may, however, use ' force' in a quite general sense to include not only the police and army but the force of public opinion, the force of principles, ideas, conscience, and so on. These agencies are rightly called forces. They make themselves felt in very different ways in different individual cases; the force of society acts on a criminal by physical compulsion, and acts in quite a different way on a well-conducted citizen. But in these very various ways there

is great force acting upon the component elements of
society; and that is the truth at the basis of Glaucon's
argument here.   What is untrue is that society, in obeying its own laws, is acting against its own will.   As soon
as society begins to obey its laws unwillingly, their
abolition is only a question of time.   The most thorough-
going despotism in the world never existed on a basis
of mere force.   If it be said that everybody would break
the laws if he dared, the answer is that if that were true,
everybody would dare; there would be no force sufficient
to frighten him from it.   This does not in the least
exclude the fact that a large number of the members
of society do obey the law from fear, and that a large
number do not obey it at all.

360 E. to
362 C.    To complete his theory Glaucon, in the third place,
undertakes to show that this inward protest of the
members of society against the supposed compulsion
exercised by law is a natural and justifiable feeling,
because the advantages of life are all on the side of
injustice.   There is no impossibility, he argues, in
imagining all the advantages of life to be secured by
the mere appearance of justice without the reality;
while the reality of justice might well exist without
a single element of good fortune.   This supposition is
put by Glaucon in a very violent way in order to press
home the question, If there is such a possibility as this
in life, in what does the real advantage of justice
consist?   It may be said that what he describes is not
altogether possible; the appearances and the reality
of justice cannot be kept separate throughout every
part of life; the consistently unjust man must somewhere drop the appearance of justice, and the man who
consistently maintains the appearance cannot always

escape the reality. But even if the picture is overdrawn, it brings out a very real difficulty, a difficulty which we cannot get away from so long as we measure the advantage of moral goodness by anything other than itself. As a matter of fact, the world is so ordered that there is no necessary correspondence between moral good and the material elements of prosperity; and so long as people expect to see such a correspondence, so long as they regard material prosperity as the proper result of goodness, they will be perpetually liable to have their theory of the world upset by facts.

In this passage and in several others, especially in the *Gorgias*[1], where the true philosopher is represented as standing in solitary antagonism to the world, we can distinctly see the impression which the death of Socrates left on Plato's mind. We find in such passages something approaching to the contrast between the kingdom of God and the kingdom of the world, with which Christianity has made us so familiar. It is true that in the New Testament the antagonism between spiritual and non-spiritual powers is closely associated, though not identified, with the antagonism between the poor and the rich, while of this latter antagonism there is no trace in Greek philosophy. But the idea of ranging all the powers that be, and all the external goods of life, on one side, and the naked principle of right on the other, is the same in Greek philosophy and in the New Testament.

We now pass to Adeimantus. The first view that he 362 D to represents contradicts expressly that which is represented 363 E. by Glaucon, but it brings out more clearly the same point that Glaucon had made, namely that the preachers

[1] See especially *Gorgias*, 521 B sqq.

of morality have always in one way or another confused it with its material results, though immoral consequences do not always follow from this teaching. Glaucon ends by showing that it is quite a possible supposition that the just should be miserable and the unjust happy; Adeimantus' first position may be briefly stated thus: justice secures happiness; therefore it should be pursued. This, he says, is the view of parents and of teachers generally. A certain prosperity, separable from goodness itself, is alleged to be the natural concomitant of goodness. Such a view is a natural distortion of a feeling in human nature that justice should have its reward. There is a kind of instinctive demand in the human mind that there should be some reward for good living, that life should be reasonable, that it should approve itself to us as just. The idea that God blesses the just man is expressed in all early literature, and notably in the Old Testament. It has nothing in it prejudicial to high morality, till in later times the principle that men are in some way better for virtue, is interpreted to mean that good men have a right to material prosperity, and material success thus comes to be made the criterion of goodness. In early times the idea is merely the readiest way of expressing belief in the righteous government of the world, but as a reasoned theory of later times it provokes the retort that good men do not always prosper. The ordinary facts of life are appealed to with opposite motives. 'Never yet saw I the righteous forsaken, nor his seed begging their bread'; the wicked 'have children at their desire and leave the rest of their substance for their babes'; each of these is an appeal to experiences which do happen, and the one appeal provokes the other. People who seek for a justification of their moral belief in observations of this kind, and are distressed if they cannot find it, commit the fallacy of resolving what is good in one sense into what is good in another; they start with a wrong expectation as to the consequences of morality. If a man complains that goodness often does not bring prosperity, there is an obvious reply: If you believe that what you understand by prosperity is the real motive and end of life, then live for it; if you do not, then why expect that it should have any connexion with morality?

This general idea of morality as connected with reward is extended by Adeimantus into a future life. The Eleusinian Mysteries have, he says, been agencies in increasing the expectation of reward in a future life for goodness in this life, and—for this is the point of the passage—this expectation of reward is made the motive of a good life. There is a great difference between saying that the soul is immortal and that it is better for it always to be good, which is the burden of the *Republic*, and saying that certain moral actions should be done for the sake of obtaining certain other desirable things.

The second view to which Adeimantus gives utterance 363 E to is the natural counterpart of the first. It is one that is 365 A. in vogue in private conversation, but poets and prose-writers may also be found expressing it. It dwells on the hardship and troublesomeness of the path of justice, and on the readiness of the gods to prosper the wicked and neglect the good. What the poets sometimes say of the indifference of the gods to justice in this life is reinforced by prophets and dealers in Mysteries. These teach expressly that sacrifices and prayers and ceremonies of initiation win the favour of the gods, for this life and the next, better than justice does. The complaint of the poets and the teaching of these prophets follow naturally from the tendency to identify goodness with material prosperity, or to make material prosperity the criterion of real success in life. There are abundant expressions in Greek literature of this belief in the injustice of Providence[1].

In the references which Adeimantus makes to the Mysteries there are two kinds of Mysteries to be distinguished. We are told first (363 C) that Musaeus and his son Eumolpus teach men to expect rewards and punishments of a gross sort in a future life. This must refer to the Eleusinian Mysteries, which were supposed to have been founded by Eumolpus. The complaint Adeimantus makes of them is simply that they encouraged a belief in rewards and punishments which tended to weaken belief in the intrinsic worth of moral goodness. Further on (364 B to 365 A) he speaks no longer of the state-recognized Mysteries, but of private mystery-mongers, who were not regular priests attached to particular places or perhaps to particular gods, but men who wandered about the country, professing to be able by spells and invocations to exercise an influence on the gods and to obtain dispensations for sin. The Mysteries they conducted were associated with the names of heroes, generally with that of Orpheus. Against them Adeimantus has a further complaint ; they encouraged the idea that the consequences of crime could be averted by some trifling payment or sacrifice[2].

Both these kinds of rites were known as μυστήρια or τέλη. The former word signifies that they involved

---

[1] Cf. Eurip. *Electra*, 583 and Fr. 293 ; Theognis (Bergk), 373 sq., with 743 sq. and elsewhere ; and the Melian dialogue in Thucydides.

[2] See *Laws*, X. 909 A sqq. and XI. 932 E sq.

secrecy[1], and were confined to initiated persons. The practice of excluding certain classes of persons from religious rites was originally widespread, and not confined to what were expressly called 'Mysteries.' Most of the gods appear at some time to have had some sort of Mysteries connected with their worship. The word τέλη is sometimes thought to refer to the payment that had to be made at the time of initiation, but it came at last to bear a reference to a sort of religious perfection or consummation[2]. These rites have left their stamp upon language in the words, bearing now a much wider sense, 'mystery' and 'initiation.'

It is generally agreed now that there was no preaching or teaching connected with the Mysteries. The Eleusinian Mysteries were religious pageants, in which Demeter and Dionysus formed the principal subjects for representation. The two main ideas which these pageants expressed were that of the earth as the place of the dead, and that of the earth as the womb of life. These were symbolized by Demeter looking for her lost daughter Persephone, and by Persephone's return. Like all symbolism, this depended very much upon the mind of the worshipper for the interpretation put upon it. In Greek literature we find evidence both of very gross and of very exalted views of the Eleusinian Mysteries. The idea which attached to them, that the future of the soul was to dwell for ever with God, was an exalted idea, but it was capable, of course, of perversion ; a passage in Sophocles which expresses it is said to have provoked Diogenes to the question whether an initiated thief was really to be better off in the other

[1] μύειν to shut the lips.
[2] τελεῖσθαι meaning both ' to be perfected ' and ' to be initiated.'

world than a hero like Epaminondas[1]. Like the Eleusinian, the Orphic Mysteries clearly had their higher and
their lower side, the higher interpretation of them expressing the idea that the life of the soul was unending,
and that it expiated in one stage of existence any crimes
it had committed in a previous stage.

There has been much discussion as to the effect of the
Mysteries in inculcating the belief in one God and the
belief in a future state. There is really no ground for
supposing that they had anything to do with the former
belief, but with the latter they had a good deal to do.
They both recognized it and gave a solemn and magnifi-
cent expression to it; and, though there is no evidence
that there was direct teaching or preaching, there is no
doubt that the Mysteries did contribute to intensify and
diffuse brighter views about the future of the soul than
had been held in the early times of Greece. It has
often been noticed that the expectation of rewards after
death for good done in the body is a late idea; the idea
of future punishment appeared earlier and took more
hold on the Greek mind. In Homer the life after death
has very little place; it is at most a negative, bloodless
sort of existence[2]. As men began to think more about
the good and evil in life, and as their views on the
subject became deeper, the fate of the soul for good or
evil not only in life but after death became a subject for

[1] See Plutarch, *Moralia*, p. 21 F, where Soph. Fr. 719 (Dindorf) occurs.
Other passages showing the higher view of the Mysteries (Eleusinian
or Orphic) are Pindar, Fr. 137 (Bergk), the Homeric *Hymn to Demeter*,
478 sq., and Isocrates, *Paneg.* 28; also in Plato himself, *Crat.* 400 C,
*Phaedo*, 62 B and 69 C, and *Laws*, IX. 870 D. Examples of the grosser
view may be found in Aristophanes, *Frogs*, 146 to 163, and *Peace*, 374-5.
[2] The Eleventh Book of the *Odyssey*, where Odysseus visits the spirits
of the departed, is generally supposed to be later than the rest.

consideration ; the interest taken in the idea of a future life was an extension of growing thoughtfulness about this life. In Aeschylus, as in Pindar, we find the idea of punishment for sin after death, but the strong belief in future rewards which we find expressed in Pindar is peculiar to him among the older poets. All the comfortable ideas about death and the future life which grew up in a later time, seem to have received expression in the Eleusinian, and still more in the Orphic, Mysteries.

In the concluding part of his speech Adeimantus 365 A to sums up what is common to the views which he and 367 E. Glaucon have put forward. They all depend upon the one belief that justice and injustice are to be sought or avoided, not for their own sake, but for the sake of something else. He proceeds to put in a vivid way the difficulty in which men like himself and Glaucon find themselves. They see the whole of public opinion arrayed upon the side of this belief ; and, further, the burden of most that they hear is that with skill and by proper devices we may commit injustice, without forfeiting the material rewards of justice. As for the gods, either there are none at all, or, if there are, we only know of them through the poets, and these poets all represent them as open to corruption. In the face of this almost irresistible mass of public opinion what is there to keep a man from injustice except weakness and want of spirit? He can only be saved from it in two ways—by some divine grace or inspiration which gives him an instinctive repulsion from injustice [1], or by his somehow coming to

---

[1] Plato is fond of using the phrases θεία φύσις and θεία μοῖρα or θεία τύχη, to express the idea of some unaccountable influence to which it is due that justice does not perish out of the world entirely. Cf. 368 A and

understand its nature better than it is generally understood now.

The cause of this difficulty is that no one has yet adequately explained what are the intrinsic good and evil which justice and injustice, whether seen or unseen, have in them. This is what Socrates is now called upon to explain, dismissing for the present all consideration of the results to which justice and injustice lead through the impression they produce on others (δόξα)[1].

This brings us to the end of the introductory part of the *Republic*; the constructive part of the work now begins.

VI. 492 A. This is also elsewhere contrasted with ἐπιστήμη, reasoned conviction or knowledge.

[1] δόξα means either what seems to me or what seems to others about me, the impression I receive or the impression I make. Here of course it is the latter.

# IV. THE MAIN ELEMENTS OF SOCIETY
# AND OF HUMAN NATURE
# INDICATED

[*Republic*, II. 367 E to 376 E.]

THE problem, which has been put before Socrates and reiterated again and again, is to show what is the effect of justice or injustice on the soul of the man that has it, or, as we should rather say, on the life of the man, and especially on his inner life. There seems at first sight scarcely any connexion between this question and the answer that he proceeds to give to it. For he begins by passing suddenly to the subject of the genesis of society. To understand the import of this transition is to understand the principle of the whole argument of the *Republic*.

To explain the method of his answer Socrates tells us 367 E to that it will be very difficult to show the effect of justice 369 A. in the inner life of the individual man, and that it will be best not to begin by an analysis of the soul but by looking at human nature where it can be seen on a large scale—'in large letters,' as he puts it—in the broad outlines of the state and of society. Beginning with the outside of human nature where it is easy to read, we are afterwards to try and read it on the inside with these 'large letters' in our mind. In other words, his method is to analyze facts about human nature which are apparent to everybody, and to examine the significance of those facts till he arrives eventually at the inmost principle of human nature of which they are the expression. The whole *Republic* is really an attempt to interpret human nature psychologically; the postulate upon which its method rests is that all the institutions of society, class organization, law, religion, art, and so on, are ultimately products of the human soul, an inner principle of life which works itself out in these outward shapes.

Plato's position is sometimes described by saying he assumes that there is an analogy between the individual and the state, and that the life of the individual is the counterpart of the life of the state; but this is not an adequate description of it. His position is that the life of the state is the life of the men composing it, as manifested in a way comparatively easy to observe. Later on, when he speaks of the justice or courage of the state, he means the justice or courage of the citizens as shown in their public capacity. The 'justice of the state,' then, is the justice of the individuals who compose it. This does not mean that justice in a state manifests itself in exactly the same way as justice in a private individual, but simply that, if there is such a thing as justice, its essential nature is the same, however and wherever it manifests itself, whether in a man's private life or in his public relations. It is true that the virtue of the state is a larger thing than the virtue of individuals; a nation is brave when its army is brave, and the army is a greater and more conspicuous thing than a single person; but the courage of the state as shown in its army is the manifestation, in the public action of certain men, of the same principle that makes men brave in all the relations of business or of private life. We must bear in mind throughout Plato's argument that there is no state apart from the individual men and women who compose it.

We have now to notice a second feature in Plato's 369 A to method; the state is to be looked at in its origin and 376 E. growth. The phrase, 'origin of society,' suggests to us at first the most elementary state of society historically discoverable; but we must put that idea aside, for that is not what interests Plato here. He is not concerned with an historical enquiry, such as how Athens came to be what she was, but with this question: Given the fact of society as it is, what are the conditions which its existence implies, what is it in human nature which makes society exist? The question is not by what stages society has grown up, but how it is that it exists at all. We gather, though he does not tell us, that in what follows he pursues not the historical order of development but the logical order. That is to say, he takes society roughly as it is and begins at what seems its lowest point, at that aspect of society in which it is an organization for the satisfaction of certain physical wants. This may be called the lowest psychological basis of society; for if man had only these wants he would be a fragment of what he actually is. Beginning then with this, Plato asks, regarding man as a creature of these wants, what there is in him to produce society. As he goes on he brings in gradually the higher elements of human nature, until he has made the picture of society complete in its main outlines; and at each stage he asks what, if any,

seems to be the principle of the good life of society at
that stage. By the end of the first section of his argument (376 E) the main constituent elements which go to
make up human life have been put before us. Given
these, we proceed to consider the development and
education of them.

We should have a modern parallel to this method if
a sociologist, taking England as it is, were to set out
from the idea that, since life would not go on at all if its
necessaries were not provided, the life of England rests
ultimately on its industrial organization, and were to
proceed to ask whether there was any principle of good
and bad, right and wrong, discoverable in this industrial
organization. But Plato has embarrassed us by the form
of his enquiry. Instead of putting the question in an
abstract way, he has put it in a picturesque way, asking
us to imagine a society of human beings engaged merely
in the most obviously useful industrial occupations. Thus
he appears to be describing an actual historical beginning,
and as a description of this, the picture he draws is open
to obvious criticisms; for instance, both builders and
shoemakers would be out of place in a really primitive
society. Of course the substance of the picture is taken
direct from Plato's own time. We may call it a *logical*
picture of the origin of society in this sense, that it
illustrates what the existence and maintenance of society
demands, and how those various demands can best be
satisfied, taking those demands in a certain logical order.

First then (369 B to 372 D) Plato sketches, in mere
outline, the elementary conditions of society so far as it
exists for the production of the necessaries of life. His
state is to be one whose function is to satisfy necessary
wants alone (ἀναγκαιοτάτη πόλις), as distinguished from

the unnecessary appetites which the luxurious state
(τρυφῶσα πόλις) aims at satisfying in addition. In this
sketch the fundamental principles of the *Republic*, which
constantly recur later in a developed form, are clearly
seen. What is the general principle which produces
human society? It is want in various forms. Society
depends upon a double fact: the fact that no man is
sufficient for himself (αὐτάρκης), and the complementary
fact that other men want him. While every man is
insufficient for himself, every man has it in him to give
to others what they have not got. This is what we may
call the principle of reciprocity; the limitation of the
individual goes along with the fact that he supplements
the limitations of others. Throughout the *Republic* this
conception is adhered to. The whole growth of society
is one great organization, resting upon this principle, for
the satisfaction of various human wants.

This passage looks at first sight like an elementary
treatise on political economy, but the principle which is
here put before us in its economic form is not to Plato
an economic principle; what economists call the principle
of the division of labour is to him a moral principle.
Nevertheless his first illustration of it is taken from
productive labour. What, he asks, are the conditions
under which production will be most successful? Production will be largest, easiest, and best if the producer
confines himself to one special work, does his own work
as well as he can, and shares the results with others.
Nature has pointed out this principle; for no two men
have been made exactly the same. The very fact of
individuality organizes men for the community; each
man wants others and can contribute something to them.

This principle results in the gradual growth of industrial

society through the specialization of productive functions.
Accordingly we find pastoral industry, agricultural industry, and mechanical industries of various sorts, practised
by distinct classes of producers.  Next we notice, arising
from the same cause, the phenomena of retail trade and
of currency; and along with these an export and an
import trade, which are the application of the same
principle to the state in its relations with other states.
These are the main constituents of an industrial community, or a community regarded as an organization for
producing the necessaries of life.  Where in all this, asks
Socrates, is justice to be found?  Probably, Adeimantus
answers, somewhere in the mutual needs of these people
(371 E).

But the answer thus suggested is not developed till
we have gone a great deal further with the organization
of society.  The mention of justice leads to the question,
how would a community such as we have described live,
confined as it is to the normal and healthy satisfaction of
elementary wants?  Socrates here describes a people living
a life of animal simplicity.  Their life would be little
better, says Glaucon, than that of a city of pigs.  Human
society cannot stop at this elementary point, in a condition of idyllic innocence in which merely these bare
wants are satisfied ; for this life of ideal simplicity devoid
of progress (like the life of the South Sea Islanders
imagined in Tennyson's *Locksley Hall*) excludes the
greater part of the elements which make up human life
as we know it ; it excludes civilization.

Plato therefore proceeds to sketch briefly the elements
of civilization, in a description of the luxurious state
(372 D to 373 E).  He describes the growth of social
refinement, of luxury, and the material appliances of

life ; the growth also, as accessories to this development, of the fine arts, the decorative arts and poetry; and, further, the complication of the conditions of health and the consequent growth of medicine. In this expansion of human nature we have seen added to the necessary wants of man further wants, capable of leading to his highest development, capable, at the same time, of leading to all sorts of extravagance and evil. We have also, as we shall find, got additional elements in human nature to consider. The state as first described exhibited the working of that element which Plato calls 'appetite,' that which seeks the satisfaction of material wants ; in the more developed state we shall see, distinguished from this, what he calls the element of ' spirit ' and what he calls the 'philosophic' element. These two elements in human nature afterwards appear to be the causes of the growth in civilization here pictured. Plato's conception of these two elements in man is only gradually put before us.

The other side to the development of material comfort is, we are told, the rise of war (373 E), for the expansion of human wants beyond bare necessity brings with it the desire of aggression. Plato, however, passes immediately from aggression, which is the origin of war, to defence, which is its justification. The function of the military organization of the state, which he now at once proceeds to consider, is to protect the state against aggression and to assist in maintaining internal order ; for conquest is nowhere recognized by Plato as the true end for which the state should be organized [1]. Having now brought to our notice the necessity for armed force in the state, he has put before us the natural elements which go to

---

[1] Cf. Aristotle, *Pol.* 1333 B, 5 sq.

make up the life of human society as it is. He has done so without distinguishing the good and the bad in them.

In the defence of the community we have clearly a social function of vital importance, and the principle of the specialization of functions will therefore apply still more rigidly here. If, as we have seen, nature has specially adapted people for particular kinds of work, and if it is important for the production of commodities to get the right nature for the right work, much more will it be important for the purpose of guarding the state. This leads Socrates to take up, as the foremost problem that concerns the organization of the state, the question what sort of nature will make what he calls a good 'Guardian' of the state. Clearly it must be a nature good for fighting, a nature possessed of 'spirit' (θυμός or τὸ θυμοειδές), the fighting element in human nature (375 A). This is not merely the instinct of aggression, but rather that which prompts to resistance; it is described as something 'unconquerable,' which makes a man in all things fearless and not to be beaten. But the Guardians must also possess in a high degree an element complementary to this; for if we imagine men entirely consisting of 'spirit' such men would simply tear one another in pieces; a society composed of them could not exist. The complementary element, which is wanted in the Guardians, is an element of attraction instead of repulsion. This is what Plato (375 E sq.) calls the 'philosophic element' (τὸ φιλόσοφον). There is even in the lower animals something which draws them to what they know and are familiar with, and this is an elementary form of the 'philosophic element' in man, which is something in man's nature in virtue of which he is attracted to whatever he recognizes as akin to him. It may be an attraction to human beings, friends, relations or fellows, or it may be not to human beings but to other objects, either beautiful things in nature or art, or truth in science or philosophy. Plato never abandons this way of looking at human affection and at human reason. Philosophy in man is that which draws him to what he recognizes, as the dog instinctively feels at home with those whom he knows. Familiarity, to put it abstractly, is the basis of affection. The real meaning of this passage where the dog is discovered to be philosophic because it likes those it knows, comes out as we read the rest of the book. It is, as is so often the case in Plato, an anticipation of what he says more intelligibly later on. In Book III he speaks of the love of beauty as a sort of recognition by the soul of what is akin to it in the world about it; the soul welcomes (ἀσπάζεται) what is beautiful from a sense of kinship. In Book VI the desire of knowledge and truth is represented as the desire of the soul to unite itself to what is akin to it in the world. Not to go further into these two passages, the point common to them and to the present passage is that the element of the soul which Plato calls the philosophic, is described as consisting in a feeling of attraction to something other than oneself and yet akin to oneself.

From the manner in which these two last elements in human nature are brought in, Plato might be thought to be describing some special form of human nature exhibited only in exceptional persons; but we find as we go on that he is really describing what he takes to be normal human nature, and that every man must have in him something of each of the three elements, the element of appetite, the element of spirit, and the philosophic element.

Thus we have given us the main elements of society without which human life as it is could not go on. It could not go on unless animal wants were satisfied, unless men could protect themselves, and unless men were somehow drawn to one another. The two higher elements in human nature are here deduced from these requirements of society. The process could equally well have been reversed, and it could have been shown that, human nature having these elements in it, the essential features of society necessarily result.

# V. EDUCATION OF RULERS IN EARLY LIFE

[*Republic*, II. 376 c to III. 412 B.]

## 1. INTRODUCTORY.

AFTER this slight introduction of his conception of the main elements in human nature which tend to bring about society, Plato passes rapidly to a discussion of the nurture and education of that nature. He has fixed his attention on one function of the greatest importance in the state, that of defence, and he has told us that those who are to discharge this function must be men in whose nature the two higher elements are strongly developed. His next question accordingly is, how such a character ought to be trained, and he proceeds to consider the education which will fit it most fully for the highest functions in the state. Nature (φύσις) and nurture (τροφή) are the two things which go to make up human character. Neither will do without the other; you cannot create the required nature, but you can by nurture do everything short of that; and without the proper nurture the best nature is as likely to turn out ill as to turn out well.

Plato's general view of education is most forcibly

expressed in Book VII [1]. Its object is there said to be
to turn the eye, which the soul already possesses, to the
light. The principle which Plato conveys by this metaphor is that the whole function of education is not to put
knowledge into the soul, but to bring out the best things
that are latent in the soul, and to do so by directing it
to the right objects. How is this to be done? First,
by surrounding the soul with objects which embody
those ideas and characteristics which are to be developed
in it. The method Plato advocates depends upon the
theory that the human soul is essentially an imitative
thing, that is, that it naturally assimilates itself to its
surroundings. His belief in the overwhelming importance to the soul of the surroundings in which it grows
up is most forcibly put in Book VI, where he represents
the human soul as a living organism, and says that, just
as a plant when sown in the ground develops according
to the soil and the atmosphere it lives in, so it is with
the soul [2]. The soul, he considers, is indestructible, but,
though ill-nurture cannot entirely destroy it, it may very
nearly do so. The problem of education, then, is to give
it the right surroundings. The chief way in which its
surroundings affect it is, Plato thinks, through its tendency
to become like the things it is accustomed to; it is, he
says, impossible to be constantly with a thing you admire
without becoming like it; and so, in the system of
education which he first describes, nothing is said of
direct teaching; the whole system consists in surrounding
the soul with objects like what it is to be, that it may
live in a healthy atmosphere. The first and most
obvious instance of this imitative tendency is the force
with which the example of other men acts upon us;

[1] 518 B sq.                    [2] VI. 491 D.

hence the importance of accustoming the soul to think about great men and to have a worthy conception of the gods it worships. But the same thing is revealed in another aspect when we come to consider the effect of art, for the soul, Plato thinks, assimilates beauty from contemplating it; and a third aspect of the same fact will be found when he deals with the education of science. The soul, then, adapts itself to its environment, and it is all-important what the environment is[1].

The next question for consideration is, What instruments of education did Plato find ready to his hands[2]? He found literature the main instrument. Every Athenian gentleman was brought up on a system of what we should call general culture, studying the standard literature of his country; there might be added to this an elementary knowledge of some art, and the rudiments of the sciences of numbers and figures. Plato also found gymnastics in common practice. These agencies he adopted, and gave them a new and deeper significance. He conceived that in early life the main instruments for bringing out what was best in the soul were, first, literature, beginning with stories for children and going on to poetry; secondly, music in our sense of the word, playing and singing; and thirdly, the plastic arts (as we should call them) in general. All these come under the head of μουσική[3].

In Books II and III Plato deals with education in μουσική. In Books VI and VII he describes a further and more elaborate system of education for later life.

---

[1] Cf. 383 C, 391 E, and 401 A to 403 C, especially 401 D.
[2] See Aristotle, *Politics*, 1337 B sq.
[3] Compare the word ' arts,' which, in addition to its ordinary use, is employed, in such terms as ' Bachelor of Arts,' with special reference to literature.

The education in μουσική would, he conceives, go on till
manhood, that is, to the age of eighteen, when it was to
be succeeded by a special gymnastic training intended
to fit the young citizens for military and other duties
which require a strong and healthy physique. Then was
to come an education in science, leading to philosophy.
The education in μουσική—and this we must remember
in reading these books which deal with it alone—would
be accompanied all along not only by a certain amount
of gymnastic training, but by elementary teaching in
science [1].

The next point to be noticed, though it does not
become apparent till this section of the *Republic* is read
in connexion with Books VI and VII, is that the order
of education is based on a certain theory concerning the
nature of the soul. The soul is reached at different
stages of its growth by different agencies and through
different media. It is affected in the first place through
certain susceptibilities which we should perhaps call
fancy and imagination. The education described in
Books II and III is an education through these, and acts
upon the soul in that stage of growth in which imagination, fancy, and feelings are the strongest things in it.
It is supplemented in Books VI and VII by an education
calculated to act on the soul when reason has begun
to develop and to require training. That which the
training in μουσική ought essentially to produce is love
of what is beautiful (ἔρως τοῦ καλοῦ), love of the beautiful
in whatever form it appears. By the education which
supplements it at a later stage, the soul is to be made
receptive of truth, as before of beauty; the object of
training in the sciences is to make the soul love truth

[1] See Book VII. 533 D and 537 C.

(φιλοσοφεῖν). The ultimate purpose of both kinds of education is to present to the soul the good under various forms, for beauty is the good under a certain form, and so also is truth. 'The good' in Book VI is that supreme source of light of which everything good, everything true, and everything beautiful in the world is the reflexion, and if education could reach its utmost aim it would be in the knowledge of this. The greatest thing a man can learn is to see according to a man's measure the presence of reason and divine intelligence in the world about him. So from its earliest stages education is a method of helping the soul to see the good, but in all kinds of different ways.

The object, then, of early education should be to present to the soul in various imaginative forms the good which it will afterwards come to know in rational forms. Through what forms and in what order is this to be done? With what does education begin? It begins with religion ; that is to say, the good is presented to the soul first in the form of a being who is perfectly good and true; and the purpose of teaching about such a being is that the soul may be as like God as possible[1]. Hence the importance of determining the true nature of God, and of putting it before the minds of children in the simplest and clearest way. Accordingly, Plato's system of education begins with stories of a mythological kind, treating of the divine nature, whose very essence is to be good and true ; stories which, though in a poetical form, are about the same object that is afterwards to be presented to the soul as a study for the reason. Beginning by presenting the gods as beings absolutely good and true, education goes on to present heroic nature, and also

[1] See 383 c, and cf. *Theaet.* 176 A sq.

human nature, in its highest and truest forms. It goes on again to present reason in the guise of beauty, whether beauty of harmony and rhythm, which is the work of music in our sense of the word, or beauty of form, which is the work of the plastic arts. The function of μουσική is to teach the soul to read the sensible world around it; it will attain its end if it teaches the soul to discern and recognize in the worlds of art, of nature, and of human life, the infinitely various forms of the good 'circulating everywhere about it' (402 C).

Throughout the discussion of education and throughout the *Republic*, Plato combines with the exposition of what he himself considers right, a great deal of criticism of existing institutions. The criticism is so constant that people are apt to miss the positive side of the discussion. Plato's views are developed by antagonism. He finds Homer, Hesiod, and other writers read and looked upon with indiscriminate reverence by the Greeks without regard to what is really noble in them, and he naturally begins by criticizing their works. His criticism may often strike us as pedantic, because the Greek poets are not to us what they were to Plato ; we do not look upon them seriously, as the Greeks did [1]; to Plato they are the food upon which the Greek mind is nurtured in youth. Plato himself is aware that in his treatment of poetry he seems to take away a great deal and put nothing in its place. As if in apology for this he tells us (379 A) that his business in this dialogue is not to write poems but to found a state, and that accordingly he is only concerned to lay down general principles for poets to observe. It is a natural result of this that his criticism should to a great extent seem merely negative.

[1] See X. 598 D sq. and 606 E.

The most obvious divisions into which the subject of early education, as Plato treats it, falls, are μουσική (376 E to 403 C) and γυμναστική (403 C to 412 B). Plato at first takes this division in the popular sense, according to which the former is the training of the soul and the latter of the body; but he afterwards corrects this, explaining that both act upon the soul, but by different means and through different elements in the soul. In the section on μουσική he treats first of literature (376 E to 398 B), afterwards of music (398 B to 400 E) and the plastic arts (400 E to 403 C). The treatment of literature resolves itself into that of the matter and that of the form of literature (376 E to 392 C and 392 C to 398 B). Here again the ground of the division does not answer to what we should understand by it. It is not what we should call literary form or style that Plato is interested in when he deals with what he calls λέξις. The prominent question still is, What is the soul to be taught? and it is only because certain forms of literature are calculated to affect the soul in a particular way that the question of form comes to be treated at all.

As regards matter, the primary subject of educational literature is the divine nature as shown in stories of the gods, from which Plato passes to the semi-divine nature represented in the stories of heroes and divine men. Parallel with this division of the subject runs a division according to the moral principles which this literature ought to inculcate, the virtues which Plato conceives should be made the basis of human character. We begin with the two fundamental virtues in which children should be brought up, reverence for parents and brotherly feeling. Then we pass (at the beginning of Book III) to the virtues no longer of the growing child but of the grown man, the two recognized cardinal virtues of courage (ἀνδρεία) and self-control (σωφροσύνη), and a third, added by Plato, truth.

## 2. ΜΟΥΣΙΚΗ: MYTHS AND THE BELIEFS TAUGHT IN LITERATURE.

376 E to
end of
Book II. Plato enters upon the subject of μουσική with the startling assertion that education must begin with what is false. He has in mind two senses in which a thing may be false. All literature and all words are in a sense false if they represent things otherwise than they actually are or have happened; in this sense mythology must be untrue—God can never have acted in the human way in which he is represented as acting in myths, and Plato tells us that the myths are all false (382 D). He purposely abstained from rationalizing the myths, as was customary about that time, and in the *Phae-drus*[1] he expressly rejects this practice as on the whole an unprofitable thing. But no writer ever used myths with greater effect than Plato, for the very reason that he knew what he was about. In the *Timaeus* he says that though he cannot tell us the exact truth about the creation of the world, he will give us an acount of it in picture-language and in a myth made as like the truth as possible[2]. When however he wished to speak most in earnest about the nature of the gods, he spoke not in the language of myth but in that of philosophy. Plato considered all anthropomorphic language about God or the gods as mythological.

But there is another sense of the word false in which

---

[1] 229 D.    [2] *Timaeus*, 29 C.

not all myths are false. That which is false in the sense of being fiction, may be fiction well done or ill done ; it is well done when it embodies a true idea of that which it is intended to represent, and in this sense it is then true. Myths which represented the divine nature as doing things which we know it does not do, would yet, if they represented as nearly as possible what the divine nature really is, be true in this sense. A myth which represented God as doing evil would be false in both senses. Plato, then, would have employed myths, knowing them to be untrue in form, but as expressing substantial truth of idea.

Accordingly (after criticizing certain immoral myths, chiefly those in which gods are represented as undutiful to their parents) Plato lays down certain outlines or principles of the way in which God is to be spoken of (τύποι θεολογίας), which will determine what is a true myth and what is a false myth. These principles occupy the place of what we should call a system of dogma, so far as that place is occupied at all in the thought of any Greek writer. The first is that God is good and the cause of good alone ; the second is that God is true and incapable of change or deceit. These two canons are directed against certain false ideas of the popular religion.

1. When Plato speaks (377 E to 380 C) of the *goodness* of God, the prominent idea is that of beneficence or doing good. We draw a distinction between moral goodness or being good, and active goodness or doing good; to Plato there was no such distinction. He rejects therefore all tales which assert that God dispenses evil to men or injures them. We may find an analogous passage to this in the chapter of Ezekiel where he declaims against

the saying, 'The fathers have eaten sour grapes, and the children's teeth are set on edge.' Against popular opinions of that kind Plato urges the simple logical deduction that, if God is good, he cannot be the cause of anything not good. In the *Timaeus*[1] we are told that God made the world because he is good and, being good, wills that everything should be as like himself as it is possible to be, by being as good as possible. Thus Plato is brought across the old problem of the origin of the world. He admits that the evil things in human life outnumber the good ; whence comes this evil ? He gives one of the commonest solutions of the problem when he tells us we must either say of human misfortunes that they are not the work of God, or that they are not really evils, but punishments for which man is the better. We must not then say that God is the cause of men's misery, and we must not call men miserable (ἄθλιοι) because they receive punishment when they deserve it[2]. This really means that evil, in the sense of misfortune, is not evil if it is looked at in the right way.

The same question is touched upon in various ways in other dialogues[3]. We are told in a number of passages that evil[4] in some sense or other is a necessary ingredient in human life and in this world as it is for man, in the physical as well as in the moral world ; only in the divine nature is evil wholly absent. How are

---

[1] 29 E.

[2] Cf. *Gorgias*, 477 E, and the whole passage of which it forms a part.

[3] See *Theaet.* 176 A ; *Polit.* 269 C sq. and 273 B sq.; *Lysis*, 221 A–C ; *Crat.* 403 E sq. ; *Tim.* 48 A and 86 B sq. ; and especially *Laws*, X. 903 B to 905 D.

[4] The word for evil (πονηρία) covers any kind of defect or blemish, moral or otherwise.

we to regard this necessary element in our life? In the
*Laws* Plato's answer comes to this : We only call things
evil because of our ignorance ; if we saw the whole
of things instead of a little fragment close to ourselves,
we should see that everything works for good. The
conception in the *Republic* of ' the good ' as the cause
of all that is, and as the highest object of knowledge
and that which man is to try to see in the world,
involves the same idea. Understanding the world is
seeing the good that is in it; to see the good in the
world is to see the reason of things. No man can
attain to this, but it is the ideal which is to guide
man's imperfect knowledge. Plato, then, has two
leading convictions on this subject. He holds that
the universe, so far as man has experience of it, is
essentially imperfect, and has evil in it ; there is an
element in the world which resists the action of
reason or the will of God [1]. But equally strongly he
holds that, the more we understand things, the more
we shall see that evil has a reason for it and therefore
is not really evil. He treats these as two ultimate facts,
and he nowhere attempts to reconcile them. It would
be difficult to say whether Plato does or does not
assume a principle of evil in the world co-ordinate
with the principle of good. On the whole the idea
of the beneficent work of divine reason is far the more
prominent in his writings.

2. The second principle laid down (380 D to end of
Book II) is the *truth* of God, and Plato takes this as
meaning two things : first, that God cannot change ; and,
secondly, that God cannot lie. (*a*) Of change, he tells us,
there are two kinds : change from without produced by

---

[1] See *Timaeus*, 48 A and 53 B, and cf. 42 D.

external agents, and change from within by the will of the
person changing.   First then, can we conceive that God
is liable to change owing to external agencies?   Plato
answers by enunciating a characteristic idea of Greek
philosophy, that liability to change imposed from without
is a sign of inherent vice or weakness.   He takes the most
varied instances, living things, the human soul, works of
art, and applies to all the same principle, that in proportion as a thing is good of its kind it is less liable to be
changed by external influences.   God then, being the
best of things, is least liable to this.   We also should
regard being easily affected by outside influences (in
a certain sense) as a sign of inferiority; the stronger
a man is, the less do changes of climate, food, and the
like, affect him, and there is no such sign of inherent
moral force as being able to stand any number of
changes without being affected.   This view contains
the germ of the idea which lies at the root of Stoicism,
that strength or virtue shows itself in the capacity
to remain unchanged by any conceivable circumstances.
As for the question whether God can change himself,
this is answered by the conception of divine perfection.
The only motive to voluntary self-change must be want,
and that motive cannot operate with God, for he is
from the first perfect and wanting nothing [1].

The divine nature, then, is constant and unchanging.
This canon is directed mainly against the polymorphism
of Greek gods, and under it Plato forbids stories,
analogous to ghost stories, by which children were
frightened; all these are in his view a degradation of
the divine being.   A good deal of polytheistic mytho-

---

[1] Cf. Aristotle, *Eth. Nic.* VII. xiv. 8, where change is connected with
πονηρία, imperfection.

logy of the sort that he is speaking of[1] survives in
modern Europe in the byways of popular religion
and superstition. Throughout this passage Plato speaks
of God without hesitation as having form and shape
(using the words μορφή and εἶδος) quite in accordance
with the ordinary language of his day ; and he speaks
indifferently of God and of gods. The principle he
lays down is essentially a monotheistic principle, and
excludes the idea of God having shape at all, since what
has shape is of course liable to change ; but when he is
speaking of education, and of how religious ideas can be
presented to children's minds in an intelligible form, he
does not scruple to use the language of the popular
religion. In the *Phaedrus*[2] he tells us by implication
that though we may think of God as having a body, this
conception of him is due to our imperfect way of thinking,
and is only our fiction about him.

(*b*) Next we come to the question whether God can
lie ; for in answer to what has just been said, it may
be objected that, though the gods do not change, they
may delude us and make us think they do ; they may,
without really changing themselves, appear to us in all
sorts of shapes. This brings us to the consideration of
lying (ψεύδεσθαι) in general. Under this head Plato
includes all modes of producing false impressions, but
in the first place he describes falsehood in a peculiar
sense of the word, a falsehood in which no being, god
or man, would, if he knew it, acquiesce. For ψεύδεσθαι,
besides meaning to make a false statement with intent to
deceive, may mean to be in a state of ψεῦδος (falsehood)

---

[1] 381 E. Cf. *Laws*, XI. 932 E sq., where laws against the pretence of
witchcraft are advocated.
[2] 246 C.

oneself, or to be the victim of an illusion. This is what Plato calls the 'lie in the soul,' which is what we might call self-delusion; and this, he tells us, gods and men equally hate. It seems at first a very strong way of speaking of ignorance. We can best understand it by comparing a passage about ignorance in the *Sophist*[1], where he says there are two forms of mental evil: vice, which he compares to bodily disease, and ignorance, which he compares to bodily deformity (αἶσχος). Ignorance, he says, means that the soul, having an impulse towards the truth, thinks 'beside the mark,' like a man who cannot guide the motions of his limbs as he wishes; and this deformity he also describes as 'want of proportion' (ἀμετρία). So in Book VI of the *Republic* he describes the opposite of this deformity as 'proportion' (ἐμμετρία) of the soul[2]. He thinks of the soul as being either proportioned or disproportioned so as to be well or ill adapted to take hold of truth, just as a hand may be well or ill adapted for taking hold of things. We mean by ignorance simply want of information, and this of course is a part of what Plato means by ignorance; but the radical sense of it with him is something far more important than this; it is being out of harmony with the facts of the world; and we may compare Plato's language about it with the way in which Carlyle constantly speaks of incapacity to recognize the 'fact,' or with the phrase in the second Epistle to the Thessalonians, 'God shall send them strong delusion, that they should believe a lie.' By truth as a quality attributed to human character, Plato means being, so to say, in a true state, a state which answers to the facts or to the order of the world; ignorance, in its deeper sense as the opposite of

---

[1] 228 C sq.    [2] 486 D.

this, is, he tells us, a thing that everybody abhors; for if it were put to any one, 'Do you wish to believe lies?' he would refuse with horror; it is a form of madness, madness being an extreme and permanent form of believing lies.

This sense of 'lying' is only mentioned here to be set aside; God cannot be conceived of as creating illusion in us because he is the victim of illusion himself. Can he then be conceived of as deluding us by telling a lie or by presenting to us deceiving circumstances? We must first ask what circumstances there are under which lying is not detestable. There are cases in which it has a remedial use, like a medicine, as in dealing with mad people; and there is the analogous case of war, in which it is assumed that lying is justifiable. Like every remedy it is in itself an evil, but in such cases it is the lesser of two evils. It is sometimes justifiable also on the ground of ignorance. When we do not know all the truth, we may represent it as nearly as we can, knowing that our representation is partly false. But none of these motives can apply to God; for he has no enemies to fear, and no emergencies like that of dealing with a madman to meet; and he is omniscient. The conclusion is therefore that God is perfectly simple and true both in deed and in word; he neither changes nor deceives. (The spoken lie is here said to be a sort of imitation of the affection of the soul; it is 'an image of later birth.' The phrase may seem to suggest that the man who tells the lie has the 'lie in the soul' first and is himself deluded, but it merely means that the spoken lie is the expression of a previously conceived false thought, not that the liar is ignorant of its falsehood.)

The passage sometimes gives people an uncomfortable

feeling that Plato considers deliberate lying not so bad
as being ignorant, but the question of moral guilt is not
raised at all in the comparison between them.  Plato
simply says that a state of delusion is a state everybody
would naturally hate to be in; he implies that most
people, if they had the choice, would rather tell a lie
than be under some complete delusion about some very
important truth; and he is probably right; how the
two compare in moral worth is a further question, on
which he says nothing[1].  In what he does say as to
the morality of deceiving others, he makes it a question
of motive and of the object to be obtained.  If the good
to be obtained by a falsehood is greater than the harm
done, and is not to be obtained in any other way, then
the lie does not matter.  In accordance with this principle
Plato, later on, justifies the maintenance among the
people of a belief known by the rulers to be false, which
he says will conduce to patriotism among those who are
not enlightened enough to appreciate the real reason for
it[2].  Such passages show us that in one direction at any
rate, where we should see a very great danger in the
mere fact of saying what was untrue, Plato did not see
it.  Nevertheless, whenever he thinks lying justifiable it
is as a compromise, a concession to human weakness.
It implies the presence of an evil which you are too
weak to deal with in any other way.  The point in
which people really differ about this is as to where
the necessity for saying what is not true begins.  The

---

[1] [The conception of the 'lie in the soul' is not returned to, but later
on Plato closely associates immorality and low aims in life with illusion
(see especially IX. 585 E sq.), and it is a fair interpretation of him to say
that to have the 'lie in the soul' in the fullest degree would be to be
completely immoral.—ED.]

[2] See 414 B sq.

greater a man is the less he finds the necessity for lying; the possibility of telling the truth under difficult circumstances is one of the greatest tests of strong character. There can be no doubt that telling the truth was not a national virtue of the Greeks, and though in the passage which shortly follows[1] what Plato says about it is strict and emphatic, we see here that he is more concerned about the being in a state of truth than about the telling of the truth[2]. A connecting link between the idea of truth as being in a true state and that of truthfulness in our sense, may be found in a quality to which Aristotle gives the name of truth[3]. This is not truth-telling in general but being true to yourself in what you say, being what you profess to be and professing to be what you are. Truth in this sense seems to have struck the Greeks as more important than what we call truthfulness. The sense of its importance goes along with the hatred of versatility and of want of personality which comes out so strongly in the *Republic*[4]. We know that some at any rate of the Greek peoples were very much inclined to a sort of aimless versatility; and no doubt it was this fact that led Plato to insist upon this matter so strongly. This too leads him to make it one of the first principles to be observed about the divine

[1] 389 B to D.
[2] [Cf. VI. 485 C, where the philosophic nature is said to be truthful in every way, and a curious motive for truthfulness is given; the philosopher is passionately desirous himself to attain the truth, and lying, it appears, will be odious to him, by a sort of association of ideas, because they remind him of false belief which he wishes himself to be free from.—ED.]
[3] In the list of virtues, *Eth. Nic.* II. vii. 12. When he discusses this quality later, *ibid.* IV. 7, he says it has no name, but the man who possesses it ἐν λόγῳ καὶ ἐν βίῳ ἀληθεύει, τῷ τὴν ἕξιν τοιοῦτος εἶναι.
[4] See especially 394 E sqq.

nature, that it is 'simple and least of all things capable of departing from its own form [1]' (380 D).

At the beginning of Book III we pass from the consideration of God himself, or the gods themselves, to that of the divine nature as it appears fused with human nature; for most of the myths criticized and appealed to are not about the gods, but about semi-divine beings (δαίμονες) and heroes, and the rest are myths in which (as in the story of Zeus and Sarpedon) gods are affected by human emotions with regard to men; we are thus moving in the borderland between gods and men. Incidentally this gives Plato the opportunity both to expound positively what he conceives to be the highest moral nature, and also to criticize negatively the current conceptions about it, suggesting what poets ought to say by examples of what they ought not to say. (This is a double process going on all through the *Republic*, and often the polemical side seems uppermost.) At the same time we pass from the foundation of education, which is to be laid in the feeling of reverence to gods and to parents and in brotherly feeling, to the specific virtues of courage, truthfulness, and self-control. These virtues are to be inculcated by setting before the soul heroic types of them, just as in the preceding passage the more ultimate principles of morality, goodness and unchangeableness, were presented to the soul in stories about the divine nature. Further, whereas in the last part of Book II Plato is speaking mainly of the education of children, in the beginning of Book III it is clearly young men and not children that he has chiefly in mind. It is necessary to look at this part of the *Republic* from all

[1] For further treatment of Plato's attitude towards truth, see Section VI, page 135.

these points of view in order to see the full scope of it. It is partly concerned with a system of education, partly with the exposition of moral principles, partly with criticism.

Courage is treated of first (386 A to 389 B). There are different accounts of the virtues in different parts of the *Republic*, and if we want to form a true estimate of Plato's ideas about any virtue we must put all the passages about it together. So we shall have to return to courage later[1]. Here, as in other cases, we start with the popular Greek conception of courage as meaning fearlessness of death; to the Greek mind (as Aristotle tells us) death is the typically terrible thing (δεινόν), and the bravest man is he who is not afraid to die. Afterwards the conception of courage, while still of course including this, is widened so as to include all holding out against anything terrible, anything from which human nature is wont to shrink. The primary sense of courage leads Plato here to make some remarks about the nature of death and the life of the soul after death. He says that a good man at any rate has no cause to think death terrible. It follows that he will not think it terrible for his friends who are good, and, both for this reason and because of all men the good man is most independent, he will bear the loss of friends better than other men. As for the terrible pictures that are drawn of the world below, though they are poetically effective and stimulate the imagination and the emotions, they are not true and they do no good. It is to be noticed how Plato always associates the truth of a belief with its expediency; he did not think they

---

[1] Cf. IV. 429 A to 430 C, 441 E to 442 C; VI. 486 A sq., 503 B to E; and with the last compare VII. 535 B.

were one and the same thing, but they were connected in his mind [1].

We pass almost imperceptibly from courage, which has been expanded to include not only fearlessness of death for oneself but fearlessness of death for one's friends, to endurance (καρτερία), the passive side of courage ; and here Plato has occasion to criticize the extravagant expressions of grief that appear in Homer, condemning them the more severely since they are put into the mouths of men and even of heroes. Is the picture of a hero rolling on the ground with grief really a worthy example? From endurance in the sense of control of grief we pass to control of excessive feeling in general. Endurance is thus the meeting-point of courage and of temperance or self-control (σωφροσύνη). It is very characteristic of Plato to be perpetually showing, as he does in this passage, points of connexion between things apparently very different ; his conceptions are never at rest in his hands, but are continually passing into one another. Throughout the treatment of these virtues we find the characteristic Greek idea that excess, whether in grief, or in laughter, or in appetite, or in any passion or emotion, is intrinsically bad. We have to remember that dignity was not a strong point of Greek character. The Greeks, or some sections of the Greek race, were very liable to violent emotions ; and hence it was that the Greek moral philosophers insisted on control of emotion as they did. The Greeks had a sort of natural want of self-respect and a tendency to forget themselves, which particularly struck the Romans as unworthy. If we do not bear this in mind, the treatment of grief in this passage will appear hard and stoical, and the mention of laughter absurd. The basis of Plato's view is not that it is bad to feel, but that excess of emotion reacts upon the character and weakens it [1].

Between the passages on courage and on self-control comes a short passage on truthfulness (389 B to D). This is here considered as a part of obedience, and in reference to recognition of authority in general. It is assumed that lying is hateful in itself unless justified by circumstances, and the circumstances which justify lying can only, Plato says, apply to persons in authority. A doctor may deceive his patient for his patient's benefit, and the rulers may deceive for the public good. To all others truthfulness is a principle without exception. For the citizen to tell a lie to those in authority is like a man's telling a lie to his doctor.

This leads up to self-control or temperance ($\sigma\omega\phi\rho\sigma\sigma\dot{\upsilon}\nu\eta$) [2], the essence of which is obedience to authority, whether to a ruler, or to the higher self within oneself (389 D to 392 A). Plato treats of self-control, first as obedience to persons in authority, secondly as the control of the appetites (and especially as to the restraint of lust and of avarice, which latter is constantly associated with bodily appetites in the *Republic*), thirdly as the control of wanton-

---

[1] Cf. X. 604 A sq., especially 604 C.

[2] [Cf. IV. 430 E to 432 A and 442 C. 'Temperance' is the word generally used in translations. 'Self-control' covers the ground better, but its defect as a translation is that it suggests effort and constraint, whereas a man is not $\sigma\dot{\omega}\phi\rho\omega\nu$ in Plato's or in Aristotle's sense, unless his mastery of his passions and impulses is so easy and assured that there is no sense of constraint about it. Aristotle expressly contrasts $\sigma\omega\phi\rho\sigma\sigma\dot{\upsilon}\nu\eta$ with $\dot{\epsilon}\gamma\kappa\rho\dot{\alpha}\tau\epsilon\iota\alpha$, the forcible restraint of oneself; and in *Rep.* IV. 430 E to 432 A the same distinction is implied ($\sigma\omega\phi\rho\sigma\sigma\dot{\upsilon}\nu\eta$ being the 'harmony' and 'agreement' of the different elements in the soul). In addition to the senses of $\sigma\omega\phi\rho\sigma\sigma\dot{\upsilon}\nu\eta$ mentioned above, one of its commonest senses in Greek is that of sanity. $\Sigma\dot{\omega}\phi\rho\omega\nu$ was also used, almost as a party name, to describe the upholders of aristocracy or of a very much limited democracy.—ED.]

ness, insolence, or pride (ὕβρις), which is illustrated by the stories of Achilles. The meaning of σωφροσύνη is best understood by its opposite, ὕβρις, which is the general spirit of setting oneself up against what is higher than oneself, whether by insubordination to constituted authority and divine law, or by the rebellion of the appetites against the law of reason. Thus this quality in some degree includes what we call humility. It is often said that the virtue of humility is not recognized in the Greek moral code, but the man who was σώφρων in regard to the gods would be the humble man, and the ὑβριστικός is the 'proud man' in the language of the Bible. The misrepresentations of the divine and heroic nature which are incidentally criticized throughout this passage are peculiarly Greek, and could easily be compared and contrasted with the misrepresentations of the divine nature which are criticized by the Hebrew prophets. The human weaknesses which the Jews attributed to their God are very different from those that appear here. The most notable are jealousy and anger, resulting in unjust revenge and the like ; as the essence of the divine nature in the Old Testament is righteousness or justice, so the human weakness attributed to God is injustice.

Now that we have laid down certain principles as to the true nature of gods, demi-gods, and the world after death, it would remain, Plato says (392 A to C), to lay down principles as to human nature and how it should be represented in literature if it is not to be falsified. As in regard to the divine nature there are principles by the violation of which tales about the gods are made false in the most serious sense, so, as to human nature and human life, there are certain true principles which popular literature and popular ideas commonly violate. We are constantly told that the unjust are happy and the just miserable, and this goes to the root of our beliefs about human life. Is it true? This question cannot be answered yet, he tells us; because it is really the question which the *Republic* as a whole is designed to answer. If we eventually find that this is not the true view of human life, that justice is not really loss and injustice not really gain, then, looking back at this question, we shall be able to say that these popular representations of human life are misrepresentations. At present we can only say it by anticipation.


### 3. ΜΟΥΣΙΚΗ: THE ART OF LITERATURE.

Plato has so far considered the matter of literature, or the question what things are to be said. The next question he asks is, how these things are to be said (λέξις), or, What is to be the form of literature? In the transition to this question we really pass to the consideration of Art, for the principles which Plato lays down about literature are carried on in his treatment of the whole of the rest of μουσική. It is a fair interpretation of his procedure to say that, regarding education as a gradual nourishment of the soul in its various stages, he passes here to a stage in which the artistic sense is distinctly developed, and therefore has to be educated rightly or wrongly. As long as education is confined either to teaching young children or to inculcating definite and simple moral qualities, the artistic sense is not called into play, and it scarcely matters in what form you represent truth. But at a certain stage this question does become important, because the soul that is being educated becomes susceptible to artistic form proper. From this point onwards the discussion

392 c to 398 b.

of μουσική has to do with this stage in the soul's growth; throughout the question of form, whether in literature or music or the plastic arts, is the principal one considered, and the susceptibility to form is being taken account of as the chief thing requiring nurture for the present.

We begin with the treatment of form in literature. First, the idea of imitation (μίμησις) is explained in its application to literature (392 C to 394 C). Then the educational requirements of a literature, which should really develop the sort of character which is worth developing, are explained (394 C to 396 B). Next, the good and bad in literature are distinguished in the light of the results thus attained (396 B to 397 C). Lastly, a judgment is passed on poetry (397 C to 398 B). It is above all necessary to realize first what is the question that Plato has in his mind. The first impression made is that he is discussing a purely literary or aesthetic question, and we naturally suppose that he will try to make out what form of poetry—epic, lyric, dramatic, &c.— is best for education. But he does not do this at all; the answer to the question, What is good poetry? is given in terms of ethical not of literary criticism. The question of form in literature becomes the question, Are the men whom we are training to be imitative (μιμητικοί), and, if so, imitative of what?

First, then, we must consider Plato's conception of imitation. The word μίμησις is used in the *Republic* in two ways, in a general and in a specific sense. In its more general sense we have already seen it applied to literature ; poets were blamed for making bad copies of the gods [1], and the use of myths was said to be that

[1] 377 E and 388 C.

they should give representations of gods and heroes which were as far as possible like them.  In this more general sense of the word 'imitation,' how does poetry imitate? One must dismiss from one's mind here the question whether a poet or artist imitates nature, or whether he originates or creates.  When Plato talks of the poet as imitating, in this general sense of the word, he is merely thinking of the fact that the poet represents things, that words are to the poet, what colour is to the painter, a medium through which he represents certain objects or events.  The use of the word 'imitation' in this wide sense was familiar to the Greeks, and its import was to put the function of the poet alongside that of other artists. 'Representation' is the best word for μίμησις in this sense.

It is important here again to remember that Plato regards the human soul as essentially an imitative thing, a thing which naturally and instinctively makes itself like to its surroundings.  When we read books or see plays or hear stories, if we are interested we do to a certain extent make ourselves like the characters in whom we are interested.  Accordingly, when Plato is talking of imitation we must think of the audience quite as much as of the dramatic poet or actor ; the spectator enters into the situation and, so far as he does so, is an imitator (μιμητής).  If this were not so in Plato's view, literature would not have such enormous importance in his eyes. Men are naturally imitative (μιμητικοί), and literature is one of the things that call out this tendency.  Now all imitation tends to become the real thing ; by simu- lating a thing one catches something of the reality ; one imitates the thing one is interested in, and one gradually becomes the thing one imitates.  With this conception of the effect of literature in his mind, Plato now asks what is the best literature for drawing out what is best in human nature ; and that is the ultimate question before him throughout this discussion.

The discussion, however, is first raised with regard to the value of literature which is imitative in a specific sense ; for while all literature is imitative, one kind of literature differs from another in manner and degree of imitation, that is to say, in the extent to which it brings before us the actual circumstances described, or, as we should now say, in the degree to which it is realistic. Here accordingly ' imitation' is used not in the generic sense, but in an emphatic sense to describe that sort of literature which imitates most, or is most realistic. The poet, Plato says, either employs narrative, that is, simply tells the story, or he employs imitation, or he does both. By imitation he here means impersonation —the poet puts himself as much as he can into the actual position of the person described. The drama is the form of literature in which this is done throughout ; epic poetry employs both kinds of writing ; certain sorts of choric and lyric poetry employ only narrative.

We must not suppose that, because this distinction answers to a distinction of literary form, Plato rests what he has got to say on grounds of literary form. Having distinguished these three kinds of literature, he at once tells us that the question is not (at present, at any rate [1]) whether we are to have the drama, but whether the men who are eventually to be guardians of the state are to be imitators. Now if the question in his mind were confined to mere forms of literature, this would mean that he was going to consider whether they should be actors

---

[1] Notice the phrase used in this connexion, ' we must go whithersoever the argument, like a wind, bears us ' (394 D).

or not; but what he actually discusses is not so much whether they are to be imitative as of what they are to be imitative; what characters they are to impersonate— with what characters, that is, they are, so far as imagination enables them, to identify themselves[1]. So the real question in his mind is not, as he first makes it appear, whether the right form of literature is dramatic or epic or lyric (that is quite a subordinate matter, and in the conclusion of the argument here nothing is decided about it), but what sort of human nature is worth imitating in literature. And that means (for we are here using imitation in the narrower sense), What sort of human nature ought to be most realistically represented, or embodied in that particular way which most stimulates imagination? Ought the poet, he asks, to represent as realistically as he can, with all the force of his genius, anything and everything that can be made impressive and exciting, or ought the poet, regarded as the servant of the state, to make a selection and throw all his force into representing realistically what is great and good in human nature? To Plato there can be only one answer. Only that in human nature which is worth making part of one's own character is worth artistic imitation of this intense or realistic kind. If the type of the greatest man was the man who could put himself indiscriminately into the greatest number of situations or characters, then the greatest poet would also be such a man. But human nature, Plato tells us, is so cut up into little bits that one man can neither imitate nor practise well more than one sort of life. Since, then, what a man imitates settles into a sort of second nature with him, he must discriminate in what he imitates. The good writer will only

---

[1] This is clear in 395 C sq.

lose his own personality in some other worthy of himself; and what applies to the writer applies also to the spectator or the reader.

This being the real question at issue, Plato gives no explicit answer to the question of the best form of literature. He has left it an entirely open question how the great poet is to fulfil the demands here made of him ; he has, he says, only to lay down outlines for the guidance of the poet. He demands of poets first that they shall be, in a sense, servants of the community ; for otherwise there is no place for them in the community. He then says to them, You are men with the genius to represent life in a vivid way, in a way that stimulates imagination ; exercise this faculty upon those things which are really worth imitating. He believes that men are extremely susceptible to the influence of literature, and that its power to affect character is very great. Accordingly, he says, not that good literature is that which moralizes (in our depreciatory sense of the word), but that it is that which represents human nature in such a way as to stimulate what is best in man. There are two sorts of poets, he says. The bad poet, though he may be a man of great genius, will throw himself into any and every character, and will thereby become extremely popular, especially with children and slaves. The poet with a proper sense of what is suitable (μέτριος ἀνήρ, 396 C), when he has to treat of the actions or speeches of 'good men' (a phrase which meant something more with the Greeks than it does with us), will throw himself as much as possible into them and will represent them dramatically ; when he meets with the weaknesses, imperfections, and failures of a great character he will give them less space ; and upon quite unworthy characters and objects—on

madness or disease, for example, or on any condition in
which man falls conspicuously below himself—he will
spend himself least of all, 'unless it be in a humorous
way' (this qualification leaves a considerable door of
escape open, and gives a place for comedy). As to what
form of literature would best answer these requirements
no clue is given us ; that is left to the poet.

Plato is writing with direct reference to certain contemporary facts and to contemporary poets, though we
have not the key to his allusions. Probably all the
instances that he takes of the abuse of imitative literature
were innovations that had come in during his time. He
describes certain new tendencies in tragedy (395 D sq.) ;
probably scores of dramatists were altering the character
of tragedy in the same direction as Euripides, but with
much less power [1]. As to comedy (396 A sq.), he refers to
horseplay on the stage, and to certain, then novel, ways of
producing broad effects, which struck him, let us say, as a
coach and horses on the stage might strike a modern critic.
The passage about imitating the neighing of horses, the
bellowing of bulls, and so on probably refers to some form
of dithyrambic poetry, perhaps parallel to the modern
pantomime [2]. From these passages, and from Book X,
and from many similar passages in the *Laws*, it is clear
that Plato felt strongly that Greek literature and music
were declining ; literature, he thought, was becoming a
mere provider of stimulants to a rather morbid imagination. The kind of aimless variation and want of principle
which he describes in contemporary art, is the counter-

[1] [Nettleship here apparently referred to Arist. *Poetics*, 1460 B, 34 sq.,
where Sophocles is reported to have said that he represented men as they
should be and that Euripides represented them as they actually were.]
[2] Cf. *Laws*, II. 669 C sq., and Aristophanes, *Plutus*, 290.

part of what, in regard to the more serious matters of life, he describes in the character of the democratic man [1].

Plato's principle is a more serious principle than most people care to apply to literature, and his attitude strikes us as austere and despotic, not only because of the limitations of his view, but still more because he takes the matter more gravely than we do. If we would really put ourselves in an analogous position to Plato's, we must not think only of drama or of romance, but of religious literature, the Bible and all that takes its start from the Bible. We shall then recognize the sort of problem which Plato has before him in this discussion of literature. And if we do take literature in a serious sense, and see in it the greatest educational power in society, the question how it should be employed becomes one which must be put, in considering how society could be made fundamentally better. But to understand not merely the serious spirit in which Plato regards literature but his earnestness about the particular points to which he directs attention, we must further remember the inherent tendency of many Greek peoples to be 'imitative men,' always posing instead of being themselves.

If we take the bare principle which Plato lays down, there is nothing in it hostile to any great literature or art (though any high and exacting standard may be said to be hostile to literature and art at their ordinary level), nor is there any reason why Plato's requirements should limit the genius of the great poet. In what particular way literature may be made to conform to the principle is another question, and one so difficult that, with the exception of certain religious bodies, no state or society

[1] VIII. 561 c to e.

has tried to find a practical answer to it. But the great poets of the world have on the whole, except in comedy, dealt with what is great in human nature. They have of course differed in their conceptions of what is the great and the really beautiful in human nature; and there never can be one definite and final answer to the question in what way this principle can be best applied. In one respect most thoughtful people now would dis-agree with the spirit in which Plato seems to apply his own principle; and in one respect the modern mind, in its highest view of art, differs widely from the Greek mind; it is, that on the whole it looks for what is great and what is beautiful over a much wider range. But, *mutatis mutandis*, there is just the same question in the minds of men now as to the limits in art between the great and the small, the beautiful and the ugly. We should think it absurd for the state, certainly for the British Parliament, to lay down canons of art, but that does not prevent us from having canons. The great artists of the world have, though of course without telling us their theory or perhaps formulating it at all to themselves, recognized such canons, and as to those canons we can see that there has been substantial agree-ment among them. In one point, and that the main point, they have acted upon Plato's principle; all the great artists and poets are ideal; that which interests them most is something above the *ordinary* level of human life. On the other hand, in one way, no poet has ever come up to Plato's requirements, for none has ever deliberately set himself to be the educator of the society he lived in. Yet if we take a very great poet like Dante, however little he may himself have contemplated the effect he produced, there can be no doubt of the strength of his influence in forming the mind of generations after him.

## 4. ΜΟΥΣΙΚΗ : MUSIC AND THE ARTS GENERALLY.

398 c to 403 c.    Winding up his treatment of literature by describing how the great dramatic genius, who can imitate everything, will be bowed out of the reformed state, Plato goes on to deal with music proper upon the same principle that he has applied to literature, namely, that it must be criticized, and approved or condemned, as an influence for good or evil upon character.

What is the ground for this principle—for we here pass to something different from the direct representation of human action and character which has so far been under consideration? It is that music and every art expresses character (ἦθος[1]) in the soul of the man who produces it, and in the soul of the man to whom it appeals.  One art differs from another in the medium that it uses, but in all there is character, good or bad (εὐήθεια or κακοήθεια). No art, therefore, can help being educational; it affects character because it expresses character.  This is a general principle which can still be held without committing us to saying in what particular way music or any art affects character.  You cannot put music into words, or pictures into words, and the attempt to do so has even been harmful ; each art uses its own medium, and has its own laws ; all we can say is that in all the forms of art soul speaks to soul ; each art has its own form of sense, and through sense soul comes in contact with soul.

In his treatment of music (398 C to 400 E), Plato must have seemed even to his contemporaries still more

---

[1] 400 E.  Ἦθος does not mean ' a moral,' it means character.

conservative and puritanical than in his treatment of literature. He not only requires the musician to recognize that he has a work to do in the state; he says definitely which of the ' modes ' or ' harmonies ' of Greek music are to be allowed (namely, the Dorian and the Phrygian), and forbids the use of any others; among musical instruments he allows only the lyre and the cithara, and (for herdsmen in the country) the Pan-pipes (σύριγξ), forbidding the use of all instruments upon which more complex effects could be produced, and of the flute; he limits rhythm, though not so definitely, to a few simple forms, rhythms which will be suitable to an orderly and brave man; and finally he insists that music is to be subordinate to the words it accompanies, that rhythm and harmony must be adapted to the words and not the words to them. As he remarks, we have now begun the purgation of the 'luxurious city,' eliminating all those elements of civilization which are not really valuable, but are simple luxuries [1].

It is not difficult to see the leading idea which runs through all Plato's criticisms of the music and of the artistic and literary work of his time. It is that of simplicity as opposed to complexity. There is a right and a wrong sense in which it may be said that art should be simple. Plato's objections to mere indiscriminate imitation of human life arise from the feeling that such indiscriminateness implies that no principle of good or bad in human life is recognized; his saying that men ought to be simple, not multiform [2], is the expression of his demand that some principle should be recog-

---

[1] For more detailed treatment of the passage on music see note at end of this subsection.

[2] 397 ε (with reference to music).

nized. So when he comes to music, he objects to those kinds of music which involve every variety of rhythm, scale and the like, evidently seeing in them the same vice which produces in literature the indiscriminate imitation of anything interesting (397 B, C). In this Plato has probably confused two ideas of simplicity. In one sense every great work of art is simple ; it is the working out, in however complicated a manner, of certain simple and great ideas. But there is another sense in which art can be simple, and in which we often speak of early art as being distinguished by simplicity. It is simple in the sense that it carries its meaning on its face ; we can easily perceive the idea it is intended to embody. There is comparatively little put into an early picture ; the attitudes and gestures in it express very obviously what they are intended to express. So with a very simple tune, we easily catch the principle on which it is put together. Early poetry, too, is simple ; we at once take in the situation. In the same way we speak of simple characters ; meaning that one easily understands their acts, and sees what are their feelings and principles. In contrast to this we say that the more civilization we have, the more complex and involved does human life become. Our art might appear confused to an early artist, but the work of a great artist of later times is not really confused ; he has his own distinct and dominating idea as well as the earlier artist, only it is harder to express and harder to interpret. So with character ; simplicity in the important sense does not vanish from life as time goes on ; great characters preserve their concentration and unity of purpose ; but it becomes harder to interpret them. Doubtless also in later times every great work of art is labyrinthine and we have to find the clue to it ; but there is a great difference between complexity in the sense of having a great number of elements combined in a harmony which it is hard to analyze, and complexity in the sense of confusion and absence of principle. The great question about a work of art is whether there is a clue to it, whether there is a unity in it or not.

It is obvious that Plato thought that the Athenians were losing their simplicity in every direction. Not that he wanted them to go back to the simplicity of primitive times. What he wanted was that there should be reality in them; that they should not become, as they seemed to him to be becoming, a nation of actors, but should assume genuine characters. Athens, as he describes it to us, is becoming like a theatre[1]. The arts, too, are afflicted with the same disease, and foster it; they are complicated in the sense of being confused; they lack principle, and admit everything without discrimination. The under-lying idea is true enough; great art, like great character, is doubtless simple in the sense of being harmonious. But we feel that in working out his idea Plato is led to advocate things which are really retrograde, things which would have the effect of arresting the development of art and of civilization generally; at moments indeed he appears to be doing away with art altogether. This is because he has not been true to his own principles, but has allowed his view to be narrowed by fixing his atten-tion too much on certain particular facts which he saw or thought he saw close to him. We find the same thing later on in his treatment of property and the family. Thus, while there is nothing in his principles which is derogatory to art or which need limit its scope, yet in his particular applications of them he does limit it. To us,

[1] See again VIII. 561 C to E.

who are interested first in his principles, he says, Let all art express something, and let it be something worth expressing ; do not let it be meaningless, or cater simply to the morbid fancies of a mob and to its desire for excitement. But on the other hand it probably seemed to his contemporaries that he was setting aside a great part of the most valuable productions of the age. We find something of the same combination in Mr. Ruskin.

In a very condensed passage (400 E to 402 C) Plato proceeds to extend his conception of the educational power of art to the whole field of art. Of the arts which he now enumerates he makes no detailed criticism. Accordingly we here pass entirely from the polemical side of his writing to his positive theory of the ethical effect of art ; this, so far from reducing the function of art to a minimum, is at once as liberal, and as high in the aim that it sets, as anything that could be said on the subject. It really contains the pith of what there is to be said about it.

He first tells us that in painting and sculpture, in weaving, embroidery, the making of pottery and furniture, in architecture, and beyond these in the whole of organic nature, in fact wherever there is sensible form, there is the capacity for beauty or ugliness, and that beauty or ugliness both of figure and of sound is associated with what is beautiful or ugly in character. He goes on to describe the effect that might be produced upon the soul if, as it grew up, it was surrounded by an atmosphere of beauty. We must not suppose that he thinks the world can be reformed by art alone, but he does ascribe to it a function, among other factors in human life, more important than perhaps any other philosopher has ascribed to it.

What was it that he thought art could do? Phrases about the 'moral' influence of art are apt to make us think of art that expressly illustrates moral principles, of didactic poetry or pictures ; but there is no idea of this here. Throughout his treatment of education, here and further on, there is present the general idea of the soul as having certain powers or tendencies which may be called out (not created) by its environment. Among the media through which these tendencies may be brought out are two most important ones, seeing and hearing, through which the soul comes in contact with the exterior world. It is through them, in the first instance, that the soul acquires knowledge, or in other words is brought into conformity with the truth of the world outside it. Amongst other aspects of that truth, the soul is through eye and ear brought into contact with the beauty of the world. For in Plato's mind the world as a whole is beautiful. There is reason in the world, which makes it intelligible, and the reason in the world shows itself also in the aspect of beauty. So in the *Timaeus*[1], Plato says that the great value of sight and hearing is that through them the soul may understand the visible and audible rhythm and harmony of the world ; the great type of rhythm and harmony was the movements of the stars ; in them the Greeks saw, so to say, the harmonious movement of reason. The function of the artist, then, is to show us the beauty of the world. We must, says Plato (401 C), look for craftsmen who have the genius to track out beauty and grace wherever they are to be found ; they are to show it to those who have not the eye to see it or the ear to hear it in the world for themselves. He regards rhythm as rational movement ; it is movement

[1] 47 A to E.

arranged upon a certain principle; beautiful form, similarly, is form arranged upon a certain principle. In all
products of art (400 D sq.) there is goodness or badness
of rhythm (εὐρυθμία and ἀρρυθμία) or of harmony (εὐαρ-
μοστία and ἀναρμοστία) or of form (εὐσχημοσύνη and
ἀσχημοσύνη), and right rhythm or right form is akin on
the one hand to the reason, the rhythm and harmony,
which is to be traced in the world as a whole, and akin
on the other hand to what is right and rational in
human character. This is the real relation between art
and character or morality [1].

In what definite way, then, is the character affected
by artistic surroundings? Plato gives two descriptions
of the way in which they influence the soul; one describes what we should distinguish as the more moral,
and the other what we should distinguish as the more
intellectual influence of art, but they are not different
in his view. He tells us (401 D) that the soul appro-
priates to itself the characteristics of rhythm, harmony,
and shapeliness. He would no doubt say that it shows
this in the actual movements of the body, in speech
and gesture and bearing, for there are certain modes
of movement which are expressive of moral or spiritual
qualities [2], and the fact that they are recognized as thus
expressive shows that there is an association between
the sense of rhythm and of form and the sense of what is
right in character. But his view of the influence of art
is best summed up in the metaphor of learning to read

[1] For the association in Plato of the highest moral state with the
power of entering into the meaning of the world, see Section X, pages
225 to 229.
[2] See 399 E and 400 B. Throughout the discussion of musical rhythm,
it is manifest that he regards it as based upon the movements of marching and dancing.

the world (402 A). He tells us that we have got to learn
to read the world about us with a view to understanding what is good. The world as it first presents itself to
our observation contains both what we call real objects,
living men and women for instance, and 'images' or
reflexions of real objects in the various reflecting media
of words, music, colour, and the rest of the media of art.
The problem is to learn to read this world. If we are
able to read the real world we must also be able to read
the reflexions ; to be μουσικός, to have the real eye for
beauty, is to be able to read both the real world and the
reflected world of art, and to discern self-control and
manliness and liberality and all other good qualities and
their opposites wherever they occur. It is possible to
learn from what we call little things as well as from
great, and in learning to recognize and to value the
reflexion of good qualities in art we necessarily learn also
to recognize and to value them in their more important
expression in real life.

We must notice further that thus learning to read
the sensible world, or the world as it presents itself to
ordinary experience, is a preparation for learning to read
the world in another way. A man who has been
educated thus will have an instinctive sense of what is
beautiful and what is ugly, and will love the one and
hate the other, before he is able to frame in his mind
a reason for loving or hating them. But when reason
comes, a man so nurtured will recognize it and welcome
it from natural kinship to it, that is to say, because
his own feelings are already in accord with it. Plato
conceived that there was a real continuity between the
education of art and the education of science and philosophy, which he afterwards requires should follow it up.

I 2

In childhood the soul of man is completely subject to the senses, its perceptions are all disordered. Gradually it frees itself from the tumultuous influences of sense, and establishes order and connexion in what it perceives and thinks. The great agents by which this process can be helped are, first, the education in μουσική, and, secondly, the education in science and philosophy. In both Plato would say there was reason (λόγος)[1]; in its earlier, sensible form it shows itself as rhythm, harmony, and shape; in its later, it shows itself as principles or laws, which are apprehended by the intelligence (understood, not seen or heard or felt).

Thus the education of μουσική is the education of eye and ear in the widest sense; it is to be accomplished by presenting to the eye and ear good works, which will interpret to the soul the beauty of the world and enable it to find it for itself. The artist, by creating for the soul a sort of atmosphere of beauty which becomes familiar to it, will develop in it the power of recognizing what is beautiful in widely different forms, and of making that beauty its own.

It is curious that Plato seems to attribute much more educational influence to music proper than to sculpture. We think of the Greeks as a nation of sculptors, and we do not think of them as a nation of musicians : we might therefore have expected him to attack the idolatry of form in the same way in which he attacks the idolatry of words[2]. But sculpture is only alluded to in a list of many arts, and then not expressly named[3]. It is

---

[1] In 401 D we have the phrase καλὸς λόγος, i.e. reason in the form of beauty.

[2] See Section XI, page 244, and Section XV.

[3] 401 A, where he speaks of 'painting and all work of that kind.'

a justifiable inference that the existence of great sculpture in Greece was not so important an educational influence as we suppose. On the other hand the Greeks were extremely susceptible to words, and, further, they must have been especially susceptible to rhythmical words; and so Plato speaks of music (rhythm and harmony), which he has treated throughout as the accompaniment of words, as having the most penetrating influence on the soul. Aristotle speaks of music in a similar way in the *Politics*, and tells us that the influence of the plastic arts is comparatively slight[1].

The discussion of μουσική concludes with the consideration of beauty of human form (402 D to 403 C). The man on whom this education has had its due effect, who is really μουσικός, and who therefore has the keenest perception of beauty everywhere, will necessarily value beauty of soul far more than beauty of body. Physical beauty which is not the expression of a lovable soul will not move him. Moreover, Plato tells us, there is no fellowship possible between this sense of beauty and the madness of animal passion. Excessive passion, he says, like excessive pain, puts a man beside himself; he considers that there is a real affinity between madness and any passion which *possesses* a man for the time being[2]. Under the influence of any passion so strong the perceptive power is almost extinguished; nobody trusts the judgment of a person under the influence of absorbing jealousy or fear or any other passion; and so, Plato says, the perception of beauty is incompatible with excessive passion. This is empirically true: it has been observed about poets that they have not often

---

[1] *Politics*, 1340 A, 28 sq.
[2] See the whole passage, IX. 571 A to 573 C, and cf. 329 C and 577 D.

written under the immediate influence of violent emotions, but usually afterwards; and there can be no doubt that the deeper is the sense of beauty, the less it is compatible with *simple* animal passion, and vice versa [1]. In this passage we find that the word μουσικός has acquired an extended and higher sense; it means a man to whom life itself is the highest art; and a little later we find that the real μουσικός is the man who can harmonize his own life, putting μουσική itself in its right place in his life in relation to 'gymnastic' and to other elements in life [2]. The use of this and other phrases derived from the arts to describe morality, may incline one to say that Greek morality was aesthetic morality; but the truth is not that Plato takes moral distinctions to be, as we should say, only aesthetic distinctions, but that he gives 'beauty,' 'harmony,' 'rhythm,' and similar words a wider sense than we do.

## NOTE ON GREEK MUSIC [3].

The Greek theory of music took account of poetry, tune, and dancing as elements in one artistic product (μέλος). Aristoxenus, a pupil of Aristotle's, is the greatest authority upon it. It fell under the heads of ἁρμονική and ῥυθμική, the latter of which at first included and was afterwards distinguished from μετρική. Ἁρμονία does not mean harmony in the sense of the simultaneous sounding of two or more tones of different pitch, but a scale, a certain sequence of tones of different pitch. Ἁρμονική means that branch of the theory of music which deals with the interval between tones and their arrangement in what we call scales or

---

[1] With this whole passage compare *Symposium*, 209 E to 212 C.

[2] 412 A; cf. IX. 591 D, and *Laches*, 188 D.

[3] [In this Note several additions have been made to the original, important works on Greek music having been published since the lecture was given.—ED.]

keys. 'Ρυθμός is etymologically connected with words which have to do with movement. The typical form of rhythmical motion is dancing. The essence of rhythm is that a certain sequence of motions or sounds is measured, according to time, into portions which recur upon a certain principle. 'Ρυθμική is that part of the theory of music into which time enters. Μετρική, or the theory of metre (μέτρον), is the theory of rhythm in its special application to language.

Plato lays it down as a fundamental principle that rhythm and harmony are to follow the words. This shows us the great difference between Greek and modern music; the former grew up as an accompaniment to words or dancing, or both. It was comparatively late that music began to develop independently of these, and Plato looks upon this independent development as a wrong development. The earlier of the great dramatists not only wrote their plays, but wrote the music for their chorus. It is stated that Euripides got others to compose the music for him, and that this was made a reproach to him. One of Wagner's leading ideas has been that of recurring to the principle that poet and musician should be the same.

According to the theory that has been received till lately, the differences between the various ἁρμονίαι, or 'modes,' were analogous to the difference between our major and minor keys. That is to say, the places in which intervals of tones and of semi-tones occurred, differed in different modes. But whereas we have only two ἁρμονίαι (supposing this to be the sense of the word), the Greeks had seven, one for each note of the scale. There seem to have been originally three main modes, the Lydian, the Phrygian, and the Dorian. On these three fundamental modes there were three variations, the Hypo-Lydian, the Hypo-Phrygian, and the Hypo-Dorian (ὑπο- in this combination meaning lower in pitch). To these must be added the Mixo-Lydian [1]. According to the received theory we get these seven modes by playing upon the white notes of the piano as

---

[1] The Ionian mode appears to have been the same as the Hypo-Phrygian, and the Aeolian the same as the Hypo-Dorian. Plato mentions also a mode called Syntono-Lydian, which is believed not to have been identical with any of the foregoing, but to have been akin both to the Lydian and the Hypo-Lydian.

follows:—Hypo-Dorian or Aeolian, A to A; Mixo-Lydian,
B to B; Lydian, C to C; Phrygian, D to D; Dorian, E to E;
Hypo-Lydian, F to F; Hypo-Phrygian or Ionian, G to G[1].
There is however another theory, according to which there
is no evidence that in Plato's time the modes, or at any rate all
seven of them, differed in the way described above, and the
main difference between modes was a difference of pitch (the
difference between one major scale and another, or one minor
scale and another, in modern music)[2].

The two modes which Plato would leave in use are considered
by him to be appropriate to two sets of circumstances, and to
have a tendency to stimulate two qualities of character, courage
and self-control. Whatever may have been the differences
between the modes, the Greeks generally attributed to each of
them a specific character which made it suitable for particular
kinds of poetry and music[3]. Modes were classified as: those
which had to do with action, and had a stimulating effect
(πρακτικαὶ ἁρμονίαι); modes which stirred emotion (ἐνθουσιαστικαί,
παθητικαί, θρηνώδεις); and modes which affected character,
especially by producing a calming effect (ἠθικαί). Naturally,
though there was a certain traditional agreement as to the
character of these modes, different writers had different opinions
upon them. The Dorian mode was considered to be the Greek
mode *par excellence*. Among the epithets applied to this mode
are ἀνδρώδης (manly), μεγαλοπρεπής (stately), στάσιμος (steady),
σεμνός (dignified), σφοδρός (forcible), and σκυθρωπός (sombre).
The Phrygian mode is called ὀργιαστικός (having to do with
religious orgies), παθητικός (expressing deep feeling), ἐνθουσιαστικός
(expressing violent religious emotions). The Lydian is called

[1] [This must not be taken as implying that the keynote of the mode was
in each case the note here mentioned.—ED.]

[2] [For the former of these two views see Westphal's works and
Gevaert's *Histoire et Théorie de la Musique de l'Antiquité*. For the latter
view see Monro's *Modes of Ancient Greek Music*; see also review of this
by H. Stuart Jones in the *Classical Review* for Dec. 1894, and the reply
to it in the *Classical Review* for Feb. 1895. See also Monro's article in the
*Dictionary of Antiquities* for an outline of all the principal theories.—ED.]

[3] See Aristotle, *Politics*, 1340 A (especially line 40 sq.), and 1341 B,
9 sqq.

γλυκύς (sweet) and ποικίλος (varied); it is also said to be appropriate to the young. If the accepted theory about the modes is correct, both Plato's view of the Dorian mode and Aristotle's illustrate the fact that the present associations of the minor key are due to a late development of musical sentiment. In the early Christian Church grandness and sternness were associated with it; and early ecclesiastical music inherited the characteristics of Greek music.

Upon the subject of rhythm the Greek writers are still valuable. The Greeks had an extraordinary sense of rhythm, and expressed the true principles of it in a final way. In a general sense all spoken language is rhythmical; every one observes unconsciously a certain rhythm. This becomes rhythm proper when treated artistically and brought under laws. For this purpose we require units of measurement, the units in music being notes sounded for a certain time. These units are combined in music into bars, in verse into feet; and a dactyl or an iambus, or any other foot in metre, is best thought of as the equivalent to a bar in music. Each bar in music and each foot in metre is made into a unity by having a certain accent or stress on one of its elements (the use of accent in metre being a development of the use of accent in speech, where stress is laid on a certain part of every non-monosyllabic word, and again on a certain part of every sentence). Poetry then is rhythmical because it is divided into feet of a certain length, and there is a certain stress recurring in each foot. Here comes in the connexion between poetry and dancing. In dancing the foot is put down with a certain stress at equal intervals of time —the simplest possible illustration of this kind of rhythm being military marching. The Greeks called the stressed part of every foot of metre θέσις or κάτω χρόνος, and the unstressed ἄρσις or ἄνω χρόνος; these words referring to the putting down and taking up of the foot in marching or dancing. So (400 c) Damon, the philosophical musician, is said in his criticisms of metre to have in mind the motion of the foot no less than the rhythm of the words. Modern writers apply the words arsis and thesis in the reverse way, meaning by arsis the raising, and by thesis the lowering of the force of the voice. All the metres of poetry are a development of these simple principles.

A hexameter line is a larger unity composed of six smaller unities (feet), each of which can be resolved into four beats, four units of time, which are the ultimate elements of the metre. A stanza again (e.g. the Spenserian) is a larger and somewhat more complicated unity, divided first into lines, secondly into feet, and lastly into beats. In Pindar we find a rhythmical system still more subtle and complicated, but still founded upon the same principles.

Just as different modes seemed to the Greeks appropriate to different subjects, so did different metres or times. Plato does not say definitely, as he does in the case of modes, what form of rhythm he would allow, but he lays down the principle that rhythms must be admitted or rejected in accordance with the character they express. He mentions the three great classes into which metres were divided. To understand this division we must remember certain facts. Ancient metre is based upon quantity, that is to say upon the length of time which is taken in uttering a given syllable. Modern metre is based upon accent, stress or ictus, that is the increased loudness of the voice on a given syllable. There is quantity in modern language, for you can quite well distinguish long and short syllables, and quantity does enter into metrical effect; but the quantity of a syllable and the amount of stress upon it are distinct things; and while in modern languages it is the difference of stress on different words and syllables which is most noticeable and by which metre is governed, in ancient Greek and Latin it was quantity. The fundamental principle in which musical rhythm and metre come together is that a short syllable answers to a unit of time in music. Remembering this, and remembering that the Greeks divided every foot of metre and every bar of music into two by distinguishing θέσις and ἄρσις (the stressed part and the unstressed), we shall understand the following simple classification of metres or times, to which Plato alludes. There is the ἴσον γένος of time, our four time, in which the stressed and unstressed parts are equal. Of this the dactyl and the anapaest are types; each represents a bar of four beats (quavers), and is divisible into two parts of two beats each, of which parts one is stressed and the other unstressed. There is next the διπλάσιον γένος (our three time), in which the stressed part is to the unstressed as 2 to 1. The iambus and trochee are types of this. There is lastly the ἡμιόλιον γένος, 'one and a half' time (our five time), in which the stressed part is to the unstressed as 3 to 2. Plato does not give instances of this, but the type of it is the paeon. Throughout it must be remembered that a short syllable answers to a single beat of the music, and that a long syllable equals two short.

In modern musical accompaniments to words, the composer does what he likes with the metre of the words; he subordinates it to his own rhythm, and does not make every short syllable correspond to a beat. But the earlier we go back the more we find that the time of the tune corresponds to the natural time of the words. This was not universally the case in Greece, as Plato thought that it should have been. The parody of Euripides in the *Frogs*[1] of Aristophanes makes a single syllable spread out over many beats.

Plato requires that the instrumentation of music should be of a simple kind, as well as the rhythm. The 'panharmonion' which he would exclude is a stringed instrument on which all the modes could be played. In his preference of stringed to wind instruments he is following traditional Greek feeling, which associated wind instruments with excitement and emotional effects, and stringed instruments with the sense of form and precision. The stringed instruments in use were mainly varieties of the harp, and not like the modern violin.

### 5. ΓΥΜΝΑΣΤΙΚΗ AND DIGRESSION ON LAW AND MEDICINE.

It remains to consider 'gymnastic,' which has been 403 c to said to mean the training of the body, but in discussing 412 B. this Plato diverges into widely different subjects. The order of his thought is briefly as follows :—(a) The principle which he lays down for the training and management of the body is the same that he has laid down for the arts ; .

---

[1] 1309 sq.

it is simplicity. Simplicity of life leads in one direction to bodily health, and in another to sanity, self-control, or temperance in the soul (σωφροσύνη). The one is to the body what the other is to the soul, and there ·is a close connexion between them (403 C to 404 E). (*b*) This leads to the consideration side by side of two analogous phenomena of Athenian life, legal proceedings and medicine, of which the former had always been prominent, and the latter evidently had entered upon a new development. Constant recourse to law and to medicine are evidences of the same fault in civilization, and Plato lays down corresponding principles with regard to each, especially contrasting the modern habit of valetudinarianism with the simple ways of ancient times (404 E to 410 B). (*c*) By the way, he shows a difference in the conditions necessary to the training of a good doctor and of a good judge, which is based on the distinction between soul and body (408 c to 409 E). (*d*) The consideration of body and soul side by side leads him finally to the thought that μουσική and γυμναστική are both really means of influencing the soul, though on different sides. He tells us that the ideal of education is to harmonize the two, so as to produce a harmonious character; and he points out the evils of a one-sided education (410 B to 412 B).

(*a*) Plato considers first the kind of physical training that is fitted to produce a good citizen soldier. He finds in vogue an elaborate system of training which aims at producing professional athletes, and which seems to strike him as a part of the general complexity of modern life. He criticizes it on the ground that it does not produce that habit of body which befits a soldier. In the first place it produces a sleepy habit, broken only by short periods of great and abnormal activity ; in the second place it produces a habit of body which cannot stand changes of diet and climate and the like. This criticism is substantially the same as Aristotle's [1]. In bodily training the most important thing is simplicity of diet. Syracusan dishes, Sicilian subtleties of flavour, Athenian confectionery, and the rest of the luxuries that were introduced into the state when it passed above its most elementary stage [2], are condemned. Here Plato observes the close connexion between health in the body and self-control in the soul. The relation he sees between them consists in something more than the fact that intemperance produces disease. We are apt to think of the soul as something which is inside the body as if in a box ; in Plato, we have to remember, ' soul ' means primarily the principle of unity and move-ment in the body which makes it an organic and a living whole.

(*b*) When disease in the body and 'intemperance' (ἀκολασία, the opposite of σωφροσύνη) in the soul abound, then Law and Medicine hold their heads high. Plato criticizes the recent development of these, as he has criticized that of art. He tells us that to have con-stantly to go to law is a sign of want of education (ἀπαιδευσία καὶ ἀπειροκαλία), and so is the inability to keep oneself in health without the doctor. This shows us in what a wide sense Plato understands education; the educated man is the man who knows how to manage his own life physically and morally. He writes with great animosity about the growth of medicine, regard-ing it as a luxury of the rich who can afford to give up their work for the sake of nursing their health. If

[1] *Politics*, 1338 B, 9 sq.        [2] 373 A.

a man is radically diseased and cannot go about the business of his life, he had better die, as a poor man in such a case has to, and doctors ought not to be allowed to keep useless folk out of the grave. The general idea of the passage is that, except in comparatively rare cases of accident and the like, a man ought to be able to keep himself in health without the aid of doctors. This is a sound enough idea, within limits, but no doubt Plato's remarks about medicine are far too sweeping. The craving for simplicity in life leads him to a good deal of cruelty, as it has led him to austerity in regard to art. To many of his contemporaries his treatment of medicine must have appeared altogether retrograde, and as a mere refusal to avail himself of the advance of civilization. This is one of the cases where the spirit of the reformer, of which Plato had a good deal in him, does not harmonize with the philosophic temper, and where impatience of what he thinks abuses vitiates his theory. The principle that the man who can be of no use had better be let die (as the incurable criminal ought to be put to death) would of course be an extremely dangerous one to act upon at all. No means have yet appeared by which it could be carried out as it was intended; and not only so, but we rightly feel that it rests with people themselves to decide whether they are justified in keeping themselves alive when their usefulness is gone. We rightly feel, too, that the existence of the sick and incurable calls out a great deal of virtue which would otherwise be latent.

(c) Incidentally Plato asks whether great experience of bodily disease in the one case, and of vice and crime in the other, is not necessary to make a good doctor and a good judge? He answers that the two cases are different. The good doctor must not only have scientific knowledge (ἐπιστήμη) of disease, but wide experience (ἐμπειρία) of it ; and it is best that he should have experienced ill health in his own person, for his own physical weakness will not affect his soul, the organ by which he acts on others. But in the case of the judge, to have experienced the mental disease of vice in his own person does not mean that the soul, the organ with which he acts upon others, is impaired. He goes on to say that the apparent cleverness of a man who has had much personal familiarity with wrongdoing is limited to cases where he has to deal with persons of similar character and experience to his own ; he judges only by the examples (παραδείγματα) which have come within his own experience, and will be at a loss when he has to judge of the motives and conduct of a different sort of people. This is what distinguishes empirical knowledge, which is confined within the limits of a certain number of experiences, from knowledge which is based on principles (ἐπιστήμη). The application of this is that, in order to get real knowledge of the good and evil in human nature, the soul must be kept healthy from the first. The man who has grown up amid healthy surroundings and with a healthy mind, will come to understand the evil which he sees in other people comparatively late, but will then understand it better than the man who begins by personal experience of evil. Plato is not to be supposed to mean that an innocent simpleton is a better judge of character than a man who has knocked about the world ; the issue he raises is this : Supposing people of equal ability, is it better for this purpose that they should have had a large amount of evil experience, or that they should have kept their souls free from evil, and have studied the evil in the world late in life when their characters were formed? It is best, Plato decides, if you wish to have men trained for the function of judges, that you should aim at developing what is good in them morally and intellectually to the highest pitch, and then trust to their insight. What this implies is that no line can be drawn between the intellectual and the moral nature; what is called knowledge is not an entirely separate part of the mind unaffected by other parts, and a man cannot be affected by moral evil in one part of his soul and retain intellectual insight into its nature with another part[1]. We are sometimes inclined to suppose that a man can keep his intellectual judgment apart from his personal character; to this Plato emphatically says no; if the character is affected the organ of judgment is affected, because the soul is one and continuous. We shall find in Books VI and VII, that his whole conception of the philosopher and of philosophic education is based on the close relation which he asserts to exist between the intellectual and the moral powers of the soul.

It may be asked how far experience bears out Plato's theory of the possibility of understanding things in human nature of which one's own experience is slight. With average men it would be difficult to show that it is true; but it proves true if you take only the greatest men and those who have shown the greatest knowledge of, and insight into, human nature. Men of genius get their knowledge of the world nobody knows how; Shakespeare, for instance, cannot have had personal experience of more than a fraction of

[1] Cf. Aristotle, *Eth. Nic.* VI. xii. 10.

what he wrote about. In fact, genius is the power of getting knowledge with the least possible experience, and one of the greatest differences between men is in the amount of experience they need of a thing in order to understand it[1]. There are some people, especially women, who seem able to understand other people's characters by instinct. The greatest of all instances of such a power is the instance of Christ, of whom it is said that he understood all human nature without having personal experience of evil in the ordinary sense. But the chief psychological question which this passage raises is how far one part of one's nature can act independently of others, how far intellectual judgment can act apart from character. This is a matter in which men vary very much, some being able to isolate the parts of their mind much more than others.

(d) Returning to μουσική, Plato makes a final statement as to its relation to γυμναστική. One is said to deal with the soul and the other with the body, but both really have to do with the soul; for misdirection or neglect of physical training has a direct influence on character, no less than the misdirection or neglect of culture. Both are required to develop the elements in the soul which are essential to a good Guardian. The training of gymnastic acts upon 'spirit'; this when rightly trained shows itself in courage and manliness; if trained to the neglect of the rest of the soul, it degenerates into hardness and brutality. The training of literature and the arts affects the philosophic element, the gentle element in man which is susceptible to attraction. This if rightly developed makes a man temperate or self-controlled; if over developed it makes

[1] Cf. Section XIV. p. 321.

him soft, effeminate, morbidly susceptible, unstable and weak in character. The problem of education is to harmonize these two sides of character, and he who best deserves the name of musician (μουσικός) is the man who can thus tune human nature [1].

[1] Cf. the description of the art of the statesman in *Politicus*, 305 E to end.

# VI. PRINCIPLES OF GOVERNMENT
# IN THE IDEAL STATE

[*Republic*, III. 412 B to IV. 427 E.]

PLATO has now finished his outline of the education
of the rulers up to the age (about twenty, as we afterwards learn) at which a man enters public life. The
*Republic* is a representation of the gradual development
of the soul in society ; and the subject we have before
us in the section which now follows, and in which an
outline is given of the institutions of the ideal state,
·is that stage of the growth of the soul in which the
young citizen becomes aware for the first time of his
true position in, and his duty to, the community. It is
introduced by the question, Upon what principle are we
to select, from among those whose training has been
described, those who are to be in public authority, and
whom the others will have to obey ?
This question at once indicates the leading fact about
this new stage in the development of the soul ; when
it first enters upon practical life it will have to recognize
its subordination to authority, and to act upon principles
which it accepts from authority. The question brings

K 2

out also a fundamental fact about the state, which will
have to be considered a good deal in the course of the
discussion; there must be in the community authorities
who impose δόγματα, beliefs or principles, upon those in
subordination.

412 B to
414 B.How the governing class are to be constituted depends
upon the question what should be the spirit of those who
are to rule the state. Their function is to be Guardians
(φύλακες) of the state, and that man will guard the state
best who most fully believes that the interests of the state
are identical with his own. This, then, is the test that
we must use to discover whether those whom we have
been training will become fit to rule; we must observe
whether under all circumstances they hold fast the belief
that the thing that is best for the community is the thing
for them to do. This is to be their δόγμα, something,
that is to say, which he who holds it accepts without
understanding all the grounds of it; for the attitude
of a man entering public life must be that of accepting
certain principles from others. We have got to discover
whether they are 'safe guardians of this creed,' and that
means whether they can resist the influences which are
calculated to make them give it up. Such a belief may
be 'stolen' from us, that is, given up either in the lapse
of time from intellectual indolence, or because some one
persuades us out of it. Or it may be 'forced' out of us
by suffering or painful toil. Or it may be 'juggled' out
of us by pleasure or fear—'juggled,' because both
these feelings affect us by producing illusion, or making
us see things in a false light. These, therefore, are
the influences by which those whom we are educating will have to be tested at all stages of their career.
The test will show whether they are good guardians

of themselves and of the 'music' which they have
learned, whether the rhythm and harmony have become
a law to them. Those who stand the test best must be
made to rule. This in outline (τύπῳ) is the principle
upon which those in authority are to be chosen—the
outline will be filled in later[1]. Those who have stood
the tests well to the end will, when they are older, be
Guardians in the full sense (φύλακες παντελεῖς); the
younger members of the service will be 'Auxiliaries'
(ἐπίκουροι) to the Guardians, and will carry out the
principles they lay down (δόγματα).

In this passage two simple principles are put before
us in combination with a proposal of certain machinery
for carrying them out, which is strange to us. On the
one hand we find the principles, first, that a man will
serve the community well in proportion as he is ready
to devote himself and give up his own interests to it,
and secondly, that men should be promoted in the public
service in proportion as they show that they can bear
responsibility. On the other hand we find the idea
of a system by which the state can continue the education of childhood into later life, and test its progress
at each stage. Such an idea, which is repugnant to
modern ideas generally, is perhaps particularly so to the
English mind. Something analogous to what Plato
proposes exists in the system of the Jesuits.

The young citizen of the upper class has now been 414 B to
placed in his proper position, under authority. The ⁴¹⁵ D·
question next asked is how authority is to be established
in, and made acceptable to, the community at large.
The two essential things which have to be maintained
are the unity of the whole society, and the distinction

---

[1] See 503 sqq.

of classes, that is of social functions, within it. What
will be the basis upon which patriotism (the sense of
belonging to a community) and submission to authority
will rest in the minds of the bulk of the community?
Plato's answer, when rationalized, comes to this, that the
mass of the people really cannot understand the reason
of these principles, and that therefore they can best be
maintained by being associated with a myth, a story
of past events. They are to be taught to believe in
a myth[1] which will make them regard the country
they live in as their mother, their fellow-citizens as
brothers, and the social order with its distinctions of
classes as a thing of divine institution. There will,
Plato indicates, always be persons in the community
who know that this myth is not true, and that
patriotism and subordination have their sanction not
in historical events, but in the constitution of human
nature; but the rest are to be encouraged by a myth
to hold a belief about the order of the community,
which is somewhat analogous to the belief in the divine
right of kings.

The social organization which Plato thus seeks to
invest with a divine sanction, might at first be compared
to that of caste. But in the caste system birth absolutely
determines a man's position, while Plato's system is
based, not on birth, but on capacity and attainments.
He fully recognizes that children do not always follow
their parents in character and ability, though there is
a general tendency for them to do so; and he insists

---

[1] The materials for this myth are partly supplied to Plato by the
belief, which he found existing, that there were actual αὐτόχθονες, or men
born from the soil, and partly perhaps by the belief in a 'golden,' a 'silver,'
and an 'iron' age, which had succeeded one another in the past.

that every man is to be assigned to the rank and
function for which his character and abilities fit him,
whatever his parentage may be[1]. He insists, accordingly, that provision must be made for cases where
children are fitted either for higher or for lower social
functions than their parents. To him, as to Aristotle,
the hereditary principle seems to hold good as a general
rule, but he wishes to provide a corrective for occasional
cases in which it works ill.

With regard to the use of mythology which Plato
here proposes, there is no doubt that there are great
dangers in acting upon the principle that historical truth
does not matter as compared with truth of ideas. But
we should not forget the fact that suggested Plato's
proposal. It cannot be denied that truth is held in
different forms by different people; that religious,
political, social, and scientific truths take very different
shapes in unlearned or undeveloped, and in learned or
developed, minds. This fact Plato has recognized. We
might say in criticizing him that it is the duty of
society, while recognizing this inevitable fact, to be
always trying to do away with it, by raising the
intellectual level of the lower classes. This duty is
in theory admitted now. But whatever has yet been
done to remove the fact, the fact remains; and there
would not be any real difference of opinion among us,
that it is often justifiable to allow people to retain
beliefs which contain a substantial truth, although the

---

[1] [See 415 B and C, and cf. 423 C, D; but the system, as later
developed in Book V (where Plato relies on attention to breeding to
keep up the standard of the ruling class), would apparently not admit of
promotion from the lower class, but only of degradation to it. He is
evidently apprehensive of the tendency of aristocracies to degenerate ;
cf. VIII. 546 D.—ED.]

form in which it is put is not the truest. We have to recognize the differences of form in which truths are held; we have at the same time to try and make the form as adequate as possible, to make the truest truth true to everybody. This is the real function of education.

415 D to end of Book III. The Guardians and Auxiliaries, as we have seen, are to be watched and tested throughout their public life to see how well they retain the principles which their education has formed in them; their promotion will depend upon the results. The next point which concerns their development is that the external arrangement of their lives shall be conformable to the principles of their education. The way of living now described is to be the complement of the system of education (416 C). Its ultimate object is the same; the man is to be made to realize that he is first and foremost a servant of the community. That is the way in which Plato first introduces his communism, which is more fully developed in Book V, and which we shall have to discuss later. His principle being that a man's happiness consists in doing his work as well as he can, it seems to him to follow logically that we should make it as hard as possible for a man to do otherwise. Therefore these young citizens, when they enter public life, are to have no inducements to neglect the public interest; they are to have no houses, land, or money of their own, but to live under a kind of military monasticism. The theory of mediaeval monasticism might in effect be expressed thus: You are going to serve God; let the external organization of your life express that; do without everything that is not really necessary to the service of God. Plato's theory is the same, with

the substitution of the community for God. Both
theories have in common the belief that a great deal
can be done for human character by depriving men of
material facilities for doing wrong, and by compelling
them to live externally a certain kind of life. How
much can really be done in this way, and whether it is
not better for society, having given its members education, to leave them free as far as possible, is a question
which in one form or another, and in different degrees
of intensity, is continually reviving. For many centuries
in the history of Europe what Plato proposes in this
passage was literally carried into effect. Whatever harm
the system did, it is certain that it also did enormous
good, and it is questionable whether, under the circumstances under which it arose, the same good could have
been done in any other way. In Plato's own time there
were in some Greek states, especially Sparta, partial
examples of what he proposes ; and this must have
prevented what he says from seeming altogether paradoxical to his readers. Throughout the Republic we
often find a fusion between the Spartan principle of
absolute discipline and the Athenian principle of culture.

The proposal that has now been made leads to the Book IV to
question what account we are taking of the happiness 421 c.
(εὐδαιμονία) of this ruling class. Here are men with
brains and power; is it sensible to propose to take away
from them all the elements which are generally supposed
by such people to make life worth living? According
to what has been said they cannot travel, or keep
mistresses, or entertain their friends, or offer private
sacrifices of their own ; they are not even to be paid
money, but only to be given the provisions they need.
Plato's answer is that we are not yet in a position to

consider this question; for the present we must proceed
on the principle on which we started, that each man is
a part of a whole, the community, and cannot escape
from that fact; it is futile to ask how we can make the
part happy without considering the whole.  He takes
a simple and good illustration to make his meaning
clear : if you were painting a statue you would not think
it artistic to paint the eye purple, because you thought
purple a beautiful colour.  And why not? Because
beauty is not an abstract thing; it always means a certain quality of something in relation to something
else ; so you cannot start in painting with abstract
beauty of colour, for there is no colour which will not
look hideous in certain combinations.  In this case you
must start by considering the eye in relation to the
body.  Now apply the same principle to happiness.
People talk as if certain things, fine houses and so forth,
were absolutely worth having; but they are not absolutely good; whether they are good or not depends on
who it is that has them.  As for our Guardians, then, it
is of no use to say that as they are the best men in the
state they must have the best things.  It will not be
surprising if it turns out (as it does in Book V [1]) that they
are the happiest of men, but the present point is to fit
them for their function in the community ; for it is owing
to their function in the community that they are what
they are, as the eye is made what it is by its function
in the body.  Our object, then, is to give not to the
Guardians but to the whole state as much happiness
as possible.  We must leave the happiness of each class
to be determined by nature ; by which Plato means,
by the operation of those principles in the human soul

[1] 465 D to 466 C.

of which his state is the expression.   The question of the happiness of this or that class has in fact no sense until you have determined the functions of the class in the state.   If you take agricultural labourers or potters and put them in fine clothes, and tell them they need not work any more, you will not, as we should say, be making gentlemen of them, you will simply be unmaking them as members of the community; it will no more be for their happiness than it will be for the advantage of the community ; and the same applies to all classes.

This incidentally introduces us to a consideration 421 c to of some of the duties which, in governing the state, the 422 A. Guardians will have to discharge.   The application of the principle just laid down to the industrial classes makes us aware that it is injurious to them in the discharge of their functions to possess either too much wealth or too little.   The former makes them indolent, the latter destroys their efficiency.   The principle is therefore laid down, though the means of carrying it out are not considered, that the Guardians will have to keep both riches and poverty out of the state.

This raises a difficulty, for is not wealth the strength 422 A to of the community, which, we must remember, will have 423 B. to fight for its existence with other states?   This suggestion Plato answers by a bitter satire on the present condition of Greek states.   His citizens will fight against theirs as trained athletes against fat plutocrats ; for though, as this comparison reminds him, the rich young men of Greece do often know something of boxing and other forms of athletics, they are generally, it is implied, getting physically degenerate, and they are all ill-trained in the art of war [1].   But what is more important is, that

---

[1] Cf. *Meno*, 93 c to 94 D, and *Rep.* 404 A.

a really united state could divide any one of these states of Greece against itself by offering one class the goods of another[1]. Not one of them can really be called a city; you want a larger name for them, for each contains at least two cities, one of rich and another of poor. You will hardly find a state, Greek or barbarian, which has a force of a thousand fighting men and which forms a really united body.

423 C to D.    To preserve the unity of the state, the Guardians will not only have to keep out excessive wealth and poverty, they will have to see that the state remains at its proper level of population. It must neither be too great to be really united, nor too small to be able to supply its own needs adequately. Harder still, they have to take care that the system upon which the social classes are divided is maintained upon the basis of merit, and not of birth solely.

423 E to 425 A.    These, Plato says ironically, are easy tasks for the Guardians; then, dropping the irony, he declares that all these things will be comparatively easy to them if the one essential thing, education, is maintained. If they have once been educated in the principle of devotion to the community, they will easily recognize the consequences of that principle. In enlarging upon this text Plato expresses an idea which we very seldom find in him, that of a natural tendency to progress; if the constitution is once started upon a right basis and with a right spirit, it will go on with accumulating force, like a wheel increasing its speed as it runs. 'The guard-house of the Guardians must then be built in μουσική;' without that, legislation is useless. In a strong, paradoxical way he tells us that the fashions of music can

_____
[1] Cf. Thucydides, III. 82.

nowhere be changed without consequences of the gravest importance to the state. The spirit of lawlessness grows from tiny beginnings. When it begins to appear in music, it may do no harm at first, but it gradually filters into the minds of men and becomes in time a great subversive force. The utmost care, therefore, must be taken that even the amusements of our Guardians shall be instinct with the spirit of law [1].

Plato's belief that changes in the fashion of popular music are signs of great political change seems exaggerated merely because it is stated so simply. A modern writer would establish the connexion between these things at greater length, but the idea is certainly not foreign to modern thought. It cannot be doubted that great political changes have their precursors, if we could only see them, in trifling changes of this order; and after the event of a great revolution, people often set themselves to study these precursory symptoms, as M. Taine has done in writing about the *Ancien Régime* and the French Revolution. But the mental and moral state of a population of millions cannot be observed in the same way as that of a small independent community in Greece might have been. If a community something like a University were an independent state, it would be far more true than it is now that every change in such things as musical taste was a thing to take account of; and in a state like Athens a few prominent people, such as Alcibiades, who adopted new fashions, could produce a change which was very noticeable and very important.

Plato next tells us, in accordance with what he has just said, that it is not worth his while as a political ₄₂₅ A to ₄₂₇ C.

---

[1] Cf. *Laws*, III. 700 A sqq., and VII. 797 A sqq.

philosopher to go into the details of legislation upon
any subjects which he has not yet dealt with.  Among
the subjects of legislation he mentions not only matters
of police, commerce, and political organization, but
matters of social behaviour, dress, acts of politeness,
and the like.  In a state like Sparta, though there was
little written law, nearly all such things were regulated
by custom, which had the force of law.  All these
questions of legislation, he says, will settle themselves
if only the Guardians carry out the laws he has already
laid down upon the subject of education.  If, on the
contrary, the right spirit has not been created by education, no legislation on minor matters will cure the evils
of the state.  There remains one subject of legislation ·
which he has not dealt with, which does vitally concern
education, and that is ceremonial religion (427 B).  This,
however, is a matter he does not understand; all questions about it must be settled by the oracle at Delphi,
the πάτριος ἐξηγητής—the interpreter of divine things to
the Greek nation [1].  This is an illustration of how conservative Plato was, though in matters of religious belief
he was unsparingly revolutionary.

The mention of political legislation leads him to
satirize the legislative reformers of his own time (425 E
sqq.).  They always act upon the idea that the principle of the constitution must not be touched, but that it is
a good thing to be constantly tinkering the constitution
in details.  According to Plato, the one thing necessary
is to change existing political institutions radically in
their principle and in their spirit, and when that is once
done to keep them as they are; the legislative reforms

---

[1] This is what the epithet πάτριος implies; the word for an ancestral
institution of the Athenian people would be πατρῷος.

that statesmen now deal in are all of them quack medi-
cines. The thought and the metaphor are the same as
in the chapter of *Past and Present* ('Morrison's Pills')
in which Carlyle satirizes the reformers of his day.
If we ask what is Plato's principle in all that he here
says of legislation, we find at first a paradoxical result ;
he would leave untouched all the things about which
we legislate ; he would legislate about things which no
one would think of asking Parliament to settle, for the
'laws' (425 E), which he says it is important to make,
concern the great principles of education, the principles
which should regulate artistic production, and the like.
According to him, the function of government as a
legislative power is to lay down certain general and
elementary principles of life, and to establish a social
ἦθος (character) which people shall take in as naturally
as the air they breathe. If that be done, legislation
on the details which our legislation touches will be
superfluous, as merely formulating and putting on parch-
ment what everybody naturally does. If that be not
done, legislation is ineffectual, as merely altering little
points in life and leaving untouched the spirit within.
Aristotle is quite at one with Plato in maintaining that
the great problem for statesmen is to keep up a certain
character among the citizens[1]. It is difficult to apply
that idea to a modern state, because the function of
legislation in a modern state is different and its scope
more limited than in ancient Greece, where the lines,
which now separate law and custom, government and
public opinion, had not been drawn as they now are.
However important questions of what we call politics
may be, it cannot be denied that of the most important

[1] Aristotle, *Politics*, 1310 A, 12 and 1287 B, 8.

things in life comparatively little is touched by Parliamentary measures; and it is an admitted principle with us, that government must keep its hands off many things which are of vital importance in the life of the nation. On the other hand, what we call 'public opinion' does to a great extent perform the functions which the Greeks, unlike us, attributed to legislation. We differ from Plato and Aristotle not in our view of what is fundamentally important to the community, but in the line we draw between things with which the state can interfere to advantage, and things which it should leave alone. Every age and every country must draw that line differently, and though we are never likely to assign to the legislature proper such duties as the Greeks would, there will always be an opposition between those who deprecate every attempt to regulate life by legislation, and those who would say, Let legislation do as much for the improvement of life as it can. There is a feeling among us which is expressed in the formula, that the object of all legislation should be ultimately to make legislation superfluous; it may be said that the more perfect a state of society is, the less it will need laws and the more will a few elementary principles suffice for it. On the other hand, there is a feeling that in a free community the amount of things that can be regulated well by law is a great test of the general *morale*; it would indicate a very high *morale* in a community that it should allow a great part of its life to be governed by laws laid down by the wisest people in it. The force of both these principles is recognized in Plato.

# VII. STATEMENT OF THE PRINCIPLE
# OF JUSTICE

[*Republic*, IV. 427 E to end.]

THE remainder of Book IV falls into three divisions. (1) In the first of these Plato determines the virtues of the state, with the special object of discovering justice among them (427 E to 434 D). (2) He then investigates the nature of the soul, and shows that the virtues of the state are merely expressions of the inward conditions of the soul (434 D to 441 C). Finally (3), he applies the results of this investigation in determining the virtues, and among them the justice, of the individual.

1. The outlines of a good community have now been IV. 427 E traced, and the question arises, Where is 'justice,' to 434 D. which we started to seek, to be found in this community, and what is it? In answering this question Plato simply continues further the analysis of the conception of a good community, stating the problem of the main elements of a good community in this specific form: What are the virtues of such a community? He starts, as elsewhere, with accepted ideas; goodness shows itself in four main

VOL. II.                    L

forms, the cardinal virtues of the Greeks.  Every nation
and every epoch has its own idea of virtue and its
own way of expressing it, and the Greeks conceived of
complete virtue as showing itself under these four
principal aspects :—wisdom (σοφία), courage (ἀνδρεία),
temperance or self-control (σωφροσύνη), and justice
(δικαιοσύνη).  Accordingly Plato proceeds to enquire in
turn how each of these cardinal virtues exhibits itself
in the life of the state.

The method of this discussion is an example of
the genetic method which Plato follows throughout the
*Republic*; that is to say, he gradually develops certain
conceptions which have been present from the first.
The discovery of the virtues of the state is simply the
deeper analysis of modes of action on the part of the
citizens, which have already been implied in the constitution of the state.  The definition of 'justice,' when
we arrive at it, is the explicit statement of the point of
view from which the welfare of the state has all along
been considered.

In talking about the *Republic* people sometimes speak
as if the virtues of the state were qualities not of individuals but of some non-human entity, but Plato (as
has already been remarked) means by them qualities of
individual men.  The reason why he speaks of them as
virtues of the state is that they are virtues which certain
persons in it exhibit in their public functions.  When
you talk of a state as being well governed, you are
describing a certain quality of certain persons in it,
namely those who govern it.  What quality, Plato here
asks, do we imply when we say that a state is wise or
brave or self-controlled or just, and in whom is that
quality to be found?

He begins (428 A to 429 A) with wisdom (σοφία or φρόνησις). This is some kind of knowledge; but what kind of knowledge makes a state wise? The people of a state may be clever in agriculture or in making wooden articles, but we should not therefore call it a wise state. We should call it wise when it showed knowledge not of this or that particular branch of life, but of how to conduct itself generally in the whole of its domestic affairs and of its relations with other states. The essence of wisdom is good counsel or deliberation (εὐβουλία). If therefore we ask in whom it resides, the answer is that it must be looked for in those who exercise the deliberative function of government. The deliberative faculty is very rare; there will be many good smiths in the state, but not many good statesmen. Plato therefore asserts as an important principle that very few ought to take part in the deliberative function of the state. It seems to him a law of nature that only a very few men are so constituted as to be able to embrace in their minds the good of the community as a whole. The wisdom of our state will reside in the full Guardians (τέλεοι φύλακες), the deliberative body that forms the legislature and directs the executive of the state. We have already seen that these Guardians in the full sense were to govern all, and that the whole function of the younger Guardians or Auxiliaries was to accept upon their authority and to carry out certain δόγματα, of which the sum was that the interest of the community was supreme. What was implied in this conception is developed in what is here said of wisdom and, afterwards, of courage. Wisdom, then, is the virtue of the Guardians, their knowledge of the good of the community as a whole.

Next (429 A to 430 C) comes courage (ἀνδρεία, i.e.,

L 2

etymologically, manliness).  If we want to know whether
a state is brave we must look at its army, not because
the soldiers are the only brave people in the community,
but because it is only through their conduct that the
courage or cowardice of the community can be manifested.
From the external manifestation of courage, however,
Plato at once turns to its inward nature, and defines it
in a surprising way, not as bravery in the field of battle,
but as the preservation under all circumstances of a right
opinion as to what is, and what is not, to be feared.   In
a former passage (413) he has already described exactly
the same quality that he here calls courage ; he there
enumerated the influence under which a man is likely to
give up the beliefs that he holds ; the young Guardians
were to be tested as to their power of holding fast under
all these influences the belief (δόγμα or δόξα) that the
interest of the community is supreme.   Here we are
told that they must have held fast under all influences
a right opinion (ὀρθὴ δόξα) as to what is to be feared
(δεινόν).  Δεινόν means anything calculated to excite
fear, and the typical δεινόν is death ; but there are many
other things that we naturally shun ; all forms of pain or
deprivation of pleasure are in their degree to be feared.
Courage accordingly, the power of resisting fear, is not
confined to the one form of bravery in battle.   That is
its typical form, but such bravery is ultimately based
upon the power of sticking to what one believes to be
right, and of holding in their proper estimation the
things that might make one shrink from one's duty.
This, then, is courage.   For the state to secure servants
who possess this courage great care is necessary.   Just
as a dyer, if he wishes a wool to take the right colour
and to hold it, must choose the right material carefully

and take pains in preparing it for dyeing, so we must first choose the right nature to train for our purpose, and then take great pains in preparing it by early education, in order that afterwards, by the process of obedience to the law, the belief which the law expresses may sink into it past washing out. From this courage of the citizen Plato distinguishes the courage of the brute and the slave, which do not express any such character as he has described; they are not the result of education, but are blind and irrational, and not subservient to law. In leaving the subject, he indicates that his account of courage is not final, and does not tell us all that complete courage would involve. What does this mean? Courage, as he has here described it, implies an authority which imposes the belief that is to be preserved; and there must be a kind of courage which shows itself in holding fast beliefs which result from one's own reason and conviction. Such a virtue is briefly described later (486 A, B). Starting, then, from a narrow conception of courage, Plato widens it to include everything that we should call moral courage, and represents the courage of the soldier as a particular instance of this more general moral principle.

We should notice here and further on how Plato calls virtues 'powers' (δυνάμεις). One is apt to think of virtues as abstractions, or as, so to say, appendages hung on to a man. He emphatically represents them as forces, powers to do something; a man of great virtue in Greek means a man with a great power of doing certain things.

The next virtue (430 D to 432 B), 'self-control' (σωφροσύνη), has been implied in the constitution of the state, with its distinction between higher and lower orders and the recognition by the citizens generally that this is a right distinction. Appealing to the popular usage of the word, Plato finds that σώφρων means 'stronger than oneself' (κρείττων αὐτοῦ), or, as we might say, master of oneself. This phrase seems a contradiction in terms. It can only be explained by the conception that the self is not simple but complex, and that there is in it a superior and an inferior part. In using the phrase we imply that one part of the self ought to rule the other. Turning to society, where do we find this self-control showing itself on a great scale? We find that the superior elements in the soul are chiefly developed in the minority who are fit to rule, and the inferior chiefly in the masses. For a state to be called self-controlled there must be a distinction of the naturally superior and the naturally inferior, and the former must rule. But this is not enough; there must also be agreement (ὁμόνοια) between the classes, and a general recognition that this constitution is right. The inferior might be subordinate without this agreement; but a really self-controlled community like our state is unanimous as to who should rule and who obey. We may then call self-control, whether as seen in the public life of the state, or as seen in the way an individual man regulates the different parts of his own nature, a sort of harmony or symphony, because the essence of it is a unity of different elements; and we cannot say that it resides in any one class of the community more than in the rest, any more than in a concord the harmony resides in one particular note.

Lastly (432 B to 434 D), what is justice? Really, Socrates exclaims, the principle of justice has been tumbling about before our feet for some time. At the very beginning of our examination of society a principle began to appear, at first in its economic form, afterwards in a more general form, that each man should devote himself to that one function in the state for which he was by nature best fitted. That principle in some form must be justice. Popular language confirms this idea by representing it as typical of the just man that he 'does his own business' (τὸ τὰ αὑτοῦ πράττειν). But to establish this we must ask what element of goodness remains in the state after we have eliminated from consideration the other three virtues, for the remaining element must be justice. There remains that which enables the other virtues to exist and maintains them in existence, and it is the principle which has just been indicated. We may perhaps explain what Plato means in the following way:—One can imagine a community in which there was a spirit of intelligence, hardihood, and of general agreement; but unless the classes and the individual citizens of that community had in addition the power to do, each of them, their own duty and to concentrate themselves on their own work, intelligence would not develop into wisdom or governing capacity, nor hardihood into disciplined courage, and the tendency to general agreement would remain a tendency and not produce a really unanimous state. Justice, in Plato's sense, is the power of individual concentration on duty. If a soldier is just in this sense, he is of course a brave man ; if a man in a subordinate position is just, he of course accepts and maintains authority, or is 'self-controlled.' Justice therefore, though it has been spoken of as one among other virtues, and though it manifests itself in many particular actions which are called in a specific sense just, and to which the names of the other virtues are not applied, is really the condition of the existence of all the virtues; each of them is a particular manifestation of the spirit of justice, which takes different forms according to a man's function in the community. In modern phrase it is equivalent to sense of duty.

Plato proceeds to confirm himself in his idea of the nature of justice. The quality that has just been described as justice is certainly fit to compete with any other virtue in its beneficial results to the community. Again, this quality corresponds with the principle upon which it is acknowledged that justice should be administered by judges; this is that every man should have what is properly his own, which is a particular application of τὸ τὰ αὑτοῦ πράττειν. Lastly, we cannot imagine a greater harm to the state than a thorough carrying out of the opposite of this principle (πολυπραγμοσύνη), which would mean that every one neglected his own business and meddled with that of others. Apparently then, if we take what is implied by popular phrases, the idea that justice means doing your own work and not meddling with what belongs to others, and if we apply this idea in its deeper sense, we shall find in it the principle that we were seeking for.

434 D to 441 C.    2. Plato, however, will not yet pronounce finally what justice is. Retaining this idea, we turn to the analysis of the individual soul to see whether the same conception will apply. If it does we shall take it to be true. Each of the virtues that are found in a well-governed state has an external and an internal side. Each expresses certain observable facts about the public life of the community; we can see whether or not there is in it governing capacity, military efficiency, public unanimity, and a general tendency for all classes to perform their

own social functions.   On the other hand, each virtue expresses a state of mind or feeling, on the part of certain persons, underlying and producing these facts. This is what interests Plato most, and this is the meaning of the question, What is justice in the soul? He wishes to continue his analysis of a good community till he finds its ultimate roots in human nature, showing how all these public virtues depend upon certain psychological conditions in the members of the community.

The connexion must be shown by an analysis of the soul.   In this Plato develops the psychological view, of which we have already seen something in his treatment of education.   He begins (435 B) by enquiring what are the different forms of soul, or parts of the soul, present in each individual man.   What is the exact point from which he starts in this enquiry, and what place does it take in the development of the argument of the *Republic*?   Analysis of society has already shown us that there are three main social functions, the deliberative or governing, the protective and executive, and the productive ; and the good of society has been seen to depend upon these functions being kept distinct and upon each being rightly performed. Can we discover any deeper reason for this organization of society?   Is the distribution of functions dependent on the constitution of human nature?   If so, shall we not find that the right performance of function on the part of society is dependent upon a corresponding performance of function on the part of the souls of individuals, and that justice and the other virtues, which, as we have so far seen them, consist in certain relations between certain kinds of men in the state, are the expression of corresponding relations between certain elements in the soul of man? Justice, Plato lays down, must be the same so far as its form goes (or, as we should say, must be in principle the same), whether it is manifested in the state or in a single man; that is to say, we may expect to find in the right performance of function by the soul some similar principle to that which governs the right performance of function by the state.

In beginning this discussion Plato tells us that he is dissatisfied with the method by which he is seeking to define justice, and further on in the *Republic* he comes back to this passage (504 A sq.). However, the method is in accordance with that of other parts of the book; it consists partly in appealing to popular conceptions, refining on them and developing them, partly in applying a preconceived principle of his own by which he criticizes them. In the first place, he tells us, it is a truism that the character of a nation or a state is the character of individual men in it. Men belonging to the various nations, which came within the field of his observation (Greeks, Scythians and Thracians, Phoenicians and Egyptians), exhibit the dispositions and the characteristic activities which are the marks of the several classes of which the state is composed. The real question, he says, is whether in the various activities or functions of the soul, which are characteristic of particular classes or particular nations, the whole soul is active, or only a form or part of the soul. What makes him think this question so important? If it turned out that the whole soul was equally involved in each of these various activities (each of which is specially characteristic of the functions of one social class), the

question would arise whether any one soul could not
equally well be employed upon any one of these social
functions, and whether any one˙ man could not equally
well be a governor or a soldier or a trader.  The whole
structure of society, as Plato conceives it, is based upon
the fact that the activities in question are activities of
different 'parts' of the soul, and that, though each of
these parts is present in a degree in every man, the
different parts are very differently developed in different
men.

   To determine this question Plato first (436 B sq.) lays
down a general principle, which is an application of
what is sometimes called the Law of Identity and Contradiction, and which he formulates thus: the same
thing cannot act or be acted upon in the same part of it
and at the same time in opposite ways.  To apply
this to the soul; do we find in it certain forms of
action or reaction taking place at the same time
and towards the same thing, which are mutually exclusive and opposite to one other?  Appetite generally,
he answers, may be defined as a form of assenting to
something, drawing something to ourselves, or reaching out towards something; if, then, we ever find in
the soul an activity, the direct opposite to this, manifested at the same time and in regard to the same
object, we must infer that there are two different
agents present, two different forms of soul.  Now as
a matter of fact we are familiar with this phenomenon.
We often find ourselves, for example, desiring to drink
and at the same time reflecting that it is better not to, and
we must conclude that the element of desire or appetite
(ἐπιθυμία, or τὸ ἐπιθυμητικόν) which attracts us to the
drink, and the element of reason (τὸ λογιστικόν, or ᾧ λογί-

ζεται ἡ ψυχή) which holds us back from it, are two
distinct parts or forms of the soul[1].

So far the observation of admitted facts has led us to
distinguish two forms of psychical activity, appetite and
reason. Can we further say that what we have already
called 'spirit' (θυμός or θυμοειδές or ᾧ θυμούμεθα) is a third
form distinct from either (439 E sqq.)? Plato observes
that when a man is conscious of having acted against
his better judgment in consequence of the stress of
appetite, he is angry with himself and with the appetites
which have made him go wrong; men have been heard
to swear at their appetites at the moment of yielding
to them; whereas when a man follows an appetite which
he thinks he is right in following, he feels no such anger.
Further, he observes that when a man thinks that he is
in the wrong and has to suffer for it, the nobler his
nature the less he is capable of feeling indignation; while
conversely, if he thinks he is unjustly treated, the nobler
his nature the more his blood boils. These facts lead
to a double conclusion: first, that 'spirit,' which is that
in us with which we feel anger, is not convertible with
any form of appetite; secondly, that there is a sort
of natural affinity between 'spirit' and the better self
—not indeed that it is never wrong, but that it has
a natural tendency to side with reason rather than with
appetite. On the other hand, it is obvious that 'spirit'
is not convertible with reason, for we sometimes find
it rebuked by reason, and we also find it present in
a high degree in children and in the lower animals.

This passage (435 B to 441 C) is sometimes appealed

---

[1] [There followed in the lectures a discussion of difficulties in the argument leading to this conclusion; but the passage has been omitted, as it
was not found possible to reproduce it with the necessary exactness.—ED.]

to as the one complete and authoritative statement of Plato's psychology. It is not so ; it is only a link in the argument, and brings out a single point, the inconvertibility of certain psychical functions. What those functions are is not completely stated here, but must be gathered from the whole of the *Republic* ; and the clearest and, on the whole, most satisfactory statement on the subject is at the end of Book IX. (*a*) We find that Plato's conception of 'spirit' covers three great facts which seem to him to have a common source. First, it is the fighting element in man, which makes him resist aggression, and also makes him aggressive. Secondly, it is something in man (not itself rational, but seeming to have an affinity with his better self) which makes him indignant at injustice, and again leaves him a coward when he feels himself in the wrong. Thirdly (in Book IX), it is that which makes a man competitive and ambitious. (*b*) The rational part of the soul (here called τὸ λογιστικόν, and elsewhere generally τὸ φιλόσοφον) has two totally different functions. It is intelligence, the element in man which enables him to understand things. But in Plato's mind this is inseparably connected with a form of love (which is what the φιλο- in φιλόσοφον indicates). The philosophic element, as it first appears in Book II, is something in man which makes him fond of what he understands, and again makes him want to understand what he is attracted to. Accordingly in Book III it is this which makes man capable of understanding literature and art, and makes him love what is beautiful ; the understanding and the attraction go together. It is this again which holds society together, attracting men to one another and enabling them to understand one another (we also associate these two things together; to like a person you must understand him, and to understand him you must like him or sympathize with him). In Books VI and VII the same element in man is the source of science and philosophy; these arise from the fact that there is something in man which draws him to nature and makes him want to understand it, or that, in other words, there is a sort of affinity between the soul and nature. In the present passage the philosophic element or reason is described merely as something which is found in certain cases to oppose certain kinds of appetite. (c) The appetitive part of the soul here consists in what we should call bodily appetites, and the desire for wealth (436 A) as the means of satisfying them [1].

When Plato suggests that a difficulty might be raised on the ground (apparently) that appetite or desire is for something good and therefore is never unqualified attraction to the particular object desired, he is on the point of passing from ἐπιθυμία in this narrower sense, which is best conveyed by our word 'appetite,' to ἐπιθυμία in the wider sense of any desire, any consciousness of a want. Taking the word in this latter sense it is difficult to apply the opposition between reason and desire on which he bases his conclusions. In every desire there is an element of rational activity, and in the most reasonable direction of our activities there is an element of desire. So we may say that the real conflict is not between reason as such and desire as such, but between different kinds of desires, and accordingly in Book IX we find that each of the three forms of soul has its own special ἐπιθυμία. Plato, however, generally keeps to the nar-

[1] Cf. IX. 580 D, E.

rower sense of the word ἐπιθυμία, the kind of desire in
which the element of simple attraction is most prominent,
and the element of reason or thinking is smallest; and,
in that sense of ἐπιθυμία or appetite, the opposition,
which he adopts from popular phraseology, between it
and reason is quite intelligible. (The division of the
soul into three parts, three forms or kinds of psychical
activity, is an anticipation not so much of the division
of 'faculties' (the 'will,' the 'reason,' &c.) as of Aristotle's
distinction of kinds of soul in the *Ethics*[1].)

3. It remains to apply this analysis of the individual 441 C to
soul so as to confirm our supposition as to the nature end of
Book IV.
of justice. The manner in which it will be applied is
obvious; but what does it mean, what is the distinction
between the virtues of the state and the virtues of the
individual, and what is the advance that we make in
passing from one to the other? The virtues of society
consisted in the ways in which different classes of men
with certain functions in society performed those functions. The organization of society, owing to which they
had these functions in it, depended upon the fact that
certain characteristics were dominant in certain men,
just as different nations too are distinguished from one
another by the predominance of one or other of the
same characteristics, the fighting spirit being dominant
in one, the commercial spirit and the desire for material
prosperity in another. But while different classes and
races of men thus differ, there is no human being in
whom these characteristic things exist alone; no human
being is all appetite, or all 'spirit,' or all philosophy.
And so morality, beyond implying the performance
by each individual of the function in society to which,

[1] *Eth. Nic.* I. xiii. 8 to 19.

in a well-ordered state at any rate, the dominant element
in his soul assigns him, means also certain modes of
action and certain mutual relations on the part of these
fundamental forms of psychical activity in the individual.
A happy instinct, Plato says, has from the first led us
on the track of justice. We dreamt that the principle of
'doing one's own business' (τὸ τὰ αὐτοῦ πράττειν), spoken
of first in its simple economic sense, was justice. It
proves to have been an 'image,' an outward expression
of justice. Real justice means not the mere doing of
one's own business in the state, but such outward doing
of one's own business as is an expression of a corresponding mode of action within the soul; if the outward action
is really just, it means that the soul is just within, that
like a just state the whole soul and the several parts
of it perform their proper functions in relation to one
another. In all points the virtue of a well-constituted
state is shown to be identical in principle with the virtue
of a healthy individual soul. When we call a man wise,
we mean he has the power of understanding what is for
his real interest as a whole man; when we call a state
wise, we ought to mean that the men who have the gift
for governing have their understandings entirely set
upon the interest of the whole state. Again, a brave
man is one who has the courage of his opinions, that is,
one who will carry out his principles, whether those
principles are the result of his own reason or received
from others; and a brave state is one where the men
who have to defend it, have the courage to carry out
the laws and principles imposed by constituted authority.
Again, by a temperate or self-controlled man we mean
not merely one who governs his appetites, but one in
whose soul there is harmony and no internal conflict

between different parts of his nature; and by a self-controlled state we mean one in which social order. is not merely preserved by the army and police, but rests upon general agreement. Lastly, a man is found just in all relations of life in so far as the different elements of his nature are doing their own business, in so far, that is, as he is really one man and not many; and a state is just when it is a united whole, in which each class is set upon doing that which (looking at the interests of the community at large) it can do best. Thus the virtues of the state, which are the modes of action of the citizens in their public capacity, are, when traced to their source, the expression of a certain condition of their souls, which Plato calls justice in the soul. And further, this inward condition of the soul and the constitution of society, which is its outward expression, are so far one in principle that each consists in the proper discharge of function by distinct parts in a single whole.

Under all the forms which the argument in the later Books of the *Republic* takes, the chief object in which Plato is interested is to work out this conception of the healthy constitution of the soul.

# VIII. COMMUNISM AND DIGRESSION
# ON USAGES OF WAR

[*Republic*, V. to 471 C.]

BOOKS V to VII form a section of the *Republic* which
is clearly distinguished by its subject-matter from what
comes before and after, and is described at the beginning
of Book VIII as having been a digression. Some
critics have thought that these Books were written later
than those that follow them, and were inserted into the
original work, because it would be possible to read
straight on from the end of Book IV to the beginning
of Book VIII without noticing any break in the subject
or any great difference in the philosophy or psychology.
The tone of Books V to VII is also different from that
of the previous Books. There is more bitterness, a deeper
conviction of the evils which beset mankind, and a
stronger feeling of the difficulty of reform. Socrates is
represented as feeling at every step that he is in direct
antagonism to public opinion, as almost afraid to say
what he has to say, and yet as convinced and prepared
to face the scepticism and ridicule with which he knows
he will be met. It is impossible to prove any theory

as to how Plato composed his work, nor does it matter
so long as it is clear that there is a real logical connexion
between the subjects of the different parts. It is conceivable that the first four Books were published first,
and that criticisms which fastened on the most obviously
paradoxical suggestions in them induced Plato to work
out at fuller length the consequences of his conception
of an ideal state. But it is quite possible also that
Plato intended from the first to compose the work in its
present form. There are in the earlier Books indications
of his feeling that there was a great deal more to be said
about certain points that he raised by the way [1]. In
a modern book a writer might announce his intention
of treating his subject first in a general and superficial
manner, not because he was unaware of the consequences
to which his principles led, but because he preferred to
reserve till a later stage a fuller discussion of those consequences: writing as Plato does in a dramatic way
he brings in again at this point certain personages of
the dialogue, and makes them criticize the procedure
of Socrates and insist on his returning to a point which
needs further working out.

To show the connexion between Book V and the
earlier Books, we must sum up the results that have so
far been reached. Plato has been seeking to discover
the principle, if there is one, by obeying which human
life in society will become the best that it can be. He
has found it in the fact that on the one hand no soul is
self-sufficient, but each requires the help of society, and
on the other hand every soul can contribute something to
the social whole of which it forms part. It results from

---

[1] See, for example, 414 A, 435 D: and see Book V. 450 B, 453 C,
472 A, 473 E; Book VI. 497 C, D, 502 E, 504 A, B.

this that the ideal of human society is a collection of
souls so organized that each may contribute its best to
the whole and get from the whole what it most wants;
everybody in such a society would do what he was best
fitted to do, and the result would be that everybody
would do both what was best for himself and what was
best for others.  The principle upon which such a society
would be based is, according to Plato, that in which
justice consists.  His perfect state is substantially the
same in its conception as St. Paul's perfect Church or
perfect spiritual community, and each represents his ideal
under the figure of a perfect human body (462 c).

The particular point, in the description of a state
based on this principle, which forms the connexion
between Books IV and V is the proposed community
of wives, accompanied here by the proposal of community of pursuits between men and women.  It has
been laid down in a cursory way (423 E sq.) that the
family along with private property would cease to exist
among the guardians of the ideal community, and this,
it now appears, was meant to imply further that men
and women should both take part in the public life of the
community.  Paradoxical as this suggestion is, it is not
thrown out casually; it is simply the most startling of the
consequences which to Plato himself seem to follow from
the principle which governs the ideal community.  The
ideal community would be one which was literally and
indeed a *community* (κοινωνία), and every member of it
would be absolutely a partaker in it (κοινωνός); he would
have nothing private (ἴδιον); he would not be content
with doing certain external acts of a common life, but
would literally feel that he was one with other men.  In
fixing upon this point, community of wives, as deserving

further discussion, Plato is forcing himself to carry out his fundamental principle in detail and to the fullest consequences which, he thinks, can be drawn from it. But Book V goes on to a subject which has little apparent connexion with this. The divisions of the Book correspond with three difficulties which Socrates has to face in succesion, three 'waves,' each more overwhelming than the one before it. The first difficulty is to show that men and women should have the same education and partake in the same public functions (451 C sqq.); the second, that the family as it now exists should cease to exist amongst the highest classes, and that they should form instead one family (457 B sqq.); the third, that the salvation of society, and its only salvation, lies in the sovereignty of philosophy (473 B sqq.). The simplest way of expressing what is meant by this last contention is to say that human life would be as nearly ideal as it is capable of being, if it were regulated by the best possible knowledge on all subjects, and that it follows from this that the ideal of society would be realized if statesmanship were combined with the most profound knowledge. We should observe that Plato speaks of this idea as one that he has had before him all along but has been afraid to express; it is the ultimate consequence of the principle upon which the ideal state was based. He speaks also as if there was a close connexion in his mind between this idea and that of communism; so that the three 'waves' of the argument form one series. One naturally wonders at first what connexion there is between the two subjects. The connexion in Plato's mind is an idea that if society were governed by real knowledge and if men saw clearly what their real interest is, they would see that they

could only live at their best by living a perfectly
common life. He finds in the constitution of human
nature something which makes common life possible to
man; and this is the highest thing in man, that which
makes him human and that also in which he partakes of
the divine [1], the philosophic element. The more it predominates the better; its complete predominance over
the lower elements in man would involve a perfectly
common life, and, conversely, perfect community would
only be possible through its complete predominance.
To look at the matter from the other side, all the evils
of life appear to him to arise from selfishness; and
selfishness is simply seeking one's own satisfaction in the
wrong way, seeking it in the lower instead of the higher
elements of one's nature. Unselfishness, which enables
a man most completely to live a common life with
others, is one and the same thing with the predominance
of the philosophic element, the highest element in
man's own soul. Thus communism and the sovereignty
of philosophy, which together form the subject of this
Book, appear together to Plato as the ultimate consequences of the principle upon which his ideal state is
based.

We may notice at once two aspects of the general
idea which is in Plato's mind, when he makes this
proposal that philosophy should by some means be
made sovereign in the state. (a) The philosophic element, which is in the first place that which enables
man to understand and to live with his fellows, is also
what we sometimes call the 'speculative element,' the
instinct of free thought which makes men wish to get
to the bottom of things. To a certain limited extent

[1] Cf. IX. 588 D and 589 D.

this exists in every man, and without it he would not be a human being ; but in the majority it is present only in a subordinate form. It enables them, perhaps, to obey certain precepts of reason which society has taught them, and to feel that they are right in obeying them. But it only exists in a few people as a really philosophic or speculative impulse. It is clear that Plato was very deeply impressed by the evils resulting from the aberration of this impulse in the men in whom it is by nature strongest. If wrongly developed, he believes it is the greatest instrument of destruction in society; the majority of men do no great good and no great harm in the world, those who do great evil do so by reason of a perversion of the philosophic element in them. The good of mankind requires that this, which is inherently the best thing in human nature, should not be allowed to become a destructive force, but should be enlisted in the service of man. It has already been attempted, in the ideal state, to enlist the artistic instinct and the fighting instinct in that service ; let the power of thinking, a still more potent force in the world, be so enlisted too. (*b*) Again, the philosophic element in man answers to what we should call the 'spiritual' element ; and mediaeval and modern analogies to the idea of a state ruled by philosophy may be found in the idea of a ' spiritual ' state, which has been entertained, though in different senses, by many people. One result of this idea at its best was the mediaeval Catholic Church, and in England in the seventeenth century many men had the idea of a state in which religion should literally rule.

Of the particular consequences which the true idea of the state seemed to Plato to involve, the form of communism which he advocates is the most remarkable.

With regard to this, we should guard against the misunderstanding that communism means to him the
sacrifice of the individual. As we have seen, the simple
and inevitable result of the conception of a *community*
in the real sense of the word seems to him to be that
the individual should lead a completely common life;
but he certainly does not think that the individual would
be sacrificing himself to the community in leading this
life. On the contrary, when he demands that the best
should be done for the community, it is not in order
that the individual man may be nothing, but in order
that he may be the most that he is capable of being.
The highest life for each individual is that in which the
greatest number of people share, and the lowest that in
which the least number share.

Communism has been advocated from many different
points of view. As advocated by Plato, it has hardly
anything in common with the communism of this
century; it is not suggested by the evils of poverty,
and it only applies to the highest classes in the state.
The one point common to all systems of communism
is, that all profess to meet certain assumed evils by the
external regulation of human life in whole or in large
part. Plato introduces communism as supplementary
machinery to give effect to and reinforce that spirit
which education is to create. Nobody has insisted
more than he on the comparative uselessness of legislation when the souls of men are not in a right state,
but he also feels strongly the logical necessity that the
external order of life should be made to contribute its
utmost to the moral education of men. We have already
in the earlier Books seen indications of the attitude of
mind which makes him think that for this end the

abolition of the family is devoutly to be wished for. In his treatment of the arts, despite his intense artistic sympathies, he adopts a theory which might easily lead to the extirpation of art from human life. Two feelings struggle in him, the feeling of what art may do for men, and the feeling of the evil that is often associated with it; and the result of the conflict is the idea that art can only be made serviceable in the world by limiting it. In the same way, when he deals with property and the family, starting from the idea that the more a man leads a common life the higher life he leads, he becomes filled with a sense of the enormous evils which attach to these institutions; they appear to him as the great strongholds of selfishness. There can be no doubt that selfishness has, in fact, found in these two institutions not its cause but its most pernicious expression. To Plato, writing in the spirit of an enthusiast for social reform, this fact seems to prove that in order to bring about a common life we must cut away these along with all other inducements to selfishness.

Two distinct ideas therefore are combined in this part of the *Republic* : the idea that the highest life is a common life and that, so to say, in losing himself a man finds himself; and the idea that men had better be stripped of all inducements not to lead this life. The latter idea will always attract more attention. There seems to be a perpetual conflict in the world between two feelings. One, of which Plato may be considered a type, is that the way to bring about an ideal state of things is to do away with all occasions of evil. The other is, that the way to make the best of human life is not to begin by taking away opportunities of evil, but to use everything that human life offers in the service of the ideal principle, whatever we may take it to be. This latter feeling, we may say roughly, is represented by Aristotle. It is by no means the opposite of idealism ; Aristotle has a more ideal conception of human life than Plato. The principle of pressing everything in human life into the service of what is highest is harder to carry out, and it may easily sink into a principle of 'accommodation' with evil, but it is the most ideal conception of life all the same. Plato's theory may be compared with the idea upon which monasticism rests, that a man can only serve God by avoiding certain temptations which tend to prevent him from serving God, and that therefore, as it has sometimes been put, a man should live outside the world. Those who hold an opposite view would say it is a harder thing and a higher thing to serve God in the world. At the same time it must be remembered that it *is* a harder thing, and there is no doubt that people living in the world constantly justify by their behaviour those who would seek refuge in monasteries; for they fail to make use of their circumstances in the world. Great men have been impressed sometimes by the thought that most people make the worst of the circumstances surrounding them in ordinary human society, sometimes by the thought that the only way to mend this is to make the best of circumstances, not to evade them.

451 C to
457 B.
1. To come to the various sections of the Book, Plato first discusses the question whether men and women are to share in the same education and the same pursuits in life. He begins (451 C to 452 E) by laying down the principle that this question must be decided with reference to the functions which women are qualified to fulfil in the community. The name

Guardians which he has given to the rulers (for it is the women of the ruling class alone that he is considering) suggests to him the analogy of watch-dogs.  In their case sex makes no difference to the function for which they are employed ; is there any good reason why it should in the case of human beings ?  If there is not, then women must be trained for and employed in the service of the state, like men.  The consequences may at first appear ridiculous and grotesque, but no regard must be paid to this feeling ; everything must give way to the one consideration of the good of the community.  This is the principle of the *Republic* from beginning to end. Plato is intensely ' utilitarian ' in the sense that he puts the good of the community before everything else, and we have in this passage the strongest expression of his utilitarianism.

Assuming this principle, we have first to ask (452 E to 456 C) whether it is possible for men and women to share in the same occupations, for if it is possible, Plato has no doubt that it is expedient.  May he not be confuted upon this point out of his own mouth, since he has all along insisted upon differentiation of functions in the state and attributed all evils to the neglect of this principle ?  This argument, he says, though it sounds so logical, is only superficially logical.  It is a specimen of the art, not of reasoning but of wrangling, of the mere verbal logic, which sticks to the word and is verbally consistent but disregards real differences of kind.  To say that men and women are different and must therefore have different public functions, is like saying that long-haired men and bald men are different and therefore cannot both be shoemakers.  For ' different ' is a wide and vague term, and the point in question is not whether

men and women are different, but what the particular
kind of difference between them is, and whether it affects
their capacity for the functions we have in view. This
is a question of fact. Is there, asks Plato, anything
for which men, as men, and women, as women, are
respectively gifted by nature? He answers no; men in
general show superiority to women in every pursuit;
there is a general superiority on their side, but no
specific natural gift on either side. If this is so, we
shall expect to find between woman and woman the
same varieties of natural endowment as between man
and man, some women specially fitted for philosophy,
some for war, and so on. So far then from being
contrary to nature, the state of things now being advocated is the natural one, and the existing state of
things is unnatural.

So much then as to the proposal being possible. As
to its expediency, Plato argues (456 C to 457 B) that
no one can doubt that it is the interest of the state
that the women in it and the men in it should be as
good as possible, and that if a certain course of education produces good men, it will also produce good
women. So the studies and pursuits that have been
prescribed for the rulers must also be followed by
their wives. Here Plato repeats the principle from
which he started; there is only one thing beautiful,
that which does good, and only one thing ugly, that
which does harm.

In this discussion the consideration of the 'rights
of women,' the modern aspect of the question, does not
appear at all; it is a question solely of their duties to
the community, and Plato does not make his proposal
in the interest of women as a class whom he supposes

to be wronged, but in the interest of the community. Whether his proposal would have struck an Athenian as favourable to women is doubtful; it might very likely have seemed to be dragging them out of a position in which they would rather be left. Hardly any one would dispute Plato's position that the real good of the community ought to prevail over every other consideration in this matter. Most people too would accept his view of what the good of the community is; they would agree that the more co-operation there is in a community and the more every one contributes to the common life, the better. The great question is that of the best way to carry out this conception of public good in this case. Plato's view of the way in which men and women can co-operate together for the public good is a comparatively narrow view. The main public functions he has in view are the deliberative and administrative and the military; but, as it might be put now, there are thousands of ways of contributing to the service of society besides being a Member of Parliament or a soldier. One has, then, to distinguish between Plato's principle and the particular application which he makes of it, which is to a certain extent determined by the circumstances of his time. His position that the more co-operation there is between men and women, the better, is irrefragable. As to his application of it he has himself told us the point of view from which it must be criticized; we cannot refute his conclusion by merely saying that men and women are different, we require to consider thoroughly the question in what respect they are different. Aristotle, when he deals with the question, starts from the principle that the difference between men and women is one which fundamentally affects their social functions; they ought not to do the same things, but to supplement each other[1]. From the point of view which he adopts[2] it may also be said that the analogy of the lower animals to which Plato appeals would prove nothing, for even granting that in certain kinds male and female are not widely differentiated in character, this is due to the fact that animals are not so highly developed as man ; in man, the most highly developed animal, the differentiation of the sexes is greatest.

457 B to<br>466 D.

2. The second 'wave' of the argument is the discussion of the proposal to abolish the family among the ruling class. A state family is to be substituted for it, and the most important section of the state made literally into one great family. Here, as often, we are apt to be struck by the incongruity between Plato's principle and the machinery by which he proposes to realize it. The principle he appeals to is as high a principle as a man could have, the machinery makes one realize forcibly how barbaric much of Greek civilization was[3]. But what he says cannot be dismissed with a laugh or by merely saying that the proposal is impossible ; if he does go wrong, it is worth while to make out where he goes wrong. He puts forward this

---

[1] *Eth. Nic.* VIII. xii. 7. Cf. also *Politics*, 1264 B, 1 sq.

[2] *Hist. An.* 608 A, 21.

[3] It is not clear whether Plato intended unpromising children and children born unlawfully to be put to death. 459 E seems to mean this, but the other references to the matter (460 C and 461 C) are obscure, and in the summary given of part of the *Republic* in the *Timaeus*, the expression used is τὰ δὲ τῶν κακῶν εἰς τὴν ἄλλην λάθρᾳ διαδοτέον πόλιν (*Tim.* 19 A), i. e. they are to be brought up as traders, artisans, &c. It is quite possible that in 459 E τρέφειν is used in the emphatic sense of educating as Guardians and Auxiliaries, as it is in the *Timaeus* (ibidem), and in that case the sentence does not imply that their children should be destroyed.

proposal upon two distinct grounds. First, it is part of a system for regulating the number of children born to the community, and still more for ensuring that they shall be well bred. Secondly, it is a means for increasing the common spirit or *esprit de corps* of the community, by extirpating the various forms of selfishness which he conceives to arise from or attach to the present institution of the family.

(*a*) First then (458 E to 461 E) he takes, as before, the analogy of the lower animals, and asks why we should not take the same care about the breeding of human beings as we do about the breeding of domestic animals. If the breeding of animals is important, much more so is that of men and women. Accordingly he devises an elaborate system by which the production and rearing of children of the ruling class is to be brought under state control, and regulated upon scientific principles. Nowadays the question that Plato raises occupies many people's minds very seriously. It is evident that the conditions under which members of the community are born are most important, and the evils which result from .entire disregard of this elementary fact are enormous. But to what extent is it possible, men and women being what they are, to regulate marriage? Plato admits that his proposal could only be carried out by an organized system of deception, without which it would be unendurable. Now the reasons which would make it unendurable to those who had to submit to it are really sound reasons. On the one hand, there never would be in any community people so much wiser than the rest that they could safely be trusted to regulate other people's lives in such a matter. On the other hand, to place men under such a control would be to treat them like animals, to ignore their reason. To put the matter in another way: in breeding domestic animals man clearly determines the purpose for which they are bred; this may or may not be better for them, but the end of their existence is in man. To introduce such a scheme into a human society would imply that certain persons in the community were to determine the end for which other persons, the majority, were to live. Slavery has been considered the greatest wrong that can be done to humanity, because it is treating men like lower animals, ignoring the right, which belongs to every reasonable being, to make his own life; and the systematic breeding of slaves would be carrying this wrong to the extreme point. In any system in which one set of men assumed such an authority as this over the lives of others, we should feel that the same wrong was being committed.

(*b*) It is more important to consider the second argument (461 E to 466 D) by which Plato supports his scheme, for in this he sets forth in the most striking way his whole conception of the relation of the citizen to the state. It is often said that his radical fault in this and in his preceding argument is that he ignores individuality, or sacrifices the rights of the individual to the community. But these phrases do not truly indicate the point where the fault lies, or the advance which has been made since Plato's time. We have not come to believe, any more than he did, that an individual has a right to do just what he pleases with himself or his property, or a right to disregard absolutely the interests of the community in respect to the children he produces. Every right which he possesses depends on the recognition of others and is held on certain conditions; in other words, it implies a κοινωνία. Individuality and community, we ought to recognize, are not mutually exclusive things, as the antithesis of 'the individual and the community' suggests. The contrast expressed by this antithesis is really a contrast between different forms of individuality, or between the less comprehensive and the more comprehensive ends with which a man identifies himself. There is no such thing as an individual in the abstract, a human being literally independent of all others. Nor, conversely, is there such a thing as a community which is not a community of individuals, or a common life or interest which is not lived or shared by men and women. Nor is individuality, in the true sense of the word, diminished by participation in this common life or interest. A public servant who devotes as much of himself as he can to the public service does not cease to be an individual; he puts as much of *himself* into his work as does the most selfish miser. When a man so completely throws himself into the common interest that he can be said to live for others, he does not lose his individuality; rather his individuality becomes a greater one. In this sense it may be said that what Plato had in view was not the abolition of individuality, but the raising of it to the highest possible pitch through *esprit de corps*.

It would be instructive in this connexion to examine two common expressions, the phrase *esprit de corps*, and the saying that 'corporations have no conscience,' which seems to contradict the notions that we attach to *esprit de corps*. By *esprit de corps* we mean a spirit which is felt and possessed by individual men; a member of a regiment who is stimulated by it does not feel it to be something outside himself. As we all know, a man at

times does in the strength of this spirit things which
he could never do without it, and when he does so he
certainly is not losing his individuality. On this fact
Plato has seized. He practically says that the ideal
of human life would be realized if every man lived
perpetually in the feeling which all. men under great
excitement at great national crises do feel. We may say
that this is impossible, but then so is every ideal, and
it is none the less noble an ideal for that. Aristotle
however says that Plato's scheme for abolishing the
family and re-creating it on a larger scale would not
accomplish the result it aims at at all. It would not
really re-create family feeling on a larger scale; the
family affection which it would diffuse among members
of the community would be but a 'watery affection'
(ὑδαρὴς φιλία)[1]. This is a true enough criticism, and it
brings us to the considerations which have made people
say that corporations have no conscience. It is an
undoubted and humiliating truth that when a number
of men act together their sense of responsibility is often
weakened instead of being intensified. Here again the
fact of acting together with others does not destroy
a person's individuality, it simply means that he so far
assumes a new individuality; in the supposed case this
new individuality is lower than his customary individuality, in the cases mentioned before it is higher.
Such observations as 'Corporations have no conscience,'
or 'What is everybody's business is nobody's business,'
bring out an important fact—that human nature is
limited in the degree to which it can really lead a
common life. What is more, if human nature is over-
strained in this way, it does indeed live a common life

[1] *Politics*, 1262 B, 15.   See also the whole passage beginning 1261 B, 33.

in a sense, but it does so at the cost of its own higher individuality. When it is said that Plato ignores the rights of the individual, the real point is that he has not seized upon this half of the truth. We may now apply this remark to the particular case of the family. There can be no doubt that the various evils which Plato associates with the family are all to some extent real. He regards the family as the centre of mean and petty selfishness. So it often is. Take for example what is implied in our word 'nepotism,' or consider how many of the greatest evils in history have been due to dynastic interests, which are simply family interests on a large scale. Nowhere does the selfishness of man come out more obviously than in matters connected with the institution of the family. But also nowhere does the unselfishness of man come out more obviously. Some of the noblest things that have ever been done, as well as some of the basest, have been associated with the love of man and woman or with the love of parent and child. In fact the individuality of men here asserts itself in its intensest form, both for good and for evil. That being so, the problem raised by Plato's proposal is this: there being certain elementary and ineradicable instincts in human nature, capable at once of being the most selfish and the most unselfish, what is the best way to deal with them and with the institutions which are their result? Plato says that it is best in the first place to remove as far as possible all opportunities for the selfish development of these instincts, and in the second place to give them scope in such a sphere and on such a scale that they must be unselfish. We might answer: The latter part of this idea is impossible, and the attempt to carry it out

N 2

would only result in the 'watery affection' that Aristotle
describes; the right way to deal with the instincts which
create the family is not to attempt to resolve them into
something higher, but to make the best of them as they
are and use them as a preparation and education for
something higher: we cannot make the state a gigantic
family, but we can make the life of the family a preparation for the service of the state; for the family may be
an institution in which people learn from their earliest
years an unselfishness which is not limited by the family.

Aristotle in his criticism of Plato's communism puts
the most obvious and far-reaching objection when he
says that Plato's fundamental fallacy is an exaggerated
conception of the virtue of unity.   This criticism, however, would be expressed more truly by saying that
Plato has a one-sided and defective conception of unity;
he does not realize enough that unity in human society
can only be obtained through diversity.   The ideal state
of society-would be one in which there was the greatest
scope for individual diversity, and in spite of that the
greatest unity.

To return to Plato's demand that the production of
children should be regulated, perhaps most people who
thought about it would agree with him that the production
of children is one of the most important factors affecting
the welfare of the community, that it ought therefore to
be governed by the best knowledge that can be had
about it, and that individual members of the community
ought to feel their responsibility in this more than in
most things.   But Plato goes on to say that the way
to accomplish his end is to entrust the regulation of the
matter to a few highly trained and all-powerful persons.
Now we, on the contrary, should probably all agree that

Plato's object can only be accomplished in one way, namely, by the diffusion throughout the community of that knowledge and that sense of responsibility which Plato would have concentrated in a few people.  This of course could only be a matter of slow growth.

At this point in the argument there follows a digression 466 D to upon the usages of war, by which Socrates evades for ⁴⁷¹ C. a time the question whether such a state of society as he has sketched is possible.  He first describes how children are to be brought up to be soldiers (466 D to 467 E), and then treats of the bearing of citizens towards one another and towards their enemies (468 A to 471 C).  There are here several curious anticipations of mediaeval chivalry. Young people are to serve as squires; love is made a motive to military prowess; poetry is to be the handmaid of war; and there is a general fusion of sentiment and policy[1].  Again, hero-worship, to which emphatic recognition is given, takes the form of a regular canonization of great men[2], in which the Delphic oracle may be said to take an analogous position to the Church, as the ultimate authority.  The Delphic oracle is prominent in the *Republic*; Plato conceives it to be a centre of unity to the Greek race, and one of the agencies which counteract its disintegration.  Here the oracle is made to regulate to some extent the usages of war[3].  Plato lays down that no one is ever to allow himself to be taken alive in battle, and that any one who disgraces himself in battle is to be degraded to a lower social

---

[1] Cf. especially 468 B with 458 E ('We will make the nuptial union as sacred as it can be, and it will be most sacred when it is most useful').

[2] Thuc. V. 11.

[3] Of such canonization as Plato speaks of there is a famous historical instance in the worship of Brasidas at Amphipolis.

182 LECTURES ON PLATO'S 'REPUBLIC'

class. As to the treatment of enemies, no Greek, he
insists, ought ever to be enslaved by a Greek. He
has in mind throughout the unity of the Greek race,
and the natural antagonism of Greece as a whole to
the barbarians. This feeling determines his attitude
towards the usages of war, and makes him forbid not
only the enslavement of Greeks but other usages which
tend to perpetuate and intensify enmity between Greeks,
the offering of arms in temples, the ravaging of the land,
and the burning of houses. The war of Greeks against
Greeks should be regarded not as legitimate war but
as civil (στάσις)[1], for the Greeks are one race. What
he says reminds us that, as we find in Thucydides,
the Peloponnesian War acquired, as it went on, more
and more of the character of a social war between
class and class, and that horrible results followed from
this. Some of the principles which Plato lays down
appear to have been recognized by the Spartans. The
spoiling of the dead beyond a certain point was for-
bidden; so in Plutarch's *Apophthegmata Laconica*[2]
we have a saying, attributed to Lycurgus, which closely
resembles what Plato says upon the subject. The
Spartans also differed from the rest of Greece in not
hanging up arms as offerings in temples, which again
is the subject of a saying of Cleomenes in the *Apophthegmata Laconica*[3]. The refusal of leave for the van-
quished to bury their dead was very rare in Greece
and a sign of bitter hatred. Leave was refused to
the Phocians in the Second Sacred War (B.C. 353).

[1] Cf. Callicratidas in Xen. *Hell.* i. 6. 14.
[2] p. 228 F.
[3] p. 224 B. The reason there given for the practice is very different
from Plato's.

Lysander also was reproached for leaving the Athenians unburied at Aegos Potami.

Having dealt with the usages of war between Greek and Greek, Plato concludes in a very Greek way by putting the barbarians in quite a different category ; to them Greeks may behave in war as they now do to one another.   It is a striking instance of how limited a conception some of the greatest men have had of the rights of humanity.

# IX. PHILOSOPHY AND THE STATE

[*Republic*, V. 471 C to VI. 502 C.]

471 C to
474 B.

AFTER this interlude Socrates can no longer postpone meeting the third and greatest of the 'three great waves' of the argument: All that has been said of the ideal state is excellent, and we can say a great deal more about it ; but is it possible?

Before revealing the paradoxical secret which he has got in store, Socrates makes some preliminary remarks on the relation of ideals generally to reality. An ideal, he tells us, is none the worse for being unrealizable. We started with asking, What is justice? and that means, What is justice in itself or as such? Now we must not expect any human being whom we call just to be, so to say, embodied justice, but must be content to regard justice as a παράδειγμα or pattern, to which the justest man approximates most nearly, but only approximates. In other words there will always be, in Plato's phraseology, a certain difference between things as they are in themselves (τὰ ὄντα), and things as they come into existence in our actual experience (τὰ γιγνόμενα)[1].

[1] Cf., for example, 485 B.

The same difference may be expressed as the difference between the ideal and the actual. Justice being of the nature of a pattern for human action, we may say boldly that what we decided to be the ideal community is the truth of human life; true human life would be as we have described it. All actual forms of human life are to a certain extent falsifications of the truth; they fall short of it. When we are asked to show the possibility of an ideal, we must first lay down that no ideal is actually possible, and that to expect it to be so is to misunderstand it. For it is in the nature of things that action should get less hold of the truth than words (λέξις), or, as we should rather say, than thought. This is a general principle applicable to all ideals. Accordingly in the *Laws*, in looking back to the *Republic*, Plato still insists that the true pattern was what he had there drawn; but he says that it was only practicable for gods or children of gods[1]. In the *Republic* he abates nothing of his ideal; he is simply content to exhibit it as an ideal; when challenged as to its possibility, he feels bound to show, not how human nature can realize this ideal, but how it can approximate to the realization of it.

This task resolves itself into the question, What is it in human life, as it is, which prevents it from realizing its ideal, and what is the least change in things, as they are, which would enable it to do so? (It is implied that the questions of the ideal good of man and of the source of evil in man are really the same.) There is one change, not a small one but still possible, which would bring about the ideal of human life; and, again, there is one great source of evil in human life. The change would consist

---

[1] *Laws*, V. 739 B sqq. Plato there proceeds to show what he thinks the nearest practicable approximation to the institutions of *Rep*. IV. and V.

in making philosophy sovereign, or, in other words, in
the union of political power and philosophical insight;
and the radical source of all the evils of mankind is the
divorce between these two,factors.  This union of political
power and philosophical insight would involve negatively
the exclusion from power of most of those who now
have it, and from philosophy of most of those who now
pursue it.

This negative requirement is of course what will
excite most opposition and outcry.  It touches at their
tenderest point most of the leading men of the time,
whether political leaders or leaders of thought; and this
explains why in what follows Plato is at such pains to
defend his position.  In his defence he addresses himself
rather to the leaders of thought than to the leaders of
politics.  He is more impressed by the evils which
result from the waste or wrong use of speculative genius
than by those which result from the comparative ignorance of governors.  Book VI is full of the tragedy which
is continually going on in the ruin or uselessness of the
most gifted men; for by philosophers he does not understand merely what we understand, he means men of
genius in the fullest sense of the word; and whereas we
mean by 'philosopher' a man with one special kind of
gift, his description of a philosopher enumerates all the
qualities which go to make up a great man.

From this point to the end of Book VII there is no real
break in the argument.  It is a continuous development
of what is involved in the position just laid down.  (1)
The first obvious section is that in which it is shown what
is meant by philosophers (474 B to the end of Book V).
(2) The second section (VI. 484 A to 487 A) shows that,
if this is what we understand by philosophers, they should

logically be the only persons fit to rule, because all the gifts and excellences, required of the perfect man, follow from the conception of the philosophic nature. These two sections together put before us Plato's ideal of the philosophic nature, and show us what philosophy ought to mean; and accordingly (3) the next section gives us the converse of the picture and shows us what philosophy does mean as a matter of fact. Here (487 A to 497 A) Plato tries to explain the admitted and glaring contrast between the ideal of the philosophic nature and the actual facts about it. The result is to show that these facts are due to the want of adjustment between the philosophic nature and its environment, that it is society itself which is to blame for these facts, for society corrupts or makes useless its noblest natures. (4) The next step therefore is to point out how society can adjust itself to philosophy, and how the environment of the philosophic nature is to be made favourable (497 A to 502 C). This finally leads us round again to (5) the question of education; for the adjustment of the soul to its surroundings and of its surroundings to it, is a question of education in the large sense of that word. Therefore, starting with a new and enlarged conception of the philosophic nature, we have to ask what education implies over and above the education of μουσική which has already been considered. The nurture of the philosophic nature through a training in the sciences, which leads eventually to the study of what we should call philosophy, is the subject of a section extending from VI. 502 C to VII. 534 E. The philosophic nature in its essence is that in man which seeks to understand things, which draws him to ask questions of the world about him and to try to find himself at home in it. The sciences represent the efforts of man to understand the world, and by being trained in them the soul comes to understand the world. They are the product of the philosophic spirit, just·as art again is the product of it in another phase or stage; and as, in the part of education previously described, art was used to be the nurture of the soul, so here the sciences are used to be the nurture of the soul in another stage. (6) The last section of the argument (535 A to the end of Book VII) accordingly deals with the practical application of this idea and the actual distribution of the educational life of the Guardians, the order of studies and the time spent on each.

474 B to
end of
Book V.

I. First then we come to Plato's analysis of the philosophic nature, intended to justify the statement that it alone is fit to rule. It is a passage in which we must be careful not to jump at conclusions, and must be content with what Plato actually says.

He first treats of the generic character of the philosophic spirit, and then gives us its differentia, that is, what distinguishes it from other spirits which bear a resemblance to it.

The generic character of the philosopher is deduced (474 B to 475 E) from the simple meaning of the word; he is a lover of something, namely of 'wisdom.' In English the word has lost its etymological meaning. 'Speculative,' in a general sense, is a more appropriate word than 'philosophic' to describe what is meant by φιλόσοφος, though it scarcely covers the same ground. Probably in Plato's time all that the word necessarily implied in ordinary use was a sort of higher culture and a claim to pursue some subject in a rather higher spirit than was common, so that the most different men, a statesman, an artist, a man of science, might be said

to be philosophic (φιλοσοφεῖν), not necessarily with the
meaning that they speculated or theorized on their
subject, but simply in so far as they followed it in
a higher spirit. We sometimes use the word in this
sense still; thus we might speak of a 'philosophic'
doctor or lawyer, meaning one who pursued his subject
for its own sake, and who went beyond the ordinary
range of it. Plato fixes at once on that element in the
word which in our use of the word 'philosopher' we tend
to leave out of sight, the element which signifies emotion.
ι 'Philosopher' means somebody peculiarly fond of a certain
thing.ǀ What does this fondness imply? When we
characterize a man as being essentially a man fond of
a certain thing, as a man peculiarly susceptible to beauty
(ἐρωτικός), or a born lover of distinction (φιλότιμος), or
a man with a natural taste for wine (φίλοινος), or the like,
we mean that he has a sort of indiscriminate enthusiasm
or appetite for the particular thing to which he is thus
susceptible. The man susceptible to beauty is normally
and perpetually in love; accordingly a whole vocabulary
has literally been invented in order to enable such
persons to describe the object to which they are susceptible, and to leave none of it unmarked. There is
to them a certain charm in youth which they will do
anything not to lose. So with the lover of distinction;
he has an indiscriminate appetite for honours; if he
cannot be a general he will be a lieutenant; he will be
anything rather than not get some title. (We must not
suppose that in this description Plato ignores facts about
which he is silent. He has emphasized one side of
enthusiasm for a given object, and with perfect truth;
but he has omitted to remark that all these tempera-
ments are peculiarly critical as well as indiscriminate.

The undoubted and curious fact is that, when a person
is intensely fond of a given thing, he is peculiarly critical
about it.  In the case of wine, and again in the case of
ambition, this is obviously so.  Yet, as in these cases,
the good critic must be enthusiastic about what he
criticizes.  When we call a man by a name which
implies that fondness for a certain thing is of the essence
of him, we ought to mean that this fondness is in the
first instance an indiscriminate appetite.  The best analogy
to express what he should be is the most homely; he
should be like a man who has a good and strong diges-
tion, he should be the opposite of squeamish.)

Now to apply this to the philosophic nature.  We
must not say that a man is of a philosophic nature unless
he has this indiscriminate appetite for μαθήματα.  We are
here again at a loss for a word ; for 'knowledge' is not
general enough.  Plato includes under the title φιλομαθεῖς,
people whom we should certainly not include under the
title 'seekers of knowledge'; he includes theatre-goers,
lovers of art, anybody to whom it is a keen pleasure to
exercise his eyes and ears.  Μανθάνειν means, in fact,
any exercise of mind through which we get a new
experience.

We have so far arrived at this, that the philosopher
is a person who has a boundless curiosity for new
experience ; and this is his generic character.  But it
is obvious that we cannot say that every one that has
this character is a born philosopher.  It is shared by
many whom we should not call philosophers ; by theatre-
goers, concert-goers, and intelligent artisans.  They have
some affinity with the philosopher, in having this indiscriminate pleasure in exercising their minds; but we must
ask, What is it that differentiates the philosopher from

those who share this generic character ?  The philosopher
proper is not one who likes looking at everything new,
but one who likes looking at the *truth*[1].

But what do we mean by the truth, the specific object
of the philosopher's vision, and how are we to distinguish
the truth ?  Plato proceeds (475 E to end of Book V) in a
preliminary and general way to answer this question, and
his answer brings before us, though in a statement which,
he implies, is only a brief *résumé* of something already
familiar to his hearers, his conception of 'forms' or
'ideas' (εἴδη, elsewhere ἰδέαι).

The assumption with which he starts, is simply that
there are distinct kinds of things or forms of being ;
justice, for instance, is absolutely distinct from injustice,
good from evil, beauty from ugliness.  Further, whenever we speak of a 'kind' or 'form' of thing, as of justice
or beauty, we mean that it is *one*; that there is a likeness
in all the things that belong to this kind ; that justice,
for example, in however many things it may occur,
remains one and the same justice.  Each distinct form
or kind is thus a unity.  But, further, each distinct kind
of thing appears as a great many things; or, as he puts
it, these forms or kinds 'communicate with one another
and with bodies and with actions'; and thus each appears
as a multiplicity.  What are called 'forms' then are, in
the first place, the elements of unity in the manifold
objects or things which we apprehend by the senses.
Now if we go back to the people who like using their
eyes and ears, and from whom the philosopher has
to be distinguished, we find that the objects on which
they exercise their minds are just these manifold things,

---

[1] Τοὺς τῆς ἀληθείας φιλοθεάμονας,—θεᾶσθαι is the word used of spectators
at the theatre.

voices, colours, figures, not beauty as such, but this, that,
and the other beautiful thing.  Whereas the philosopher
is the man who is able to distinguish the 'kind' or 'form,'
and who loves to do so.

In order to characterize these states of mind further,
Plato goes on to show (476 D) that the philosopher has
knowledge (γνώμη), while the mere φιλομαθής has only
'opinion' (δόξα)[1].  Now when we say that we 'know'
a thing we imply that it has being—in plain English,
that it is; and the being of a thing is exactly conter-
minous with its knowableness; if you ask what anything
really is, the answer must be that it is all that is known
about it.  On the other hand what is the negation of
being is also the negation of knowableness; it is nothing,
nonentity—not a mysterious something beyond what
we know, but just *nothing*, of which we can say nothing
and think nothing.  What answers to this on the part
of the mind, as knowledge answers to being, is utter
ignorance.  (Ignorance in the full sense is blankness of
the mind, and we must not read this passage as if Plato
spoke of ignorance as a faculty, having an object called
'not-being'; ignorance is the negation of faculty, and
its object is no object.)  Now in ordinary language we
distinguish knowing from mere thinking or opinion, which
lies between these two extremes of perfect knowledge or
mental illumination and perfect ignorance or darkness.
And knowledge and opinion are both called powers or
faculties (δυνάμεις).  How do we distinguish one power
from another?  It is not something that we can see,
distinguished by colour or shape; we distinguish it only
by what it does, by its province and operation.  Know-

---

[1] Besides what we call opinions, δόξα covers what we should call
perceptions and even feelings.

ledge and opinion, we agree, are different powers; they must therefore have different objects or operations, or produce different effects. The object of knowledge is what is; or, in other words, the operation of knowledge is to produce consciousness of what is. Opinion also must have an object; we cannot think nothing. On the other hand, it cannot have the same object as knowledge. It results that the object of opinion must both be and not be. We can neither say that it is in the full sense, nor that it is not in the full sense; for if we could, opinion would not be different both from knowledge and from ignorance.

With these results let us turn back (479 A) to the distinction we found between the manifold objects which present themselves to ordinary perception, and the distinct forms or elements of unity which underlie them. There are those, as we saw, who like to use their minds on the audible, visible, tangible world and its multiplicity; this they take to be the reality, and it is the sole reality that they believe in. And there are those, on the other hand, who assume the reality of what Plato calls forms (of some principle, for instance, which constitutes beauty itself, or justice itself), in which the manifold objects participate, but which none of them *is*. If we asked people of the former sort to tell us what is beauty, justice, weight, they would answer by pointing out beautiful objects, just actions, heavy things. But if we take any one of these many things, and observe it in a different relation or position, we find that, in Plato's language, it plays double, or exhibits opposite qualities. Take a beautiful thing and put it in a different situation, and it is easily made ugly;—this is most obvious in the case of colours. Take a just thing, an act or a law;

do the act or apply the law under different circumstances, and it is easy to make it unjust. Take a heavy thing, and it will be light when compared with what is heavier still. Thus what Plato says is illustrated alike from the spheres of art, morality, and nature. Each of the many things that come under any one category holds of opposite qualities; there seems no reason for saying it is this rather than that; we can most simply express its nature by saying that it is both. It both is and is not, i.e. is and is not beautiful, is and is not heavy. It answers then to what has been said of the object of opinion. These manifold objects, which we point to if asked what anything is, are the very objects which the bulk of mankind hold to be the only reality. Opinion is thus the state of mind of most people on most things. Yet it is clear that this state of mind does not correspond to what we expect knowledge to be, nor its object to what we expect reality to be. We may therefore say generally that what appears as the reality to ordinary people in their ordinary, received opinions about most things[1] is 'tumbling about' between 'what is' (the full reality) and 'what is not' (what has no reality at all).

Returning to the point at which we started, we have defined the philosophic nature as that which loves to look at the truth, and this is now found to mean that the philosophic nature is always looking for unity in the manifold or variety of which our ordinary experience is made up. For our ordinary experience is emphatically contained in a great number of separate objects; but, when we think, we cannot but see that these many things do not satisfy our idea of complete reality, and we have

[1] Τὰ τῶν πολλῶν πολλὰ νόμιμα καλοῦ τε πέρι καὶ τῶν ἄλλων, 479 D.

to seek for some principle or law or unity underlying these many objects. Everybody, we may remark, admits this to some extent. For instance, we all must recognize, if it is put to us, that justice did not come into existence with any particular law, and does not perish when any particular law becomes obsolete ; and that there must be some more permanent principle of justice underlying the actual laws and customs of society. And the same thing is still more obvious in physical science ; the first thing we have to learn when we try to understand physical phenomena is that such things as weight are relative. What Plato here calls philosophy is the clear and complete recognition of what we all to some extent admit. To state his conception of the philosophic mind briefly, it is one which constantly looks for principles or laws or unities of which the manifold of our experience is the phenomenon [1].

Plato's conception of forms corresponds to what we have in mind when we speak of 'principles' in morality and of 'laws' in science. What he says applies alike to moral, aesthetic, and physical conceptions ; the form in every case is that which is constant under variation, and it is what the man of science is always trying to get at. To the ordinary mind it seems at first unreal, less real than the ordinary view of things as they appear, the sensible world ; but the world as it is for science, the world of what Plato calls forms, is not a second, shadowy, unreal world, it is the same world better understood.

Plato speaks in this passage of the 'communion'

----

[1] We may compare Shelley's *Hymn to Intellectual Beauty*, and stanzas 52 and 54 in his *Adonais*, and Rossetti's sonnet, *Soul's Beauty*, with the language in which Plato contrasts sensible phenomena with the unseen principles which underlie them.

(κοινωνία) of forms 'with acts and bodies,' their being communicated to acts and bodies (476 A). The meaning of the expression may be put as follows:—If you take any given act called a just act, you will see it is not the whole of justice; it only partakes in justice along with other acts. Justice may be regarded as something communicable (κοινόν) in which various acts and persons partake without diminishing or modifying justice, as the common interest of a community is shared in by all its members without being diminished, and remains something one and the same in them all. The sense in which forms are said, in the same place, to communicate with one another, is different. If you take a given act, person, or thing, you find it is the meeting-point of various principles or forms. A particular act is never merely just; it always has other qualities besides, and it may even be partly unjust. So the forms of justice and injustice and other forms meet and communicate with one another in this act. In the *Sophist* Plato tells us that one of the great ways in which scientific knowledge shows itself is in recognizing what forms thus communicate with one another, and what forms have no communication with one another [1].

Plato contrasts clear and complete perception of a truth (perception of the form) with confused perception of it, by contrasting waking with dreaming vision (476 c). The ordinary man is in a dream with regard (amongst many other things) to justice; like a man in a dream he takes the resemblance for that which it resembles, or in other words takes one thing for another with which it is so far, but only so far, the same. For, Plato says, he identifies

[1] See *Sophist*, 251 D, and 252 E to 253 C. Cf. also *Politicus*, 277 E to 278 E.

particular just laws and actions with the principle of
justice. What does Plato mean by this? Our first impulse, if asked what justice is, would be to instance some
familiar actions, precepts, or institutions. We may be
right in thinking that the main part of justice for us
consists in them; but if (to take this instance) a man
*identifies* justice with certain laws, he may be reduced
to a hopeless difficulty if it can be pointed out that the
laws become unjust or obsolete. This has always made
mankind look for principles that remain constant as the
world changes. Laws, people say, may change, but
justice remains justice. Again, if a man acts on the
principle which Plato describes, that certain actions he
is familiar with are justice, when he comes to a just
action which looks rather different he thinks it is not
just, because he has identified justice with another thing.
In this he is like a man to whom shadows and superficial
resemblances are the whole reality. This is the meaning
of Plato's insistence that the just act is not justice, but is,
as he puts it, like justice.

2. The next section of the argument is complementary Book VI to
to that which has gone before it; it develops the con- 487 A.
ception of the philosophic nature from its more ethical
side. From the general description he has given of that
nature Plato now proceeds to deduce the ethical characteristics which it seems to him to imply. If the philosophic
nature were what this deduction shows it ought to be, there
could, he claims, be no doubt that it should be placed at
the head of society.

We have reached this conclusion: first, the philosophic
nature has an indiscriminate appetite for knowing about
things; secondly, its search for knowledge is distinguished
from other kindred forms of activity by the fact that it is

always trying to get at the underlying principles or 'forms' of which the manifold and changing world of experience, as it presents itself to us, is the partial appearance. We have next to ask, What is the bearing of this conclusion on the fitness of the philosophic nature to govern? and this again brings us back to the question, What is involved in being a good ruler or guardian (484 C)?

In order to keep or guard a thing you must have a clear vision of it. If then a man is to keep or guard laws and institutions and to improve them when they want reforming, he clearly must not be blind; he must have in his mind some clear pattern or principle by which he can know whether what he is maintaining is really just and expedient, and to which he can appeal when he wants to change existing institutions. To expand what Plato says, a statesman cannot know when the existing order is failing to serve its purpose, and in what way to reform it, unless he has in his mind some definite principle to go upon as to the purpose of that order. The perception of forms or principles is therefore of vital importance for the governor; and if a man who possesses it can add to it what is called experience (ἐμπειρία) he will have the essential requisites for good government. 'Εμπειρία, whether used in a good or in a depreciatory sense, means that knowledge which comes from habitually having to do with a thing. It may be extremely valuable; it may be almost worthless. Thus ἐμπειρία sometimes denotes mere superficial acquaintance with a thing, and is contrasted with knowledge of principles as we contrast rule of thumb with science[1]. Sometimes, as in this passage, it is used to

---

[1] In this sense Plato often uses τριβή; cf. 493 B.

denote the real acquaintance which comes from practice. In all such cases, it is represented as the necessary filling up of knowledge of principle; for a man cannot carry out principles unless he knows how to recognize them in the details of life and to apply them to details. True knowledge of principles involves *a fortiori* the knowledge of details. Plato is impressed with this truth; and in his scheme of philosophic education in Book VII, the fifteen years from the age of thirty-five to the age of fifty are set apart exclusively to the special purpose of acquiring the experience which is necessary in men who are to become leading statesmen. But what is here insisted on is the supreme importance for the statesman of having a principle in his mind. Without that experience is nothing [1].

It only remains now to ask (485 A to 487 A) whether the philosophic nature carries with it the other qualities, moral and intellectual, which go to make up a good and great character. This is somewhat analogous to the question in Book II, whether 'spirit' is compatible with gentleness. In that case Plato decided that the one quality, if real, implied the other, and his answer is the same here. He proceeds to deduce from the simple conception of love of truth all the virtues which seem to him to be part of perfect human nature. He first describes afresh in emphatic language the essence of the philosophic nature. It involves the passion for reality, the impulse to get at, and to be at one with, the permanent laws or principles of things. To such a nature, he remarks, there is nothing too great and nothing too little for study, because everything is capable of leading to the truth (cf. 402 C). From such a disposition there

[1] Cf. 409, 493 B, 520 C and 539 B.

follows instinctive hatred of falsehood. Self-control
follows no less, because the love of truth is emphatically
an absorbing passion; it is an appetite (ἐπιθυμία), and
when a man's appetites are intensely set in one direction,
other desires grow weaker like a stream whose waters
are diverted. Again, any kind of meanness or spiteful-
ness or little-mindedness is inconsistent with such
a nature, for the essence of it is to be always reaching
out after the whole world, human and divine. Courage
must follow too, for the fear of death is impossible to
a mind to which human life is a mere fragment in
a greater whole, and which has its vision set on all time
and on all existence. And justice must follow, for a
mind not influenced by fear, greed, or personal passion
has nothing to make it unjust[1]. There are also intellectual qualities which will go with such a nature. It
must be quick and retentive, for a man cannot love
learning if the practice of it is constant pain to him.
It must also possess ἐμμετρία—a sort of mental symmetry
or proportion. This is a quality which makes the mind,
so to say, naturally adaptable to the nature of things[2].
(Plato is fond of representing the relation between subject
and object in knowledge as the relation between two
things which are akin to one another and like one
another. It is habitual with him to say that a soul which
easily learns is one which has a great and natural affinity

---

[1] Or δυσξύμβολος, i. e. difficult to deal with in business.

[2] Εὐάγωγος, i. e. easily converted into any required shape, is used in
the same sentence as an equivalent to ἔμμετρος. The epithet εὔχαρις,
literally ' graceful,' is coupled with them. This also is a word expressing
primarily a physical characteristic. It is equivalent to εὐσχήμων, ' well-
shaped.' In III. 400 D sq. μουσική is, in effect, said to make the mind
εὐσχήμων and εὐάρμοστος (apt or adaptable). In that passage good taste,
good manners, good feeling are what the words refer to.

to things about it. Learning is the conforming of one's mind so as to fit things; everybody finds in learning that, while most things are difficult, there are some which it is comparatively easy for him to conform his mind to ; and the mind which is well proportioned (ἔμμετρος) is the mind which is most ready to be thus conformed to most things. Thus in the *Sophist*[1], the soul is said to be liable to two forms of evil, corresponding to bodily disease and to bodily deformity ; the former is vice, the latter is ignorance ; it is described as a condition where the soul has an impulse to think, but ' thinks beside the mark ' because there is a want of συμμετρία between the soul and truth ; ignorance is ἀμετρία. The philosophic nature, then, will have a natural predisposition to get hold of things; it will naturally adapt itself to the form and nature of things.) And now, Plato asks, who would hesitate to entrust the state to people endowed with the philosophic nature, if it necessarily implies all the qualities we have enumerated ?

Plato has here described the philosophic nature, as he understands it, *in its fullness.* It is simply the ideally good nature ; human nature completely gifted, and with free play given to all its gifts. His idea of it is at variance with our use of the word ' philosophic,' but it is quite consistent with the gradual development of the philosophic element in the soul as it has been described in the *Republic* from the first. The leading idea in Plato's conception of this element is that it is that in the soul which prompts it to go out of itself and unite itself with something else which is akin to it. It is thus the source in man of very different things. It is the source of gentleness and sociability, for it is that which draws

[1] 228.

men together with a sense of the familiarity of man to
man. It is the source of the love of beauty, including
the literary and the artistic sense, for in what is beautiful
the soul finds something which it recognizes as its own
(οἰκεῖον) and in the presence of which it feels at home.
Lastly, it is the source of love of truth, and this means
the impulse to understand and be at one with the world
about us. Though ordinary English psychology would
not agree with Plato in deriving these three different
things from a single source, there are many familiar
facts which illustrate, and to a certain extent bear out,
what he says. For example, we all know that for us
to understand another person, or to understand human
nature, sympathy is the essential thing. An 'unsym-
pathetic' man is a stupid man. The great masters in
understanding human nature have been those who have
felt at home with all mankind. Similarly in studying
things, even the most abstract, we cannot understand
them unless we feel a certain interest in them, and that
is the same sort of feeling as sympathy.

The philosophic element in man, then, is the essentially
human element; it is what makes a man a man, and therefore in its fullness it implies a perfect humanity, a fully
gifted human nature. For a conception parallel to this
we should turn in modern times to religious thought.
It is to be found in the love of God and man which is
represented in the New Testament as resulting in all
virtues, and making a perfect man. There is an analogy,
for instance, between Plato's deduction of all virtues
from philosophy, and St. Paul's deduction of all virtues
from 'charity' in 1 Corinthians xiii. For in this
conception of philosophy there are combined the
scientific spirit and the religious spirit in their highest

forms. It is the desire to be at one with the laws of
nature, and to live according to nature; and as to Plato
the world is emphatically the work of a divine intelligence, being at one with nature is also in a sense being
at one with God. That is why he speaks of such
understanding in terms which we should apply to
religious emotion.

3. To the proof that the philosophic nature is fit 487 A to
to rule Adeimantus (487 A) makes precisely the objection 497 A.
which every reader of the *Republic* is inclined to make.
This sounds very logical, he says, but the facts are all
the other way; if you look at the people who are called
philosophers, who pursue the study of philosophy beyond
the mere purposes of education, the best are made useless by the pursuit of philosophy, and the majority are
either eccentric or disreputable. One may compare this
with what might be said with equal truth about the
religious spirit ; some people are disposed to say that
what is called the love of God results either in a saintli-
ness which does no good to mankind, or in a zeal which
is alloyed with ambition, cruelty, and fanaticism, or,
worst of all, in cant and hypocrisy.

Socrates, so far from denying the facts alleged about
philosophers, heartily admits them. It is the very truth
of these facts which has led him to say that the evils
of mankind result from the divorce between speculation
and action. He goes on to attempt to explain them,
considering in order the uselessness of the few genuine
philosophers, the corruption of most of those who are
gifted with the philosophic nature, and the usurpation
of the name of philosopher by charlatans.

First (487 E to 489 D) Plato puts before us, in the
allegory or image (εἴκων) of the ship, a picture of the

situation in the world of the few genuine philosophers
that there are. In that allegory the owner of the ship
who sails in it is the Athenian people, which owns the
state and is supreme therein. Plato's description of him
is noticeable: though he is the biggest and strongest
man in the ship, he is rather deaf and short-sighted,
and he is ignorant of navigation, but he is a noble sort
of fellow, good at bottom. With this we may compare
the passage further on (499 E), where he says of the
masses, 'Don't be so hard on them ; it is not their own
fault that they are so hostile to philosophy, it is because
they have never been shown what it means.' Aristocrat
as he is by birth and intellect, Plato has a kind of half-
pity, half-sympathy for the people. The men he really
hates are demagogues in politics or philosophy. The
sailors in the ship are the statesmen and leaders of
public opinion. Their principle is that in order to sail
the ship it is not necessary ever to have learnt the art of
navigation, and indeed they hold that the art really
cannot be taught at all. The one man on board who
could sail the ship, who possesses the double qualification of theoretical knowledge and skill to command,
represents the true philosopher. He is regarded by
the others on the ship as a mere star-gazer. This is the
simple explanation of the uselessness of the philosopher ;
he is useless because the world will not use him. And
it is not in the nature of things, Plato thinks, that
a doctor should go about to his fellow-citizens and ask
them to let him heal them ; the natural relation is that
those who want should go to those who can give [1].

[1] The uselessness and helplessness of the philosopher are vividly described in *Theaet.* 172 C to 176 A, and *Gorgias*, 484 C to 486 D ; but in the
former passage Plato almost glories in them, and in the *Gorgias* the

But, secondly (489 D to 495 B), this uselessness of the genuine philosopher is the least of the causes which ruin the state. A far more serious cause is the demoralization of most of those who have the gift for philosophy. Before describing this, Plato returns to his account of the philosophic nature. He repeats in stronger terms what he has already said of it, that its essence is the irrepressible impulse to get behind the manifold and penetrate to the reality; that there is a certain kinship (ξυγγένεια) between the soul and reality, and that the philosophic nature is not satisfied until the soul has become actually one with reality [1]. How is it, then, that most of those who have this nature become demoralized? Its very gifts [2] help to destroy it by drawing it away from philosophy, its true life; and the external good things of life, beauty, strength, wealth, and powerful connexions, also help to destroy it. If we look at this phenomenon as part of a more general phenomenon, and regard the human soul as one among other living organisms, coming under the same category as plants and animals, we can understand how it comes about. All these things require a certain environment to live in, and they grow according to it. The strongest of them, Plato says, suffer more serious consequences from bad nourishment than the

philosopher is declared to be, in spite of them, the only true statesman. Plato's tone in the present passage is different; he feels that the only hope for mankind lies in the reconciliation of philosophy and the world.

[1] He describes knowledge under the image of sexual love. Truth and intelligence are, so to say, the offspring of the union between the soul and reality, and the attainment of truth is the satisfaction of the pangs of the soul. So in the *Symposium*, the attainment of knowledge of the good is represented under the figure of love clasping the beautiful; and the progress by which the mind comes to desire this knowledge is represented as a gradual progress from a lower to a higher idea of beauty.

[2] The φυσικαὶ ἀρεταί of Aristotle; *Eth*. VI. xiii. 1.

weaker; and so the most gifted souls are the most
injured by noxious surroundings; and the great criminals
of the world have never been small or weak natures, but
always great natures corrupted. This being so, let us
ask what is the environment into which our supposed
philosophic soul is born. It is born into an atmosphere
of public opinion which meets it in the assembly, the
law-courts, the theatre, the army—everywhere where
men are gathered together. This public opinion is
invincible and irresponsible; no individual soul can
assert its own independence of it except by some super-
human gift of nature; it is the source of law; practically
it is the great educator, and there is no other education
worth talking about. Public opinion is the one great
sophist, and those poor amateurs whom public opinion
represents as corrupting the youth, merely repeat and
formulate the dictates of the very society that thus stigmatizes them. Here Plato's tone towards the sophists is
one of contemptuous pity; they are simply bear-leaders of
the people. The people, symbolized before by the owner
of the ship, is here described, with less good nature, but
with no actual dislike, as a great and strong beast who
lets himself be handled by his keepers provided they
study his whims and do all they can to humour him[1].

The so-called leaders of opinion, then, only formulate
opinion. They have no knowledge of the things they
speak of; and though they talk of good and bad, just
and unjust, these are no more to them than names for
the likes and dislikes of the multitude[2]. And the

---

[1] Cf. Demosthenes, *Olynth.* III. 31.

[2] They can only say, Plato adds, that the just and good are the
necessary. See *Timaeus,* 47 E sq., for the antithesis of the necessary and
the rational.

multitude can never be philosophers, but will tend to be distrustful of philosophic principles, and hostile to them. Born into this atmosphere, what is likely to become of the philosophic nature with all its gifts?

The passage in which Plato answers this question (494) is supposed to refer to Alcibiades [1]. He certainly seems to be speaking of some actual man ; and we know that it was made a reproach to Socrates that Alcibiades and others among his most distinguished friends turned out badly. Suppose, says Socrates, after describing a man born into Athenian society with every gift of nature and of fortune, that some one goes to the man so gifted or surrounded, and tells him the truth, ' that he has not got wisdom, that he needs it, and that to win wisdom a man must be a slave under the burden of that task': what will happen? If at first he shows a disposition to listen, the leaders of society will at once be up in arms, and set in motion every means to destroy the influence of the one man who could save him ; they want to use him for their own ends [2]. This is the way in which men of a nature which ought to make them the benefactors of mankind generally become its destroyers. Society, partly unconsciously and partly deliberately, corrupts those who might be its noblest members.

Thus, to come to the third point (495 B to 496 A), Philosophy is deserted by those who ought to be her followers. Yet she still retains the splendour of a great name, and the reputation of a philosopher remains an object of ambition and competition. From this state-

---

[1] Cf. with this passage *Alcibiades Prim.* 105 B, 132 A, 135 E.

[2] There is a certain likeness in this passage to the saying of the New Testament : ' How hardly shall they that have riches enter into the kingdom of heaven.'

ment one may gather, as one may also gather from
Isocrates[1], that philosophy was a name over which
people fought, men of different kinds claiming for themselves the title of philosopher, as a title conveying
distinction. (There is no English parallel to this
name; but, though the word 'culture' has not the same
grand associations, it has been the subject of similar
contention.) Plato was one of those who aspired to bear
this title, and to exhibit a true conception of what
philosophy should be, and in developing that conception
he necessarily fell foul of others. Doubtless in contemporary literature he was called a sophist, and denied the
name of a philosopher; but on the whole it was Plato
who did most to fix the meaning of the word in its
highest sense. He now proceeds, in a most picturesque
and powerful passage, to describe the usurpation of the
name of philosophy by unworthy aspirants. It is the
most personal passage in the *Republic*. We cannot
be certain what kind of people—no doubt a particular
set of people, known to his readers—he was thinking of.
But one can guess that they were probably inferior
lawyers and rhetoricians, who were indelibly dyed with
what we might call the professional taint. He describes
them as having their souls cramped by their trade. (The
quality of βαναυσία (the taint of the shop) which he
attributes to them, seems originally to have described
a sort of physical distortion which arose from intense
application to mechanical arts, and to which was largely
due the contempt of the Greeks for such arts. Here this
analogy is applied to men's souls, as also in the *Theaetetus*[2],

[1] For the meaning which Isocrates attached to the words philosopher
and sophist see Κατὰ τῶν Σοφιστῶν, and Περὶ 'Αντιδόσεως.
[2] 173 A.

where we are told how the slavery of the law courts gradually makes men small and crooked in soul.) Little creatures of this sort, who are smart at their own trades, take a leap into philosophy. To change the metaphor, they marry Philosophy because there is no one else to do so, so poor is she ; and the fruit of their union is seen in those misbegotten theories and ideas which circulate in the world under the name of philosophic principles. This it is which brings upon philosophy the reproach that it is not only a useless thing, but is charlatanry.

It remains (496 A to 497 A) to mention a few causes which still keep a small remnant of true philosophic natures in the service of philosophy. Sometimes a man of noble nature, well educated, is banished, and thus escapes demoralization. Sometimes a great mind is born in some petty state, and despises its political life. Some few come to philosophy from contempt of the art or profession in which they are engaged ; a few are kept from politics by ill-health ; and a few, perhaps, by a sort of divine intimation like the divine sign which keeps Socrates himself from politics. All these are abnormal circumstances, which (except the last-named) would not arise if the world were as it ought to be ; and these few true philosophers who do survive, have nothing better to do than to keep themselves as pure from taint as they can, and to wait. A man who has lived a life like this will have done something great before he dies, says Adeimantus. Yes, answers Socrates, but not the greatest thing unless he finds a city fit for him ; for in that case, he will save both himself and the commonwealth.

4. In the section which now follows, we are shown 497 A to in a general way how the divorce between the world 502 C.

and philosophy, so mischievous to both of them, may be brought to an end. The foregoing sections have shown us what philosophy really is, namely the perfection of human life, and what the actual facts of human society are; this section brings us to the reconciliation between the elements which have been so violently contrasted just before. Various incidental passages in it express the same spirit of reconciliation. Socrates and Thrasymachus are declared to have been made friends; and Socrates himself, as he rises to the height of the argument, is made to picture the work of reconciling men to the truth in this life as only a fragment of a process which extends through eternity. The world at large is declared not to be so bad as we think; the hostility men feel to philosophy arises from ignorance of it, and if they could only be shown what it means, they would be reconciled to it. The reason why the mass of mankind will not believe us is because what is generally called philosophy is an artificial jargon of words and ideas fitted together like a puzzle, so as to look consistent, whereas true philosophy is a natural harmony of word and deed, theory and practice. And, again, the so-called philosophers are men who are generally occupied in personalities; whereas the true philosopher must from his own nature be at peace with men, for he dwells in a kingdom of peace, constantly in the presence of a world where injustice is neither done nor suffered, a world of unchangeable law, which is embodied reason [1]. If then there could be found a man who could transfer the perfect law, of which he has the vision, into the

---

[1] This passage states most strongly the belief that the mind assimilates the law and reason which it sees in the world. Cf. *Tim.* 90 D; *Theaet.* 176 B–E.

characters and institutions of men, like a great artist taking human nature as he finds it and moulding it in the light of his own high conception, we should indeed have a reconciliation between the ideal and the reality. However difficult this may be it is not impossible, for it is not impossible that a genuine philosopher may be found, possessed of great power, who will escape deterioration, and it is not impossible that mankind may listen to him.

5. The question which remains after this general indication of the possibility of reconcilement between philosophy and society, concerns the course of study and the method of life by which the men who have the philosophic nature can be trained, so as to be not the destroyers but the saviours of society. 'How,' as Socrates puts it, 'can the state handle philosophy so as not to be ruined?' The form of his question gives a strong, strange impression of the double-edged and dangerous character of the force in human nature with which he is dealing[1].

[1] 479 D.   Cf. VII. 537 D to 539 c.

# X. THE GOOD AS THE SUPREME OBJECT OF KNOWLEDGE

[*Republic*, VI. 502 c to 509 c.]

THE failure of society to provide the right environment for the philosophic nature having been made apparent, we are brought again to the question of education, which forms the subject of discussion from this point to the end of Book VII. A system of education is to be sketched out which will supplement, where this is necessary, the partial education already given through μουσική and γυμναστική. What is the particular defect of this education which requires to be supplemented? It is that it provided no adequate nourishment for the philosophic nature in its more advanced stage. There is an essential continuity between Books II to IV, and Books V to VII, in their treatment of the philosophic nature; still, so great an advance has been made in the latter Books in the conception of that nature and in the corresponding conception of the education it requires, that it looks as if Plato were beginning all over again, and had forgotten or ignored what seemed in the earlier Books to absorb his whole attention.

All the very different things that are said of the philosophic nature from Book II to Book IX are bound together by a common idea. This is the conception of the philosophic element in the soul, as that which makes the soul go out of itself under the attraction of something which is familiar to it and akin to it, and in union with which it finds satisfaction. In all its various senses the philosophic element in man is the attraction to what is like oneself and yet outside oneself, whether it be attraction to other people, or attraction to beautiful things in art or nature, or attraction to truth. In these different things Plato seems to see the more and the less developed stages of a single impulse in the soul, the highest stage being that in which the soul goes out not only to human beings, nor only to what is attractive through being beautiful, but to the truth of the world about it, in understanding which the soul finds a satisfaction of the same nature as that which it finds in union with its fellow-men. The problem, then, is to find a system of education which shall provide nurture for the soul in this stage, that is to say, for those very few souls in whom the philosophic impulse is so far developed as to require further nurture. The great bulk of men would find satisfaction for this element of the soul in the active life of good citizenship in which they are engaged in common work with their fellows, but there would be a few among them driven by an inherent impulse of their natures to look for laws or principles underlying the institutions which the bulk of men accept with various degrees of acquiescence. In the case of such it is of the utmost importance both to themselves and to society that they should be trained rightly, for otherwise they will follow their impulse wrongly. By what actual method of study and life will these few become, as Plato says, the saviours of society?

More than any other passage of the *Republic*, the passage in which this question is introduced explains the relations between the earlier and the later parts of the dialogue. A criticism is made on Books II to IV, and we are told what advance on them is required. We are told that the community of wives and the appointment of rulers are two difficulties which Socrates had been conscious of all along, and of which in the earlier Books he had intentionally put off the treatment. Community of wives has been further discussed in Book V, and here we are brought back to the question of the appointment of rulers. Socrates refers explicitly to the sentence in Book III, in which the selection and appointment of rulers is said to have been dealt with in outline and not with ἀκρίβεια[1]; and the nature of the advance now to be made is summed up in the word ἀκρίβεια. This is a quality originally associated with artistic work, and ἀκριβής means primarily, not accurate or precise, but exact, in the etymological sense of finished. It is the opposite of what is merely sketched, and we constantly find Aristotle opposing it to what is 'in outline' (τύπῳ)[2]. All through this passage we find the same contrast between what is to follow and what has gone before, insisted on from different points of view. The earlier treatment was incomplete (ἀτελές), it was a sketch (ὑπογραφή), it was something without its full 'measure' (not accurately measured). Where did this want of completeness in the earlier parts of the work lie? It appeared in two principal points: in the account of the selection and appointment of Guardians, and in the

---

[1] 414 A.    [2] e.g. in *Eth. Nic.* II. ii. 3.

account (which really underlay this) of justice and the other virtues[1]. Plato begins with the appointment of rulers.

The principle upon which the original rulers were selected was that the best man to guard anything is the man who loves it most. Accordingly the supreme qualification for a Guardian of the state was that he should really love the state. The test to be applied to his qualifications consisted in exposing him to various emotional trials, pleasures, pains, and fears, which would be calculated to make him give up the belief (δόγμα) he had learned, 'that he should do in everything that which seemed best for the state.' If he showed his constancy by withstanding all these tests he would be a full Guardian (φύλαξ παντελής)[2]. But this selection was said at the time to be only provisional, and now the course of the argument has brought us back to the question who are fitted in the fullest sense of all to be Guardians (τοὺς ἀκριβεστάτους φύλακας), and we have already found that they will have to be philosophers. This involves a fuller training and a severer testing of the character of the Guardians than we at first thought necessary. It means that the philosophic element in human nature, which we saw from the first must be strong in those who are to rule, contains in it capacities for development greater than we had then any idea of. Out of this element arises the irrepressible speculative impulse in human nature with all its capacities, and this impulse is a double-edged thing. We see now that it is not enough

---

[1] What is described as want of ἀκρίβεια refers indifferently to the state of mind of the Guardians selected, and to our own state of mind or that of the supposed electors of the Guardians.

[2] See 412 B to 414 B.

merely to regard constancy of character (βεβαιότης) in
selecting our Guardians, for we have to look also for
a quality which seems just the opposite of that. The
speculative temperament does not naturally fit with the
orderly and solid and constant temperament; it is quick,
impatient, aspiring, and this side of it cannot be ignored.
And yet we cannot dispense with that constancy which
we before made the essence of a Guardian's character.
So we have again come upon the problem of how to
effect a reconciliation between contradictory qualities,
for we have to combine in our Guardians the intellectual
restlessness and aspiration of the philosophic character,
with that orderliness and constancy which is equally of
the essence of a good nature. We want, then, to fill up
the sketch of the choice and education of Guardians by
showing how to test and train this new and dangerous
element. Therefore to the tests of pleasure and pain
we shall have to add the tests of intellectual work, and
see whether the Guardian has also the sort of courage
that will stand them. We have besides to supplement
our former system of education by taking account of the
philosophic faculty, not in the sense of the love of beauty
and the like, which μουσική took account of, but in its
present sense of hunger for knowledge.

Again (504 A), there was a want in the account given
of human morality in the earlier Books. The general
principle by which we determined its nature was one of
empirical psychology. We took from observation three
main elements in the soul, and explained the four main
virtues that are generally recognized by showing that
they expressed certain states of these three elements and
certain relations between them. But, as was stated at
the time (435 D), the description then given of these

virtues was inadequate. We now want to see the moral nature of men wrought out into a perfect and finished picture. (It is to be noticed in this passage (504 D) how naturally and almost without warning the supposed Guardians, whose education is under discussion, are identified with ourselves, the parties to the discussion. This is a good instance of the fact that the education of the Guardians is primarily meant for ourselves.)

The result of this whole passage is that, whether we regard the *Republic* as a treatise on political and social reform, or simply as the exhibition of an ideal theory of human life which every one may apply for himself, it is necessary that the previous conception of what man is and needs should be carried further and filled up. And if we ask why, the answer is that there is something in human nature, at any rate in the nature of those who influence the world, which will not be satisfied with the development of character which, in the earlier Books, seemed to fulfil the requirements of morality.

The next question therefore is, What addition in 504 E. knowledge will supply the want we have discovered in the training which the earlier Books prescribed? What sort of knowledge is required to convert the previous conception of the virtues into a finished conception, and the Guardian as previously described into a Guardian in the fullest sense? The answer is: 'knowledge of the good.' The Guardians will be poor guardians of justice unless they understand wherein is the good of justice; until a man learns what it is that makes the different sorts of goodness intrinsically good, his possession of them is only the hold of opinion and not of knowledge. The knowledge of the good will fill up to their full measure all the inchoate ideas of morality which we have thus far come across. This is the highest object of knowledge (μέγιστον μάθημα), and in it all the utmost aspirations of the speculative spirit will find satisfaction. The more developed form of education which is now to be described must therefore be an education which gradually leads up to the conception of the good.

It is essential to the understanding not only of Plato but of Greek philosophy generally, both moral philosophy and the philosophy of knowledge, to realize the place held in them by the conception of the 'good.' We see at once from what Plato now proceeds to say of the good, that three ideas, which to us seem to have little concern with one another, are for him inseparable. The good is at once: first, the end of life, that is, the supreme object of all desire and aspiration; secondly, the condition of knowledge, or that which makes the world intelligible and the human mind intelligent; thirdly, the creative and sustaining cause of the world. How did Plato come to combine under one conception ideas apparently so remote from one another?

We must banish from our minds at starting the ordinary moral associations of our word 'good,' those, for instance, which attach to the phrase 'a good man [1].' Τὸ ἀγαθόν does not in the first instance involve any moral qualities; both to ordinary people and to philosophers among the Greeks the good meant the object of desire, that which is most worth having, that which we

---

[1] [The phrase ἀγαθὸς ἀνήρ as actually used in Greek seldom or never means what we mean when we call a man simply a good man. It means a man good at some work or function implied by the context, and in fact is most commonly used of a man good at fighting. The modern colloquial usage by which in discussing, say, football players, we might say 'So-and-so is a good man' is identical with the usage of the term in Greek. —Ed.]

most want. We also are quite familiar in books with the conception of the desirable as the object of human will, but we do not at once realize its meaning. The best way to make ourselves realize it is to say that the good or desirable at any given moment to any given man is that which he would rather be or do or have than anything else. If at any given moment a man will give up his life in order to get money or to save his country or avenge himself, then money, or the safety of his country, or vengeance, is to him at that moment the one good ; for it he is ready to give up everything which he can give up. Therefore what is the good to us varies every day, but at every moment there is something which we take as our good. In Greek philosophy and popular thought, it was a sort of ultimate truth that man is a being who lives for something, that is to say that he has a good. This is the most fundamental fact about man ; he is always living for something, however much he tries not to do so.

Further, to a Greek, certainly to Plato and Aristotle, this is only another way of saying that man is a rational creature. When we speak of 'a rational person' we generally mean one who does not make a fool of himself; this and other phrases, such as 'a rational being,' do not with us refer to anything so far back as do the Greek phrases which we should translate by them. To the Greeks the statement that man is a rational being meant simply that man cannot help aiming at something ; he is a creature of means and ends ; everything that he does is from the constitution of his nature regarded by him as a means to something. This is a fundamental point of Greek moral philosophy Hence the inseparable connexion in Plato and Aristotle between reason and the good. This is not an association between some particular good thing, some true end of life, and some particular kind of reason which is specially rational, as our use of the word 'rational' and of the word 'good' might suggest, but between reason as such and an end as such. The rationality of man means that he is a creature who has ideals, and who cannot help having them. An ideal is something which is not fully present at this particular moment in this particular thing, but is yet partly attained in it. The conception of an ideal involves, on the one hand, that it is never wholly realized, on the other that it is continually being realized. However much and however often the object with which man acts may change, he never lives absolutely in the present ; in the moment he is always thinking of something beyond the moment ; and it is in virtue of reason that he does so. It is owing to this that man is what we call a moral being. He is capable of morality because he has reason, and reason compels him to live for an end ; and the problem of moral philosophy to the Greeks is always, starting from this fundamental conception, to determine the true end for which man should live. It follows that to the Greek thinkers the moral life is practically identical with the rational life (in the sense of the life in which reason performs its functions most truly). The moral life can only mean that in which a man does all that he does with a view to, and in the light of, the true good. The man to whom the true good is most constantly present in all that he does is the best man. Thus the best life is the most rational life, because it is that in which action and thought are most concentrated upon, and regarded most as a means

to, the central principle or end of life, which is what the
Greeks call the good.

It is in this point that what we commonly distinguish
as the moral and the scientific views of life converge in
Greek philosophy. We say that Greek moral philosophy,
as compared with modern, lays great stress on knowledge
and gives excessive importance to intellect. That impression arises mainly from the fact that we are struck
by the constant recurrence of intellectual terminology,
and omit to notice that reason or intellect is always
conceived of as having to do with the good. Reason is
to Greek thinkers the very condition of man's having
a moral being, because, as has just been said, by reason
they understand that in man which enables him to live
for something. Their words for reason and rational cover
to a great extent the ground which is covered by words
like 'spirit,' 'spiritual,' and 'ideal' in our philosophy.
They would have said that man is a rational being,
where we should say that he is a spiritual being. It is
true, however, that Greek moral philosophy is intensely
intellectual, and that the moral and the scientific do
tend, especially in Plato, to converge.

From the point of view of the study of human life,
we have already seen that the necessity of living for
something is due to the presence of reason in man; and
now, turning from human action to nature as the object
of science, we find the Greeks assigning essentially the
same function to reason as before. For the presence of
reason in the world, which is what makes it possible to
understand things, means for them that every object in
nature or art contains and expresses some good or end.
The philosophy of morals and the philosophy of science
in Plato and Aristotle are dominated by what is called

a teleological view. In their writings intelligence and
the good are treated as almost correlative ideas; wherever there is intelligence there is a good aimed at. And
this idea is not merely confined to human life, but is
applied all the world over.

We must, however, be careful not to misunderstand
this idea. We generally mean by a teleological view
of the world one which explains nature by showing that
nature has been made to serve the purposes of men.
When popularized in this crude form, teleology leads to
the notion that nothing has any purpose, meaning, or
interest, unless it is shown to be serviceable to man;
and as our notion of what is serviceable to us is very
narrow, the so-called teleological view comes to be
an absurdly narrow and false one, against which the
scientific spirit is always protesting. But teleology in
any really philosophical sense means something very
different. Plato and Aristotle did not at all regard
man as being the highest thing in the universe, and
were therefore far from regarding the universe as made
for man. For them the evidence which everything gave
of the operation of reason lay simply in the fact that
each thing had a certain function, was calculated to do
one thing and not another, and that the various parts
of it converged to that end. If you take any complex
object (and all objects are complex), that is any object
which is a whole of parts, the only way to explain it or
understand it is to see how the various parts are related
to the whole; that is, what function each of them
performs in the whole, how each of them serves the
good or end (τέλος) of the whole. The good or end of
the thing is the immanent principle which we have to
suppose in it in order to explain it, and which is involved

in calling it a whole at all. The progress of knowledge is to Plato and Aristotle the increased realization of the fact that each thing has thus its function, and the world is, in Plato's phraseology, luminous just so far as it reveals this fact.

The best instance by which to approach this view is the simple instance of any work of art. When a man, to take the example used by Plato in the *Gorgias* (503 E), is making a ship, he does not go to work at random ; you observe that he puts the pieces together in a certain order with a certain end in view. The best ship-builder is the one who puts the parts together in that order which best enables them to serve the purpose intended. To serve this purpose is the ship's good. The good of anything is to be or do what it is meant to be or do ; and the ship realizes its good, or object, or end in sailing well. Thus it is literally true that every bit of the ship-builder's work is determined by the good, that is by what the whole thing he is making is intended to be or to do. Reason, therefore, as embodied in human art, artistic reason, shows itself in making a certain material express a certain good ; and the most artistic work will be found to be that which most, in every part of it, expresses such an end, good, or principle[1]. This is the teleological view ; that view simply consists in seeing everywhere a certain function to be exercised, a certain work to be done, or a certain end or good to be worked out. From this point of view the more we can detect the function or good of anything, the better we understand it. To a person who knows nothing about the function of a ship, it may truly be said to be an unintelligible thing. And

---

[1] It is the same fact that is pointed to when we say that the condition of good artistic work is proportion.

that of course is our attitude towards the great majority
of things in the world ; we wonder what they can be for,
we do not see the good of them.

This conception, then, is applied to all spheres of
existence, to nature, art, and moral life, because in all
of these there is present intelligence.  It is clear how
the view applies in the case of art and morality, but it
applies also under certain limitations in the case of nature.
For in regard to nature, where he does not make but
observes, man uses the same principle theoretically, which
in art and moral life he uses also practically ; his reason
works on the same lines.  Thus in regarding a plant
or an animal, he assumes from the first and unconsciously,
that it is a unity, an organism.  He begins to analyze it
into parts, and throughout the process of analyzing it and
putting it together again, he is guided by the conception
of the plant or animal as a whole, having a principle
which makes it that plant or animal.  An organism is
a natural object of which the parts can be seen to be
means to an end, instruments (ὄργανα) serving a purpose.
The conception of an organism thus implies teleology.
Accordingly modern science, however much it repudiates
teleology of a certain kind, is and must be inspired by
the spirit of teleology.  A book on botany, for instance,
exhibits this spirit in every page, for, throughout, the
problem which the botanist proposes to himself is to
discover the function of something (its ἔργον)[1].  But

[1] [In the sciences which deal with what we call, by comparison, inorganic nature, the conceptions of 'organism' and 'function' are of
course not prominent, but it is nevertheless obvious that everything in
nature is understood through the connexion of its own elements and by
the way it acts on and is acted upon by other things, that is by the part
it plays in relation to other elements in an ordered whole.  (Cf. *Hellenica*,
p. 173.)  The 'teleological view' as applied to nature generally is simply

when scientific men repudiate teleology they are right so far as they are insisting on this: that we must not interpret the postulate that everything has its function to mean that each particular thing has its end in serving some other particular thing; and that we must not allow the postulate to make us anticipate the results of investigation. It is one thing to say we can only interpret nature if we suppose it to have some meaning, and another thing to say that the first meaning we find in things is the true one.

The view then which sees everywhere means and ends is emphatically the view of Greek philosophy. This may be simply expressed in Greek phraseology by saying that the one question is, What is the good? For, to put the matter in a summary way: the word 'good' means that which anything is meant to do or to be. The use of the word implies a certain ultimate hypothesis as to the nature of things, namely that there is reason operating in the world, in man and in nature. This reason shows itself everywhere in the world in this particular way, that wherever there are a number of elements co-existent there will be found a certain unity, a certain principle which correlates them, through which alone they are what they are, and in the light of which alone they can be understood. Thus the good becomes to Plato both the ultimate condition of morality and the ultimate condition of understanding. These are not two things, but one and the same principle showing itself in different subject-matters.

To come back to human life and morality, how does this view apply to them? In the first place, it implies

the recognition of this fact. The significance of it will be seen later in considering Plato's theory of science.—ED.]

that the life of human society and that of the individual will inevitably be regarded as a certain adaptation of means to an end, and that human society and the individual soul will be regarded as organisms. Thus, as regards society, at the beginning of Book IV, where the question is raised whether we are making the Guardians happy, the reply is that you can only consider the well-being of a part when you have considered the good of the whole. So again in Book VIII the ruined spendthrift is described as seeming to be a member of the community without really being so, because he is, so to speak, inorganic[1]. And the whole decline of human society which Plato describes in Book VIII consists in its gradually ceasing to be organic. It is easy to see the bearing of this idea on virtue. Virtue is that quality of a thing which makes it good of its kind; that it is good of its kind means that it does its work well; a morally good man is one who does his work well; the man who does his work well is the man who fills the place assigned to him in the world well. The assumption, as regards society, is that every man has his place and his work. And the same idea of an organism in which each part has its place and its work is applied also to the individual soul. The virtue of the soul is that each part of it should do its work well; and what the work of each part is, is determined by the good or interest of the whole soul. Whether any given act you do is good may be simply tested by the question, Can you honestly say that it contributes to the good of you taken as a whole?

Thus the notion of the good, in its moral application, resembles the notion of principle. A man of principle

---

[1] μηδὲν ὄντα τῶν τῆς πόλεως μερῶν.  552 A.

means a man who can be said more than most men to live with a purpose, or (if you like) consistently, a concentrated man, whose acts, thoughts, and desires converge to some one end [1]. It might be said that this description would include any man who had a strong will, good or bad. We should reply that every man is really an element in a world, in a society, ultimately in the κόσμος, the intelligible order of the universe. Accordingly the purpose which dominates his life, the good for which he lives, will be good in itself in proportion as it serves a wider purpose, and ultimately the purpose or good of the order of the world. As every picture, every ship, every man's life, everything which is an ordered and organized whole, may be called a κόσμος, a little world, so the whole world, if we could see it, is *the* κόσμος, the one order or whole in which all the rest are organic parts. This idea is worked out in the *Timaeus*, and is the animating thought of that dialogue ; it is applied there primarily to the physical universe, but is applicable also to society and human life [2], and it is so applied in the *Republic*.

A man's life then is morally good in proportion as it exhibits purpose, and not merely purpose, but a purpose going beyond himself. It is good in proportion to its concentration on the one hand, and on the other hand in proportion to the amount which it embraces and the width of the interests it serves. The greater part of our lives is practically purposeless, and it is just for that reason that they come to so little. We have an idea of something of supreme value, some good, but as to

---

[1] This is what is expressed by the metaphor of harmony in 443 D. & E.

[2] Cf. e.g. *Timaeus*, 47 D, where κατακόσμησις of the soul is spoken of.

what it is we are 'in darkness'; we do not see where we
are going or what we are doing; and therefore most of
the means we use, most of the so-called good things
which are the immediate objects of our aims, are of little
profit to us (505 E). This is the case even with the
actions which we do in accordance with our views of
justice and honour.    Hence the necessity that the
guardians, whose business it is to govern others and
to direct the moral purpose of the community, should
have knowledge of the good.    A man who does not see
what is the good of justice or honour (what is the place
that it holds in the world) will not be much of a guardian
of it, for he has no firm hold of it (506 A).    We see then
why it has been said that the conception of the good is
wanted to fill up our sketchy, fragmentary view of human
life, and to give it finish (ἀκρίβεια).    The more a man sees
what he is going after, the more he will see life not as
a mere outline, but as a whole with a structure and
a plan.

   Further, the more this is the case with a man, the
more his life will become a work of intelligence on his
own part, and intelligible to other people.    We understand things just in proportion as we see the good of
them ; and the supreme good, the end to which all things
converge, is, in Plato's metaphor, the sun that gives light
to the intelligible universe.    Intelligibility is the reflected
light of the supreme purpose which pervades the world
and is reflected through various *media* to us.    Everything
in the world in its measure reveals, or is the appearance
of, the good.    We may say therefore, to give a general
statement of Plato's conception, that for a man to attain
the good, so far as it is given to man to do so, would be
for him to live in the light.    So to live means that he

should realize constantly his position in the economy of things, in the society of which he is a member, in humanity, in the world. And, seeing his position, he would realize how he can best be that which he is and best do that which he does. We see then how closely related morality and knowledge are in Plato's mind. This ideal of a man's life might equally well be described as perfect knowledge and understanding (so far as that is possible) of himself and of his own life, or as perfect performance (so far as that is possible) of his true function in the world of which he is a part. From both points of view, the conception of what we call an organic whole with a unifying principle in it lies at the bottom of Plato's conception. On the one hand to understand the world, or any bit of it, is to see it in the light of the good, that is to see how the different parts of it converge to their common end. On the other hand, to be perfectly good is 'to do one's own business' (τὰ αὑτοῦ πράττειν), which always means to do what, in virtue of what one is, one can do best, and what contributes best to the good of the whole of which one is a part.

We have seen that the good is also the end of life. When man is spoken of as living for an end (τέλος), we have to remember that the Greek word primarily means, not an end in the sense of what we come to last, but the finished or consummated work. In the case of man, the end is just to be, in the course of his life, in his imperfect way what nature has given him the capacity to be. Thus when we speak of the good as the end of life we must guard against supposing that it is any single tangible thing which a man can get and have done with. It is an ideal which cannot possibly be attained, or it would cease to be an ideal. This is just as true of

Aristotle's ideal as of Plato's; just as true of the Utilitarian ideal as of any other. Everybody means by the ultimate ideal not wealth, health, power, or knowledge, but always something which makes these good to him, as is proved by the fact that nobody is ever finally satisfied, or sits down and says, 'I have the good.' The difference between one theory about life and another does not concern this point; it lies in the particular ways in which men conceive of the ultimate good, and in the ways in which they connect this good with the rest of their lives.

The good, as we remarked at starting, is represented by Plato not only as the end of life and as the cause of things being understood, but also as the source of the being of everything in the world; it actually makes things what they are, and sustains them or keeps them in being. What Plato means by this may be seen from the passage in Book IV (already referred to) where he is answering the question whether the guardians would be happy. If one takes a human society one sees that it is literally true that a member of that society is exactly what he does in that society, just as a hand or a foot is what it does in the body. For the function or ἔργον of a thing is its being; you cannot separate the two ideas. If you are asked what anything is, every answer you give describes a function of the thing. The being of a thing is its activity. When a man ceases to do that which makes him himself, he has really ceased to be that man; if he is performing no civic function he is no citizen, just as if you cut off a foot from the body it is not a foot. This is the simple principle which makes Plato say that the good is the source of the being of things. The reality of things is what they mean;

what they mean is determined by their place in the order of the world; what determines their place in the order of the world is the supreme good, the principle of that order. Thus their very being is determined by that order; they realize their true being in proportion as they recognize that order; and so far as they refuse to recognize it they fall out of that order, and literally give up so much of their being.

The same conception of the good appears in other dialogues. The *Gorgias* has already been referred to. In the *Phaedo* the good is represented as the final cause of the world, which is what in the truest sense makes and holds together the world; it is contrasted with what are ordinarily called material causes, which Plato calls 'the conditions without which the cause would not be a cause[1].' In the *Philebus* it is represented as manifesting itself in three principal forms, truth, beauty, and proportion[2]; but under all its aspects it is the principle of the *order* of the universe. In the *Timaeus*, where Plato describes in 'picture language' the creation of the world, the creator (δημιουργός) embodies to a great extent, in a personal and mythological form, the same attributes as are ascribed to the form of the good in the *Republic*. He makes the world to be as good as possible, because he is himself perfectly good and therefore free from all envy and perfectly beneficent. Further, he makes the world as we perceive it with the senses (δόξῃ μετ' αἰσθήσεως ἀλόγου δοξαστόν) after the pattern of a world which is 'intelligible' (νοήσει μετὰ λόγου περιληπτόν); which means not that there are really two worlds, but that, as we might say, the world as it is revealed through the senses is the

---

[1] *Phaedo*, 97 B to 99 C.  [2] *Philebus*, 64 B to 65 A.

manifestation of an intelligible order[1]. At the end of
the *Timaeus* we find the distinction between the Creator
and the intelligible world tending to disappear, while
the sensible world itself becomes God made manifest to
human senses (θεὸς αἰσθητός)[2]. As in the *Republic* we
are told of the good that it cannot be explained to us
in its fullness as it is, so in the *Timaeus* we are told that
it would be impossible to speak of the gods and of the
origin of the world in exact and altogether consistent
language[3]. The two dialogues then, in spite of the
difference in form, agree in this, that the world as we
see it is represented as revealing, though revealing imperfectly, those intelligible principles upon which it is
really constructed, and that this system of intelligible
forms is represented as leading up to and depending upon
some supreme creative and sustaining power. Moreover,
in the *Timaeus* as well as the *Republic*, we are told that
the highest bliss of man consists in getting to be at one
with the universe of which he is a part[4]. In the
*Timaeus* the supreme power in the universe is described
in a personal way, in the *Republic* it is described in
what we call an abstract way. Of the two ways no
doubt Plato thought the latter truer. Though he never
hesitated to use the language of popular Greek theology
to express philosophical ideas of his own, he often lets
us know that this language did not and could not
embody the truth as it is. The 'form of the good' in
the *Republic* occupies the place in regard both to morals
and to science which the conception of God would

---

[1] *Timaeus*, 27 D to 30 B.        [2] Ibid. 92 B.
[3] Ibid. 29 B & C [where 'the gods' is seen from the context to be
equivalent to 'God.'—ED.]
[4] Ibid. 47 B & C.

occupy in a modern philosophy of morals and nature, if that philosophy considered the conception of God as essential to its system. Plato in the *Republic* does not call this principle God but form. He has assigned to a form or principle the position and function which might be assigned to God, but he still speaks of it as a form or principle. With this reserve, we may say that the *easiest* way to give Plato's conception a meaning is to compare it with certain conceptions of the divine nature, for example with the conception of the ' light of the world.'

We may now summarize the passage in which the 504 F. to conception of the 'good' is introduced to us in the 506 B. *Republic*. Certain preliminary and more or less accepted notions of the good are first brought forward. In the first place everybody allows that, whatever else the good means, it is that which gives all other things their value. We must not think of it as a thing that can be taken from or added to health, wealth, and the rest; it is simply that in everything which makes it really worth having; all men, philosophers and others alike, assume this. Plato goes on to mention two current theories as to what is most worth having in the world. Some call pleasure the good, holding that what we want is to feel pleased, to get enjoyment. Others call intelligence the good, holding that what we want is to understand things. These two theories, which form the subject of discussion in the *Philebus*, are but briefly mentioned here. Plato simply points out where they both fall short. Those who make pleasant feeling the one object of life are obliged to allow distinctions of good and evil in pleasure, and this at once introduces a standard other than pleasure. So again those who say that understand-

ing is the true good are obliged to import into their
definition the very conception that they suppose themselves to be defining; for when asked the question,
'understanding of what?' they answer, 'understanding
of the good'; so that both parties are full of inconsistency
(πλάνη). But amid all this inconsistency one thing is
certain, that people are in earnest on this matter, and that
when they talk about the good they mean something
real. Many are found quite willing to put up with the
appearance of morality; there the appearance has a certain
value; but nobody would willingly put up with the appearance of the good, for the good, their own good, is
what people really want. But it is just this real thing
about which they are so much in the dark; every soul
surmises that there is something of this sort, something
in comparison with which nothing else is worth having;
but every soul is in doubt what it is, and is without any
sure or permanent belief about it (ἀπορεῖ). And this
very uncertainty makes us miss what is good in other
things; our being in the dark about the real or ultimate
good re-acts on our ideas of the ordinary 'good things,'
commonly so called, and makes our aims uncertain.
Certainly then, this ultimate good is the one thing about
which men who are going to govern the state should not
be in the dark.

506 B to
509 C. After this preliminary survey of accepted beliefs and
diverse theories, Socrates, who has been spending his
life in enquiring into the nature of the good, is called
upon to say what he himself thinks about it. He answers
that to express what is in his mind all at once would be
a flight above his power; the utmost he can do at first
is to explain his conception of the good by an analogy:
'I cannot show you the good, but I can show you the

child of the good.' From what follows later on [1] it is pretty clear that Plato was quite serious with the notion that the world, as it is to human sense, is a manifestation, a likeness or image, of an intelligible and non-sensible order. So that the passage, which now follows, about the sun, is not merely an illustrative simile, but expresses to Plato's mind a real analogy between the phenomena of the sensible world and the non-sensible principles they express [2]. In the comparison which he draws the good

[1] Cf. the passages from the *Timaeus*, quoted on p. 232.

[2] [It is not possible to reproduce the whole of this passage as it occurred in the lectures, and the foregoing sentences as they stand might give a false impression of what the comparison between the good and the sun leads to. In order to follow the main course of Plato's thought we must be careful at first not to press this comparison at all beyond the points which he specifically uses it to bring out. The position of the sun in the visible universe here supplies Plato with imagery to express the idea that the good is the source of all knowledge and the source of all being. In Book VII the sun affords Plato more imagery for describing the stages by which man may be led up to a clear vision of the good. Now it is probable, as this passage in the lecture suggests, that Plato felt it was no accident that made this imagery available for him, by placing in the world, as seen by the eye, a visible object thus comparable to the chief object in the world as thought could make it known. He probably thought that, so to speak, it was part of the function of the sun thus to present a type of the good. Compare the language used about the heavenly bodies generally in VII, 529 C, sq., and the passage already referred to in the *Timaeus*, 47 A to E. But he does not develop this idea, and the point of this passage, in the agreement of the *Republic*, lies simply in the statement that the good is the cause of all knowledge and of all being. In the following passage (the comparison of the divided line) where this is expanded and explained, the real relation of the good to the visible world begins to appear in its main outlines, and then of course the sun does not play a part different from that of any other visible object. As we make an advance in understanding the world when we turn our attention from things as we see them to the unities or principles which underlie what we see, so we make a further advance when we rise from the principles which thought first discovers in the world to the ultimate principle of all, the good. As the varying multitude of things pre-

is said to be in the intelligible world as the sun is in the visible. He works out the comparison of the good with the sun through a theory of light and of vision which was wrong, but this does not affect the points which he wished to bring out in his conception of the good. They are briefly these. First, the good is the source of intelligence in the mind and intelligibility in the object, just as the sun is the source of vision in the eye and of visibility in its object. Truth is the reflexion of the good ; the world is intelligible and the soul intelligent in proportion as the good is strongly or weakly reflected. Just as in a sense there are colours and vision without light, so we may speak of an object and a mind as being potentially intelligible and intelligent ; yet there is not really intelligence and truth until the good shines upon the mind and the world. Secondly, as the sun is the source not only of light and vision, but also of the actual generation and growth of the organic world, so the good is the source not only of truth and knowledge, but actually of the life and being of the world.

This passage then assigns to the good its position in the world. The world as it is to sense is the image and the product of the good, and the world as it is to intelli-

sented to the senses are made what they are by laws or principles which the senses do not directly reveal, so the whole scheme of laws or principles which thought or science discovers owes its being, and the things of sense in turn owe their being, to one ultimate principle, the good. Such is Plato's account of the good as completed by subsequent passages. Looking then at the passage about the sun in its place in the course of the argument, we might say that it is not really the sun in particular, but the whole visible world, whether as seen or as understood by thought, that is the child of the good in whom its image may be traced. In the *Timaeus* the metaphor of paternity comes up again, and there it is the world, not the sun in particular, that is called the child of the creator. —ED.]

gence is also the image and the product of the good ; so, we might say, the whole world, whether as it is to sense or as it is to intelligence, whether in its more superficial or in its more profound aspect, reflects the good.

# XI. THE FOUR STAGES OF
# INTELLIGENCE

[*Republic*, VI. 509 D to end.]

509 D to the end of VI. HAVING described in a general way the position and function of the good in knowledge, Plato goes on to distinguish more in detail the stages of development through which the human mind passes or might pass from ignorance to knowledge, from a point at which the objective world is, so to say, perfectly dark and unintelligible, to a point at which it is perfectly lumi- nous. He represents to us by a very obvious symbol an ascending scale of mental states and a corresponding scale of objects of thought. Imagine a vertical straight line, and divide it into four parts. The line must be conceived of as beginning in total darkness at one end, and passing up to perfect light at the other. It is a continuous line, though it is divided into sections. Plato, in choosing this symbol, may have wished to express the continuity of the process which it represents. At any rate we have to remember that there is no sudden break between the visible and the intelligible world, which the two main sections of the line stand for [1].

[1] There is a curious uncertainty as to whether Plato wrote ἀν' ἴσα τμήματα or ἄνισα τμήματα, i.e. whether the line is divided into four

The scale which the four sections of the line represent is a scale of luminousness. It is an attempt to represent the stages through which the human mind must go if it would arrive at a perfect knowledge of the world; and, again, an attempt to represent the different and successive aspects that the world presents to the human mind as it advances in knowledge. When we speak of the objects of the mind's thought in its different stages, we should divest ourselves of the notion that they represent four different classes of real objects; they only represent four different views of the world, or different aspects of the same objects. For what we call the same object has very different aspects to different people; for example, the scientific botanist and the person who knows no botany may see the same flower as far as the eyes go, but they understand it in totally different ways;

equal parts, or into four unequal but proportional parts. As it is uncertain which he wrote, and as the line is never referred to again, it is not worth while trying to make out what might have been meant by the inequality of the parts. [I think it is clear that ἄνισα (unequal) is the right reading. Otherwise there is nothing to show what the line symbolizes; for the suggestion in the lecture that the line passes from total darkness to complete illumination is not founded on anything in the text of the present passage, but derived from Plato's use of the metaphor of light in the preceding and following passages. But if we read ἄνισα the meaning is clear. The proportion in length between the different sections of the line symbolizes the proportion in clearness or in profundity of insight between the different mental states described. Cf. καί σοι ἔσται σαφηνείᾳ καὶ ἀσαφείᾳ πρὸς ἄλληλα, κ.τ.λ., 509 D. The sentence is not brought to its logical completion, but it starts as if Plato was going to state a proportion between the mental states, as, according to this reading, he has already stated a proportion between the sections of the line. That proportion would obviously have been : ἐπιστήμη is to δόξα, in respect of σαφήνεια, what, within the sphere of δόξα, seeing real objects is to seeing shadows; and, further, within the sphere of what we have called ἐπιστήμη, νόησις is to διάνοια what ἐπιστήμη itself is to δόξα.—ED.]

to the former it is the image of all botanical laws.
Plato is anxious throughout to emphasize the difference
between these views of things. They differ in degree
of superficiality and profundity as well as of obscurity
and luminousness. This means, we may regard progress in knowledge as a progress from the most superficial to the most penetrating view of things. Hence
the relation between each higher and each lower stage
is expressed by Plato as the relation between seeing
an image or shadow and seeing the thing imaged or
shadowed. This metaphor bears a great part in his
theory of knowledge. It means that there is a great
deal more in what the mind perceives at each stage
than in what it perceives in the stage below. There
is more in the actual solid object than there is in a
mere reflexion or picture of it; and when science comes
and says that these solid objects, which we call the real
things in the world, are not the ultimate truth, that it
is the principles which they embody which are really
worth knowing, that not some particular plant or animal,
but the permanent and uniform nature which appears
in all such things, is the object of real knowledge,
then science, though it seems to be leaving the real
world behind, tells us more than the ordinary view
of things tells us.

Through these different stages all human minds which
develop their powers of understanding fully must more
or less pass; the most gifted as well as the least begins
by what Plato calls seeing things as images; different
minds advance to different distances in different stages,
and the same mind advances to different stages with
different parts of itself. Plato's ideal for education is
that, recognizing this law of mental development, it

should provide for different minds by giving them, according to the stage they are in, appropriate objects of thought, and should lead them gradually, according to their capacity, and as easily as may be, to the truest view of things of which they are capable. Want of education in this sense means that minds which ought to have advanced further remain in a lower stage, and mistake the comparatively superficial view of truth they get there for the whole truth.

The four stages of mental development are called (beginning with the lowest) εἰκασία, πίστις, διάνοια, and νόησις (later called ἐπιστήμη). The two former are stages of what has previously been described as δόξα ; the two latter are stages of what has been called γνῶσις or ἐπιστήμη and is later on called νόησις (a term which in this passage is limited to the higher of them) [1].

(1) The most superficial view of the world, that which conveys least knowledge of it, is called by Plato εἰκασία. The word has a double meaning; it has its regular meaning of conjecture, and an etymological meaning of which Plato avails himself, the perception of images, that state of mind whose objects are of the nature of mere images (εἰκόνες). There is a connexion between the two meanings ; when we talk of a conjecture we imply that it is an uncertain belief, and we imply also that it arises from a consideration of the appearance or surface of the thing in question. Plato has availed himself of both meanings of the word, so as to express a certain character or property of the object of mental apprehension and a certain state of mind in the subject ; the mental state is one of very little certitude, its objects are of the nature of ' images,' shadows and reflexions.

[1] Cf. 533 E sq.

Why does he describe this lowest group of objects as shadows or reflexions? Shadows, images, and dreams, are the most obvious types of unreality, and the contrast between them and realities is very striking to early thinkers, as it is to a mind which is just beginning to think. In what respect does a shadow differ from the real thing? It resembles it merely in the outline, and that is often very vague and inexact; the rest of the real thing, its solidity, its constitution, even its colour. vanishes in the shadow. In what respect does a reflexion differ from the real thing? A reflexion reproduces more of the real object than a shadow does; its outline is very fairly defined and exact; the colour of the object is retained to a certain extent; but a reflexion is still only in two dimensions. Any state of mind of which the object stands to some other object as a shadow or reflexion does to the real thing, is εἰκασία.

This at once opens an enormous field; but what particular states of mind had Plato in view? We may find an example of his meaning in the Allegory of the Cave, the prisoners in which see only shadows of images (ἀγάλματα)[1]. An instance of an image, in the language of that allegory, would be the conception of justice as embodied, perhaps, in Athenian law, which according to Plato would be a very imperfect embodiment. A step further from reality, a shadow of that image, would be the misrepresentation of the Athenian law by a special pleader. Suppose a man believed that justice really was this misrepresentation, his state of mind would be εἰκασία; justice would come to him

[1] VII, 517 D. Note that the εἰκόνες of our present passage (509 E) do not correspond to the ἀγάλματα of the Allegory of the Cave, but to the shadows of the ἀγάλματα.

through a doubly distorting medium, first through the medium of Athenian legislation, and further through the words of the lawyer.

We may take another example from Book X, where Plato works out this idea in his attack on the imitative arts. The effect of arts like painting is due to the fact that the artist puts before us not the actual thing, but its image (εἴδωλον) or its appearance at a certain distance. He puts things before us not 'as they are' but 'as they appear' (the word εἰκασία is not used, but it is the same idea). He is so far like a man who goes about holding up a mirror before things[1]. If any one then were so far taken in by the perspective and colouring as to think the picture before him the actual thing, he would be in a state of εἰκασία. The moment a man knows that a shadow is only a shadow, or a picture only a picture, he is no longer in a state of εἰκασία in that particular respect. But, though the arts do not produce illusion of that simple kind, Plato attacks them in Book X, entirely on the ground that they are constantly used to produce and stimulate a multitude of illusory ideas of another kind. He takes painting as the most obvious instance of imitative art, but he applies the principle which he makes it illustrate to words. Poetry and rhetoric are the great sources of the kind of illusion he has in mind. The poet gives us an image of his experience ; but, if we think we know all about a thing after reading about it, we are just as much deluded as if we took a picture for the reality.

---

[1] Like the pleaders in the Allegory of the Cave he gives us a piece of work which, in Plato's language, is two steps removed from the reality. First comes the 'idea' of the thing represented, beauty; then the first copy or expression of that 'idea,' in the beautiful human face (the actual thing) ; then comes the second copy, the artist's representation of that face (the reflexion or shadow).

When then Plato talks of 'images,' he is not thinking
specially of pictures or statues, what he is primarily
thinking of is images produced by words. Sensitiveness
to the force of words is a marked feature of Plato ; and
he seems to have felt intensely the power of evil they
may have when used by a skilful sophist [1], as if his own
great mastery over them had made him realize the possible
perversion of such skill. He looks upon language as the
power of putting images between men's minds and the
facts. He felt this about rhetoric still more than about
poetry [2], the two being closely associated in his mind,
and both being arts of using language which exercised
a great power over the Greeks [3].

But we must not suppose that Plato regarded the
power of language as only a bad thing, and incapable of
good. In Book III we have the metaphor of images
used in a good sense ; and we learn that it is one of the
functions of art (including both poetry and the plastic
arts) to put before us true images of self-command,
courage, generosity &c., and to train the mind to recognize
them [4]. The scholar, he says, who knows his letters must
be able to recognize them just as well in their reflexions
in water or in a mirror, and so the μουσικός will recognize
the types of beauty and the reflexions of virtue in art.
Thus μουσική is conceived in this passage as the education
of εἰκασία, a training of the soul to read the reproductions
of reality in art aright ; it is intended to develop rightly
that side of the soul on which it is appealed to by images,
a condition of mind which is predominant in children and
undeveloped races, and in many men throughout their

---

[1] Cf. *Sophist*, 234 B–E.  Cf. 254 A, B.          [2] Cf. VII. 517 D.
[3] Cf. *Gorgias*, 501 E sqq., where poetry and rhetoric are classed together.
[4] 401 B and 402 B sq.

whole lives.   In Book X, on the other hand, where Plato denounces imitative art and exposes its dangers, all that he says is dominated by the idea that the artist gives us *only* the external appearance of things.   His general view of art may be thus expressed : the right function of art is to put before the soul images of what is intrinsically great or beautiful, and so to help the soul to recognize what is great or beautiful in actual life ; when art makes people mistake what is only appearance for what is more than appearance, it is performing its wrong function.

We are all in a state of εἰκασία about many things, and to get a general idea of the sort of views that Plato had in mind when he spoke of shadows and reflexions which are taken for realities we must think how many views there are which circulate in society and form a large part of what we call our knowledge, but which when we examine them are seen to be distorted, imperfect representations of fact, coming to us often through the *media* of several other men's minds, and the *media* of our own fancies and prejudices.

The literal translation of εἰκασία is ' imagination.'   But it would be very misleading to translate the one word by the other; for, while εἰκασία expresses the superficial side of what we call imagination, it does not express the deeper side.   Imagination in English has two senses.   In one sense it really does answer to Plato's conception of seeing images.   When we say that something is a mere imagination, or that a man is the slave of his own imagination, we do mean to describe a very superficial view of things.   But when we say that a poet is a man of great imagination we mean almost the exact opposite.   We mean that the appearance of things suggests to him all kinds of deep truth which to the ordinary person it does not suggest at all. The great poet, while it is true that he regards things on their sensuous side, is great because he reads through what his senses show him, and arrives by imagination at truths not different in kind from those which another might arrive at by what we call thinking. Plato seems much more impressed by the possible misuse of imaginative work than by its possible use, though he himself is a standing example of what the union of thought and imagination can do. And it is an undoubted fact that we are apt to live habitually in an unreal world in which we take the image for the reality, instead of reading the reality by the image.

Plato's conception of the mental condition of the great body of men is put before us in the Allegory of the Cave; their state is for the most part such that all that occupies their minds is of the nature of shadows; it is, further, such that they firmly believe these shadows to be real and the only reality. And in this lies their illusion, for so long as a man realizes that the shadows are shadows there is no illusion[1]. Their state is also one of great uncertainty. Among the prisoners in the allegory those who are honoured and rewarded most are those who are quickest at learning to remember the order in which the shadows pass, and who are thus best able to prophesy what will pass next. This is meant to illustrate how uncertain or conjectural their judgments necessarily are. In proportion as our knowledge is not first-hand, not derived from actual contact with things, we ought to regard our beliefs as uncertain.

---

[1] We must remember, however, that the degrees of such illusion as Plato is speaking of are very subtle; there are, to develop his metaphor, many intermediate stages between taking the shadow as altogether real and ceasing altogether to be misled by it.

(2) Thus εἰκασία is conjecture, and the next stage,
πίστις, is so called because it contrasts with εἰκασία in
regard to certitude. Πίστις is a feeling of certainty.
When people have themselves come in contact with
things, they feel far more certain about them than if they
had only come into connexion with them through others,
and πίστις is the state of mind in which we know what we
call the actual tangible things of life ; these are not the
sole reality by any means, yet we feel about them a good
deal of certainty.

We must remember that both εἰκασία and πίστις are sub-
divisions of ' opinion ' (δόξα), so that what has been said of
it is true of them. To the state of mind called opinion
truth and reality exist under the form of a number of
separate and apparently independent objects, each with
a character and position of its own, whether these objects
are real or reflected. Whether, for instance, one's knowledge of justice is derived from books or from what we
are told, or derived from personal experience, it is equally
true that, so long as we are in the state of ' opinion,' the
only answer we could give to the question What is justice,
would be to point to some particular acts or laws or
institutions. Still we feel a difference when we come
out of the region in which we can only know things at
second hand, or can only imagine them, into that in
which we have to do with them ourselves. It is the
transition from uncertainty to a sort of certainty [1].

Further, just as there is a good state of εἰκασία and also
a bad state, a state which contains some truth and

[1] The state of 'right opinion' described in Books III and IV, with its
attendant virtue of courage, i.e. tenacity, is a state of πίστις. It is
a state of mind which is continually being tested by action, as contrasted
with a previous state of mind in which the soul was not in contact with
real life.

a state which contains none, so it is with all opinion.
It is important to remember this, for in Book III
'right opinion' is the sum of virtue, the virtue of the
Guardian; so that it is surprising to us when, in Book
V, Plato begins to speak of opinion in a tone of contempt. Now εἰκασία is only described as a state of
mind which we have to get out of, when it is regarded
as one which we are satisfied with and accept as final;
the harm of the shadow or reflexion arises only when
one takes it for something else; illusion is the misinter-
pretation of appearance, but the appearance which
is the occasion of illusion is capable also of being
rightly interpreted. And so with opinion generally;
it is only so far as one believes the object of opinion
to be ultimate truth that it is a thing to get rid of.
'Right opinion,' in which true principles are embodied
however imperfectly, is a state of mind which is quite
laudable, and beyond which we cannot get as regards
the great bulk of our experience. What is unsatisfactory in this state of mind is that it is bound up with
certain particular objects, and is liable to be shaken
when we discover that these objects are not so fixed and
permanent in their character as we thought, but depend
on their surroundings for their properties. Then the
mind is set to ask, If what I have known as justice, or
beauty, or weight, changes in this extraordinary way,
when seen in different relations, and is in such a continual
state of fluctuation, what can justice, or beauty, or weight
be[1]?

It is this feeling or perception that the objects of δόξα
are self-contradictory which sets the mind to ask for
other forms of truth. The sense of difficulty and em-

[1] Cf. VII. 524.

barrassment arising when what we are accustomed to believe in fails drives us to look for something else. We are impelled to search for what Plato calls 'forms,' principles or laws which make these various things what they are, or for the unity which underlies this changing and manifold world.

(3) Plato calls the stage of mental development in which he describes us as beginning to do this, διάνοια. The word itself gives no clear idea of the thing meant; it was to the Greeks what the word 'intellect' is to us. Like intellect, it has no very fixed meaning, and describes no one state of mind [1], but it was a word obviously applicable to the state of mind of which the scientific man is the best instance. Plato's illustrations of διάνοια are taken from the only sciences of his time; and, though there are differences, there is a great substantial similarity between the things he says of it, and modern ideas of what we should call the scientific habit of mind [2].

Plato gives us two characteristics of this state, without showing us the connexion between them: (a) It deals with sensible things, but it employs them as symbols of something which is not sensible; (b) it reasons from 'hypotheses.' Arithmetic and geometry are the most obvious types of διάνοια in both these respects.

---

[1] Thus in Aristotle διανοητικαὶ ἀρεταί is a name which covers ability in all high forms of intellectual activity, in art, philosophy, morality, &c.

[2] The word is often translated by 'understanding,' while νόησις, to which it is opposed, is translated by 'reason,' because these are words which have been used to describe a lower and a higher phase of intelligence. Διάνοια and νόησις or ἐπιστήμη stand in the same relation to one another as 'Verstand' and 'Vernunft' in Kant; and Coleridge gave the words 'understanding' and 'reason' technical senses intended to correspond with 'Verstand' and 'Vernunft.'

(a) The arithmetician and the geometrician, while they use visible forms, are not actually thinking of them. The geometrician is thinking about the triangle or the circle as such; he uses the circle which he draws as a symbol of this; and though, without such symbols, the study of mathematics would be impossible, the circle which he draws remains a mere symbol. Visible images such as he uses are just the objects of opinion—separate, independent, sensible things, each with a position and character of its own. The objects of which these 'real things' are symbols to him are what Plato calls forms, such as the 'form of the triangle' or 'the triangle itself,' for these two expressions are used indifferently.

What Plato here says of mathematics applies to all science whatever. All science treats the actual objects of experience as symbols. It is always looking for laws, and the sensible things around us become to it symbols of them, or, in other words, are looked upon only as the expression of principles; the botanist or zoologist has to speak of particular animals or plants, but it does not matter to him what particular animal or plant of the same species he takes. We express the same fact by saying that science is abstract. The man of science necessarily and consciously leaves out of account a great deal in the objects he contemplates, and fixes his attention on certain points in them. It is a matter of indifference to the geometrician, in investigating the relations between the sides and angles of a triangle, how big, or of what colour, or of what material the particular triangle is; it may be of great interest to some one else, but not to him; yet all these things go to make up the 'visible triangle.' In using this phrase and contrasting the 'visible triangle' with an 'intelligible triangle,' which is the object of the geometrician's study, we are speaking as if there were two triangles, and may easily be led to think of the 'intelligible triangle' as if it were another triangle which is a faint image of the sensible one. From this difficulty of language arises the greater part of the difficulty of Plato's idealism. We must, therefore, be clear what we mean when we speak of the intelligible triangle; the use of the phrase does not imply that there are two different classes of triangles, the intelligible and the sensible; it means simply that there is in the sensible triangle a property distinguishable from all its other properties, which makes it a triangle. The sensible triangle is the 'intelligible triangle' *plus* certain properties other than triangularity. These other properties the geometrician leaves out of account, or, in Plato's language, regards as merely symbolic. The phrase, which is familiar to us, that science abstracts, expresses just what Plato means when he says that science treats particular objects as merely symbolic, symbolic of something which they as a whole are not. All science does this.

We may put this in a different way so as to illustrate its bearing upon education. The study of the sciences compels us to think; it compels us, as Plato says, to let go our senses and trust to our intellects. In Book VII he insists upon this in the case of all the sciences he mentions; we have in each to set aside our senses and their associations, and to look at things with our minds; that is we have to set aside all but that particular law or principle which is our object of interest for the time being. That is why science seems at first to upset all our ordinary associations and to be less real than our ordinary experience.

(*b*) Plato tells us further that διάνοια reasons from 'hypotheses.' We mean by a hypothesis a theory temporarily assumed to be true, which we are prepared to abandon if the facts do not agree with it; a hypothetical view would mean a provisional view, awaiting confirmation or disproof. But the use of the word ὑπόθεσις in Plato and Aristotle is different from this. Plato meant by a hypothesis a truth which is assumed to be ultimate or primary when it really depends upon some, higher truth; not that it is untrue or could ever be proved false, but that it is treated for the present as self-conditioned. The point of contact between Plato's use of the word and ours is that, in both, a 'hypothesis' is regarded as conditional or dependent upon something; but Plato's hypotheses are by no means provisional theories, they are the truths at the basis of all the sciences. Arithmetic and geometry rest upon certain assumptions or hypotheses. The ultimate assumption of arithmetic is number. with its primary properties of odd and even. The arithmetician does not expect to have to give an account of this; if any one denies the existence of number, the possibility of his studying arithmetic is destroyed; but, granted number as a starting-point (ἀρχή), the arithmetician reasons from it connectedly and consistently, and discovers from it any particular arithmetical truth he wants. So with the geometrician; what he takes as his starting-point is the existence of geometrical space with a few of its most elementary properties. If, when he brings a truth back to his postulates, axioms and definitions, you deny them, he can only say it is impossible to argue with you; it is not his business as a geometrician to prove them. In the same way the physicist starts with the conceptions of matter and motion, the biologist with life, the economist with wealth, the moralist with morality. These, with a few of their most elementary forms and attributes, are the hypotheses of the sciences concerned with them, and each science has similarly its own hypotheses.

By calling such conceptions hypotheses, in the sense that they depend for their validity on some other truths, what does Plato mean? Not that they are untrue, for he speaks of them as a form of ' being.' They are hypotheses because, if we saw things wholly and as they are, we should see that being is one whole (a κόσμος), and that, as it is one whole, the various forms or kinds of it must be connected ; whereas the arithmetician and the geometrician treat their respective forms of being as if they were perfectly independent ; that is, they assume them without giving an account of them. The truths they start from await the confirmation (βεβαίωσις) of being shown to be elements in an interconnected whole[1]. It is thus an imperfection of διάνοια that its 'starting-points' are hypothetical, that they are not seen in their true or full connexions ; for the ideal of science is perfect connexion and perfect explanation. And these are the same thing. As long as you can ask Why? the ideal of knowledge is not satisfied. To ask Why? is the same as to ask What is this dependent on ? Perfect knowledge would imply seeing everything in its dependence on an unconditional principle (ἀνυπόθετος ἀρχή). The human mind, though it never reaches such a principle, is always demanding it, and, so long as it falls short of it, cannot attain the ideal of knowledge. This points the way to the description of the final stage of intelligence, νόησις or ἐπιστήμη.

[1] See 531 D sq. and 533 B sq.

(4) This, as Plato describes it, is a pure ideal; to realize it is not within the scope of the human mind. But it expresses his idea of what we should aim at and what knowledge tends towards. It involves, he tells us, first, a state of perfect *intelligence* with no element of sense in it. It involves, secondly, the absence of hypothesis; the various principles of the specific sciences would be seen not as hypotheses but as they really are, all naturally following from the fact that the world is a world of reason, each being a step to the one above it, and so leading ultimately to the unconditional principle on which they all depend.

(*a*) The statement that in perfect intelligence there is no element of sense perception (nothing αἰσθητὸν) is difficult to understand. Probably we may explain it in the following way. Take, by way of example, any object regarded by a geometrician, and used by him as a 'symbol,' say a triangle. We have seen that the real object which he thinks about is not that particular triangle, ' but the triangle as such. There remains therefore in the sensible object a great deal which is no object for the geometrician, but falls outside his intellectual vision. It is to him of the utmost importance that he should ignore it, that he should not confuse what makes the triangle a triangle with a certain size or colour. Otherwise, having seen a triangle an inch high, when he came to see another a foot high, he would suppose the properties of the two as triangles were different. In such a simple case no educated person would make such a mistake, but in more complicated things we are always making it, and it is because he thinks mathematics train men not to do this that Plato insists on their educational value. Every political economist knows

how difficult it is, even with the best intentions, to
disentangle complex phenomena in which the actions
of a number of human beings are involved; and in
ordinary life we are continually doing what Plato calls
mistaking the symbol for the reality.· Now the other
properties of the triangular object, which are ignored by
the geometrician, may of course themselves be made
the subjects of scientific investigation. The student
of optics may investigate its colour, some one else its
chemical composition, and so forth. And so with more
complex objects; every single property of any object
has what Plato calls a form; as there is a triangle
as such, or a form of triangularity, so there is colour
as such, or a form of colour. Every particular object
is the meeting-point of innumerable laws of nature,
or, as Plato says, in every particular object many forms
communicate. Suppose then that different men of
science had set themselves to work to exhaust all the
properties of an object, and that all these properties
came to be understood as well as the triangularity of
a triangle is understood by the geometrician, we should
regard the object as the centre in which a number
of laws of nature, or what Plato would call forms,
converged; and, if an object ever were thoroughly
understood, that would mean that it was resolved into
forms or laws. The fact would have become a very
different fact, a fact which, so to say, had a great deal
more in it, though none the less a fact; the object as it
is to an ignorant person would have disappeared. Therefore in perfect knowledge there would be no element
of sense; not that anything which our senses tell us
would be lost sight of, but that every sensible property
of the object would be seen as the manifestation of some

intelligible form; so that there would be no symbolic or irrelevant element in it, and it would have become perfectly intelligible. As the geometrician sees the various properties of a triangle and fixes his eyes on triangularity, disregarding everything in the sensible properties of his symbol that could cause him illusion or confusion, so, if he understood the whole object perfectly, he would see all its properties in the same way. It would not be to him a confused collection of pro- perties which seem to be constantly changing and constantly contradicting themselves, but a meeting-point of various permanent and unchanging forms or prin- ciples. That is to say, it would take its place in an order or system of 'forms'; it would be seen in all the relations and affinities which it has. This is an ideal; but we do know that everything has relations and affinities with everything else in the world, and the only way in which we can represent to ourselves perfect intelligence is by supposing a mind to which all the properties of everything, all its relations and affinities with other things, are thus perfectly understood. This remains a true statement of the ideal of our intelligence, though of the great bulk of things our experience must be always to a large extent 'sensible.'

(*b*) In perfect intelligence there would moreover be no hypothesis. To describe how the world would pre- sent itself to a perfect intelligence, Plato uses a figure; it would present itself as a sort of scale or series of forms of existence, each connected with the one above it and the one below it, and the whole unified by one uncon- ditioned principle, the good. The good is that on which they all depend, and that which, to use another figure of Plato's, is reflected in them all; or, again, the position and function of each in the world are determined by the supreme purpose of the world, the good. To a perfect intelligence it would be possible to pass up and down this scale of forms without any break, so that from any one point in the world it could traverse the whole. In proportion as we do understand one fragment of truth, one subject, we find it possible to start anywhere and to get anywhere in it and in the subjects most closely connected with it; and a very fair test of how far one understands a thing is the extent to which one can develop any given point in it. Such a state of mind in its perfection would be νόησις or νοῦν ἔχειν in the fullest sense of the words.

And here Plato introduces a new term, of which we shall have to consider the meaning. The power or faculty, he tells us, by which such a state of intelligence could be brought about is that of dialectic (τὸ διαλέγεσθαι, elsewhere διαλεκτική). This term he eventually uses to describe knowledge as it would be if perfect [1]; and the passage in which he then introduces it throws light on the passage before us. Speaking of the application of the various specific sciences in his system of education, he says that if the study of them is to be made profitable to the end in view we must try to see their relations with one another. This is a principle to be borne in mind throughout the more advanced part of the education in science which he proposes ; the points of contact between the sciences must be perpetually brought out. The test, we are told later, of whether a man has the dialectical nature is whether he is συνοπτικός, which means whether he has the power of seeing together at one view the relationships (οἰκειότητες) between the various specific branches of

[1] 531 D sq.

knowledge[1]. Now this brings out strongly, what is hinted at in the passage before us, that progress in knowledge is progress in the perception of the unity of knowledge. A man who has a gift for perceiving this‘ is a natural dialectician, and dialectic in the fullest sense is simply what knowledge would be if this possibility of seeing the affinities and communion between the different branches of knowledge (not, of course, only the particular sciences to which Plato refers, but all branches of knowledge) were realized. In this use of the word dialectic is equivalent to perfect knowledge. Later on we shall have to consider this conception in more detail.

[1] 537 C.

# XII. EDUCATION IN SCIENCE AND PHILOSOPHY

[*Republic*, VII.]

## I. THE EXISTING WANT OF EDUCATION.

AT the point which has now been reached in the argument, Socrates says that he will describe by an image what is the actual condition of mankind ' in regard to education and the want of it.' The description is given in the passage known as the 'Allegory of the Cave.' To see the place which this passage fills in the argument, we must recall the course of the discussion in Book VI. It had been shown that the philosophic nature was the gift which most fitted men to rule human society, but that there were inherent in it certain dangers and causes of difficulty. We were thence led to consider the question how this nature is to be educated, and how its full development can be secured, so that it may really prove the saviour of society. The answer was that the knowledge which would satisfy all the requirements of education would be the knowledge of the good ; the relation of this knowledge to the rest of human knowledge was pointed out ; and a sketch was given of the stages of the advance by

S 2

which the world becomes more intelligible and the mind more intelligent.  Now Plato turns round and asks what is man's actual position in this scale of intelligence. He is here no longer dealing with an ideal community, but describing as they are the facts about the human race ; and they are exactly what they ought not to be. So far from progressing from darkness to light through the stages which have just been described, men, as he here represents them, practically remain in the lowest stage of intelligence.

We need only notice a few points in the allegory (514 A to 518 B).  In the first place we are told that the state of the human race at large is one of εἰκασία. Instead of passing out of this initial stage to some truer understanding of the world, most people abide in it all their lives.  If any man rises out of it, it is not by his own doing, nor is his liberation due to any method of education or any help which society gives him, but it comes φύσει, no one knows how (515 C).  The prisoners see only shadows and hear only echoes of the truth, and each is tied fast to his own shadowy experience.  In other words, the view of men generally with regard to themselves and the world around them is a view distorted by falsifying media, by their own passions and pre- judices, and by the passions and prejudices of other people as conveyed to them by language and rhetoric. And there is no advance in their view, they are perma- nently in the state of understanding in which children are, except that they believe in the truth of what they see and hear with the force and tenacity of grown men. This is not the state of a few miserable outcasts, it is our own state.

In the second place, not only is this the normal condi-

tion of men, but it is one from which they do not desire
to escape.  They have no idea of anything better beyond
it, for the bonds in which they are tied keep their faces
perpetually turned away from the light, and there is no
system of education to free them from their bonds.
Moreover, the few who do get free find that every step
in their progress towards true knowledge is attended
with pain.  In the third place, if here and there a
prisoner from the cave does get up to the light, and
then, being filled with pity for the other prisoners, returns
to tell them what he has seen, they laugh at him and
perhaps kill him.  In other words, instead of co-operating
with the leading minds that arise in its midst, society is
either indifferent or actively hostile to them.

These are the main points to be noticed in the allegory.
The prisoner set free from the cave and gradually accustomed to bear the strongest light passes through a series
of stages which correspond generally to that which was
symbolized by the divided line in the preceding section
of the argument.  The stage in which he is turned round
from the position in which he was originally bound and
made to face the light is that in which a man is forced
to face the real world and see things as they are, coming
out of the false preconceptions which fancy and hearsay
and prejudice have made for him.  This is represented
as a painful process.  The second stage is that in which
he is led to take a scientific view of facts, and that too is
represented as painful.  It would be pressing the allegory
too closely if we tried to find definite stages in education
corresponding to the steps by which the released prisoner
is led to look at the sun.

Such being the actual facts of man's condition, the
passage (518 B to 519 B) which immediately follows the

allegory draws a contrast between the true theory of education ‑ and the actually prevailing theory. Education,
we are told, is not like putting sight into blind eyes, it is
like turning the eye to the light. And further, it is as if
this could only be done by turning the whole body
round; education means not merely illuminating the
intellect, but turning the whole soul another way. For
the great causes of the blindness of the mind are the
appetites and pleasures which overpower the soul;
these are compared to leaden weights with which the
soul is encumbered at birth, and which must be cut
away before it can lift up its eyes from the ground.

Next (519 C to 521 B) we are shown what ought
to be the relation ‑between society and its leading
minds. The facts that have been described make
it quite natural for those who have been freed and
have got to the⁻ light to wish to stay there and to
stand aloof from the · world ; for they owe nothing
to society. But the relation between society and
those who can serve it in any' way ought to be just
the opposite; it ought to be one of reciprocal service
between society and its members, each contributing
to the other ‑ something that the other wants. And
this principle, which has already been applied to minor
matters, ought *a fortiori* to be applied to the relation
of society to great minds. They should be made to
feel that they are not sprung from their own roots, but
owe their nurture to society, and are therefore bound
to society. In a state which does give philosophers
the nurture which they need, it will be no wrong to
them to tell them that they must rule and take an
active part in society. They will do it willingly
because they will feel that it is a duty which they owe

in return for their nurture; and they will govern well because they will feel that they have already something better than any of the rewards which generally accrue to office, for that state will be best governed whose rulers rule, not from any wish to enrich themselves, but simply from a sense of public duty[1].

## 2. EDUCATION IN THE SCIENCES.

The question which has now to be dealt with is, How are we to escape from the state which has been sym- bolized by the position of the prisoners in the cave; how are those who are to rule and save society to be brought up from darkness to light? In the first place, What are they to be taught? Socrates begins by re- viewing very briefly the education which the Guardians have already received. They have been trained in μου- σική and γυμναστική; and the former of these will have produced a sort of .harmony and rhythm of character, by means of habituation, for the soul has had the order and beauty of the world put before it in such a way that it cannot but unconsciously assimilate them. ⁻ But in all this there was no learning in the true sense of the word (μάθημα). What then are the studies or branches of learning (μαθήματα) by which the soul is to be led to the knowledge of the good, the greatest thing to be learned (μέγιστον μάθημα)?

Here (522 E sqq.) follows the important passage in which Plato points out that the sciences are the proper

[1] Notice also (520 C) that the philosopher when first he turns back from philosophy to the life of the world sees badly, like a man going back from the light into the darkness of the cave; but with practice he will come to have a far better insight than others in practical affairs, because of all that he has seen in the clear light. (Cf. VI. 484 E.)

instruments to mediate between the state of mind which the previous education of the rulers has produced and the perfect intelligence which (as far as may be) they must possess. In this passage he describes the beginnings of thinking (νόησις), showing how the soul passes from sense-perception (αἴσθησις), and such certainty as that can give it, to thought. There are, he begins by telling us, two sorts of things that we perceive by the senses. The first are objects which are adequately apprehended by the senses, so that they do not provoke thought. For instance, as he says, if we see three fingers, the perception which we get through sight raises, as a rule, no further question; there is nothing in this mere perception to impel the ordinary mind to ask what is a finger. Such perceptions constitute the state of mind called πίστις. Here what a man knows consists of a number of separate objects (πολλὰ ἕκαστα), and up to a certain point the mind rests satisfied with them, and is not anxious to find out any connexion between them. But at a certain point the soul becomes conscious of things like quantity, and such qualities as hardness, softness, &c. The separate sensible object (αἰσθητόν), which was at first regarded as a whole thing, then seems to break up into a number of attributes, and these are the objects that provoke thought. For suppose we observe the size of the three fingers, or their hardness or softness, or their colour, these are also sensible things, as the kind of objects previously mentioned are, but with this curious difference, that sense no longer adequately perceives them ; the attributes have no fixity, and pass into their opposites ; we find the same finger in different relations great and small, hard and soft, &c. It is the sense of this contradiction which sets the mind thinking upon the question, What is each of these qualities which the senses report? If each of them is one distinct thing it cannot also be its opposite, and when we see each of them thus confused with its opposite the question arises what hardness, or greatness, or the like really is. So we are brought to the distinction between the object of thought (νοητόν) and the object of sight (ὁρατόν), or of the senses generally (αἰσθητόν). There is magnitude as seen in a separate visible object in this confused and self-contradictory way, so that a thing is both great and small in different relations; and there is 'the great,' 'the small,' which is apprehended by thought and is quite clear and definite, so that the great is never small and the small never great. And thus we get to the point of view which was described as that of διάνοια, in which the objects with which the mind is occupied are not the sensible things that happen to be before one, but the various intelligible principles which can be apprehended through the objects of sense, magnitude, weight, and the like.

What is here said about the objects of sense corresponds exactly to what was said in Book V. 479 about the objects of opinion. It applies, of course, not only to the perceptions of simple sight or sound or touch, such as are here instanced, but also to our perceptions of what is pleasant or painful, good or bad, and the like. The passage must be taken as an attempt to describe the way in which the soul passes from a state of *unreflecting* perception, through a state of perplexity and bewilderment (ἀπορία), into a state of more or less developed intelligence. Sometimes, from various causes, the mind becomes dissatisfied with the condition of mere opinion and mere feeling in which it finds itself. It is, of course, generally in the sphere of morality that we first feel keenly how, as Plato observes, the objects of opinion contradict themselves. Thus, further on[1], he describes the position of a man brought up in certain beliefs about justice and honour, to whom the questioning spirit comes, asking him, What is justice, What is honour? When he gives the answer that he has been taught, reason confutes him and shows him that what he calls just may also be unjust. Then, unless he knows how to deal with this new spirit of questioning, he gets to think that there is no such thing as justice or honour, and the commonness of this result is one reason of the general discredit of philosophy. Plato describes this in order to show the necessity of that constancy to which the Guardians were trained while still in the state of mere opinion, a constancy which, in spite of difficulties, holds fast what it has been taught, till further knowledge comes to take its place. The bewilderment which he thus describes as arising in regard to moral ideas is of the same kind as that which has been shown to arise with regard to the physical properties of sensible objects. It is to meet this difficulty, in the minds in which it occurs, that the sciences take the place in education which Plato proceeds to assign to them. If a man has the sort of mind that is going to think, it is most important that it should be trained to think in the best way and on the best method.

What has just been said of the tendency of certain kinds of sensible objects to arouse thought has now to be applied to the problem of education (524 D to 531 D). The question is what particular studies are,

[1] 537 E to 539 A.

from the nature of the objects that they deal with, suited to provoke and stimulate thought. Take first the object with which arithmetic deals, number. We find that every sensible object is both one and infinitely many, like a chain which is one but consists of many links. Thus, since unity and multiplicity co-exist in the same thing, to sense the one is many and the many are one. Yet if you said this to the arithmetician he would laugh at you, and say that a unit is always a unit, and can be nothing else. Clearly therefore the arithmetician is not thinking of a sensible unit but of something else. The same thing is shown to be true of geometry, astronomy, and harmonics. In each the object as it is to sense seems to contradict itself, and the object as it is to thought is distinct and self-consistent. Thus the sciences by compelling the mind to think, that is to disentangle and see through the confusion and contradiction of the senses, are or ought to be great educational instruments, in fact just the instruments we want to facilitate the transition of the soul from mere perception to intelligence; and it is with this end constantly in view that the sciences are to be studied.

Of the present manner in which the sciences are pursued, Plato speaks in a very depreciatory way, rebuking the practice of studying them merely for what we should call utilitarian purposes. He does not say that these uses of the sciences are not extremely valuable; on the contrary, he insists more than we should on the value of geometry for a man who is going to be a soldier; he wishes that such men should cultivate the geometrical sense. What he does say is, in effect, simply this: the study of the sciences, if it be confined to the limited objects of trade, finance, the arts, and so forth, is not

really educational, or educational only in an infinitesimal
degree ; and so, until people are encouraged, by the state
or otherwise, to a further study of the sciences than
is required for these purposes, the standard of education
will be very low.   Useful the study of the sciences ought
to be ;  but useful for what?   Plato is a thorough utilitarian ; but, he says, trade, navigation, and the like, are
not the end of life ; the end is to do the best for the soul
you can, to make the best man you can ; and the object
you have in view will make a great difference to the
spirit in which you learn.

What, according to him, is the real value of the study
of the sciences ?  It is twofold.   Their first great function
is to teach us to think.   Thinking means asking questions
which difficulties and apparent contradictions in our
experience force upon us.   Now science.owes its origin
to the fact that the soul has found such difficulties in
its sensible experience, and has felt a certain necessity
to clear them up.   Science is the result of thought
exercised on sense.   If men never felt in their experience
such bewilderment as Plato has described, or were
never impelled to find their way out of it, the spirit
of enquiry which creates science would not exist.   There
could not be a science of arithmetic, for example, till
some one was driven to form a clear conception of unity
as apart from particular single objects ; and there can be
a science of any subject only so far as the subject-matter
can be thus clearly and separately conceived.   All
sciences then have originated in difficulties of this kind,
and result in the solution of such difficulties.   Naturally
therefore the sciences which already exist form the best
instruments for training the mind to think ; for in studying them each man's mind is led to do over again

what has been done by the minds that have made them.
They are embodied διάνοια, representing the results
of thinking. If you want to learn to think, study the
sciences in which past thought is embodied, for you
cannot do so without being compelled to think yourself.
That, according to Plato, is the first great function of
science in education.

The most elementary ἀπορία of all is that which
concerns the one and the many; therefore Plato puts at
the bottom the science of number, which is the result of
thinking upon this antithesis. Next to arithmetic, the
study of number, comes plane geometry, the study
of space in two dimensions; then solid geometry, the
study of space in three dimensions; then astronomy,
the study of solid bodies in motion; and, lastly, harmonics, the study of the motion of bodies as producing
sound. This is the order of his scientific course. Each
step adds something to the complexity of the subject
studied, and in each case he reiterates that, along with
simple observation by the senses, the *mind* has got to
be used on the subject.

As yet we have only seen the most obvious use of
the sciences in education. There is another, to Plato inseparable from the first. If their first use is that they
train the mind in thinking in general, the second is that
in studying them the mind comes gradually to understand certain principles or forms of being which are a
first step towards understanding the good, the principle
which governs all being. It is puzzling to us that Plato
should speak of these sciences as putting the mind on the
track of the good, and we naturally ask what the study
of number, or of space, can have to do with the final
cause of the world. The answer is that each of the

sciences deals with a particular branch, kind, or form
of existence; that existence is one, forming a κόσμος;
and that the ideal of knowledge is to be able to pass
freely from any one point in the system of existence to
any other; so that, though number, space, and motion
are not directly manifestations of the good, and the very
abstract sciences which deal with them have no moral
influence in the ordinary sense, yet, as everything in the
world is ultimately a manifestation of the divine intelligence, even in these abstract sciences we are really on
the ladder which leads up to the good.    Let us translate
this into modern language, such as many modern philosophers have used:  The study of the laws of nature,
which begins with the laws of number, space, and motion,
is already the study, though in a very elementary form,
of the reason of things; nature does everywhere reveal
reason, that is God, so that all the laws of nature are
laws of God, and even the study of number is a study of
the laws of God.

Education in the sciences has then in Plato this double
function:  first, it is a sort of mental gymnastic; and,
secondly, it introduces the mind to positive knowledge
about certain elementary forms in which the presence of
the good in the world is manifested.    It is, as he puts it,
the 'prelude' to the study of 'dialectic'; in it we hear
the beginning of that great music of the world which the
human race has to learn (531 D).

In Plato's treatment of each of the sciences that he
mentions, we are struck directly by the strong distinction
that he draws between those aspects of things which are
sensibly perceived and something which is not seen or
heard but thought or understood; and we observe that
he treats the latter as more real than the former.    Our

first impulse on a superficial reading of the *Republic* is to say that Plato altogether ignores what we call observation and experiment, and writes as if we could construct laws of nature simply by thinking out certain axioms to their consequences. We think so because, coming to Plato with certain expectations, derived from what we know of the methods of modern science, and with a certain modern phraseology in our minds, we apply these to him. Really he says nothing which has not been practically confirmed in its spirit by modern science [1].

The most striking examples of his view occur in his discussion of astronomy and harmonics, for we are apt to accept what he says of arithmetic (524 D to 526 C) and geometry (526 E to 527 D). No one denies that arithmetic is concerned with the nature of number as such. If we said we saw or touched a number, we should know we were speaking in an inaccurate way ; when we use counters for numbers we recognize that the visibility and tangibility of the objects reckoned with are accidental, not essential, and that these objects are merely symbolical and suggestive of number as apprehensible by thought. As to geometry, what Plato says might perhaps be disputed. His position simply is that the visible and tangible triangle, for example the diagram on paper, is not the real object of our thought, but a symbol suggesting the real object, triangularity, which is not seen and touched, but thought. This position can not be disputed. But of course triangularity in its essence, though it can only be *thought*, is still the result of thinking about what we can *see* and *touch*. On this ground objection might be taken to

---

[1] Cf Whewell's *Philosophy of Discovery*, especially Appendix B. Remember, however, that facts and theories are not opposite and mutually exclusive things, as Whewell implies.

Plato's antithesis between sensible experience and thought. He does not, however, really ignore this fact, and, if we are to dispute whether the language which he uses is justifiable, the whole question at issue will really be what exactly we are to call *sensible* experience. When, however, Plato comes to astronomy and harmonics, the way in which he writes of them seems strange at first. He makes Glaucon say that astronomy (527 D to 530 C) will have a grand educational influence, because it compels us to direct our minds upwards; and he makes Socrates laugh at him for supposing that star-gazing can enlighten the soul. He proceeds to say that a man might gaze at the stars all his life and yet find out nothing of their movements. Now he does not say that the truths of astronomy can be arrived at without observing the stars ; and he often says that knowledge can only be arrived at through the eyes and ears[1]. The question here is, Could we ever get at the truths of astronomy by simply looking? Newton would never have thought of the law of gravitation if he had not had eyes, but if we chose to say therefore that Newton *saw* the law of gravitation in the falling apple we should be giving the word 'see' a meaning different from its usual meaning, and to be consistent we ought to adopt a new phraseology altogether.

Plato goes on to distinguish the visible motions of the heavenly bodies from their true motions, but he does not mean that the former are, in the ordinary sense, untrue or unreal. He contrasts apparent motion with real motion, as we do. No one can say that simple observation of the movements of the sun tells us the truth about them,

---

[1] Cf. especially *Timaeus*, 47 A sq.

for no one now believes that it moves as it seems to do ; and yet no one supposes that the simple observation that the sun occupies different places in the sky at different times of the day is not a true observation ; it is a real fact, it is what we see. The question is how we are to interpret this fact. This interpretation is an act of thought ; we put together this simple observation and many others, and correct one appearance by another until at last we arrive at a hypothesis which will account perfectly for them all. We all believe that the truths discovered by Kepler and Newton are truer than the casual notions of persons ignorant of astronomy. How are they truer (for in one sense every experience we have is equally a fact and equally real) ? What is the difference between one fact and another ? The most real facts are those which contain most, the widest and deepest ; the most superficial facts, mere 'empirical' facts, are those which contain least. The laws of motion are facts ; so are the things that I myself observe in the sky. The difference between these facts lies in the amount which they enable people who know them to say. My fact of observation of the sun's position tells me very little about the sun ; but the fact of observation is not denied or ignored by the greatest astronomer, it is used along with a great deal more. There is no hard-and-fast line between empirical facts and ultimate laws; a fact is empirical so far as it is isolated. A great generalization, such as that of Newton, is a stupendous fact, it connects and contains innumerable facts ; it is simply a very large fact. What Plato says then is that the apparent motions of the heavenly bodies are to be used as examples (παραδείγματα) or symbols which suggest to us to think out the real motions ; not that they are unreal, for they are not visions, or illusions, or untrue [1].

Harmonics (530 C to 531 C) is one of the branches of the science of motion. Plato says that motion has many branches, but he takes only two, the motion of heavenly bodies which are seen by the eye, and the motion of bodies which produce sound to the ear. Here again he begins by laughing at those professional musicians who think that the science of sound can be discovered by, and consists in, what we actually hear, and that the person who has the finest ear and is capable of appreciating the smallest intervals knows most of the laws of sound. Next he criticizes quite a different class of people, the Pythagorean theorists. The great discovery that musical intervals are mathematically expressible was attributed to Pythagoras, but it does not seem to be known exactly what he really discovered, or what was discovered by other Greek theorists on music. Plato speaks with approval of the Pythagoreans in that they have investigated the principles of harmony, but he also criticizes their enquiries as superficial. They have confined their investigations to intervals and concords which can be heard, and for these they have found numerical expressions, but they have not gone on 'to ask, in general, what are harmonic numbers, and what are not, and what is the reason for each being such.' He means that, though they have worked out the numerical expression of the ordinary intervals of the scale, they have not raised the question what harmony

---

[1] In the passage where he speaks of the absurdity of supposing that mere star-gazing will reveal the laws of the stars, Plato is very likely thinking of Aristophanes, *Clouds*, 171 sqq., where Socrates is represented as hoisted up in a basket gazing at the sky.

itself is, and what is the ultimate law which explains why sounds harmonize at all. This is a question that has exercised the minds of some of the greatest thinkers. Here again Plato does not say, Music is trifling, it ought to be resolved into harmonics. He does say, If you think that, because you have a delicate ear, you necessarily understand the science of sound, you are very much mistaken, for no amount of listening to sounds will show you the principles upon which the musical scale is based.

So far, we may say, Plato understands the real principles upon which all science is based ; his language, if pressed, is hardly less true than Mill's in speaking of the same subject. But he has expressed himself at least in a dangerous way in speaking as if real motion were another kind of motion from that which we see. The laws of motion are the truth of the motion we see. A person who fully understood the laws of any sensible phenomenon would, in apprehending the phenomenon by sense, also understand it, for these would not be two separate acts. If he understood all the laws of the phenomenon there would, in Plato's language, be no sensible (that is, *merely* sensible) element in his apprehension of it, for whatever he saw, heard, or touched, would be to him the expression of laws he could not see or hear or touch. And yet, we may say, his thus understanding the phenomenon which he had first apprehended by sight or hearing or touch would mean that he would know that if he put himself in certain other positions he would have certain other sensations of sight or hearing or touch. We must therefore, in reading Plato, guard against that sort of bastard Platonism which resolves experience into two worlds, the

sensible and the intelligible world, of which the intelligible world, if you ask what it is, can only be
described as a fainter reproduction of the sensible.  He
certainly often gives occasion to this misunderstanding,
but he does not himself draw a sharp line between the
sensible and the intellectual ; for he constantly calls the
sensible the appearance of, the image of, the suggestion
of, what is intelligible ; the one is essentially related to
the other.  What he does is to realize and work out
powerfully the fact on which all science and philosophy
is really based, that it is by thought and not by simple
sensations (as the term is ordinarily understood), or any
amount of combinations of them, that truth is really found,
and that therefore truth is, so far, an intelligible, not
a sensible, thing ; it is an interpretation of sense, or, as
he would say, sensible experience is a symbol of it or is
a reproduction of it, or participates in it.

The difficulty in appreciating this idea is to know
what exactly is given by sense and what is arrived at
by thinking.  Language leads us to believe that first
there are certain well-ascertained facts given us by
observation, and that then we theorize on those facts [1].
But really there is one continuous process of ascertaining
going on from the most elementary sensible observation
up to the highest generalizations of thought, a process
in which, in one meaning of the words, we may be said
to get away from sense, but in which all the time the
more elementary facts are not done away with, but are
explained by being taken gradually into wider and wider
connexions.  As Plato says that what is sensibly perceived is the symbol of the intelligible truth, so we
might say that we do not see or hear the laws of motion

[1] See the work of Whewell, already referred to.

or sound, but that what we see and hear are parts of the facts which those laws express. The progress of what he calls thought or intelligence means that experience gets more and more clear to us as we go on, the world as it is known to us at first by the senses being very confused. We may represent that progress to ourselves by comparing the sort of impression which we get, if we have no musical education, on first hearing a chord struck, with what we experience when, by practice or otherwise, we have come to hear the different notes distinctly and to know the intervals between them. The difference between these two experiences, carried out further, may give us some notion of that process of clarifying confused things which Plato calls the work of thought.

In any fuller enquiry into the relation of sense and thought everything must turn on these questions : First, what is meant by 'sense'? Secondly, how much do we really experience in sensible experience? Thirdly, what is the nature of the change that takes place when we come to understand better the thing we have experienced? (Every one would agree in the one point of calling this change a process in which thought becomes clearer.)

### 3. DIALECTIC.

The system of education in the sciences is a prepara- 531 D to tion for 'dialectic' (διαλεκτική or τὸ διαλέγεσθαι), and will 534 E. be of use so far as it enables the Guardians to become 'dialecticians' (διαλεκτικοί). There is for several reasons a difficulty in understanding what Plato definitely means when he talks of dialectic in the *Republic*. In this, as in other cases, and notably in that of the doctrine of ideas, he takes for granted a great deal which he has developed elsewhere, so that here, as often, what we are told in the *Republic* is rather an indication of his meaning than an actual account of it. Further, he repeatedly uses the word to describe an ideal science, and, as to what that would be, he could only give us a general idea—an idea the filling up of which must be left to one's imagination and to the progress of the human race. Moreover, the word is used in the *Republic*, as elsewhere in Plato, in other senses besides this.

The word itself means originally the art or process of discourse, of asking questions and giving answers; it is equivalent to διδόναι καὶ δέχεσθαι λόγον, to be able to give an account of a thing to another man, and to get from him and understand his account of a thing. This is a standing phrase in Greek for reasoning, and διδόναι λόγον[1] is to give an exact definition of the thing you are speaking of. A man who understands a thing can give an account of it to others, and on the other hand you cannot give an account of a thing unless you understand it. The faculty of doing this attracted the attention of ordinary people in Greece, and in Aristotle it becomes a large part of the subject of logic. The *Topica* is an elaborate treatise on practical logic in this sense, logic as used in society for conversational purposes, in the pursuit of science, in the law courts, and the like. But the art of giving an account of what you yourself think is scarcely more important than the art of extracting from others their opinions or beliefs (λόγον δέχεσθαι or λόγον λαμβάνειν). To know how to put a question is just as hard and as important as to know how to give an answer to one; and a process analogous to that

----

[1] More fully—λόγον τῆς οὐσίας.—534 B.

of questioning others goes on in the mind of the single
enquirer.

In Xenophon's *Memorabilia*, Socrates says that the
word διαλέγεσθαι came from the practice of men meeting
together to deliberate, διαλέγοντες κατά γένη τὰ πράγματα,
'laying apart the things they discussed according to
their kinds'; everybody, he says, ought to practise this
and fit himself for it, for 'this is what makes men the
best men, and leaders of men, and masters of discourse'
(ἀρίστους καὶ ἡγεμονικωτάτους καὶ διαλεκτικωτάτους)[1]. This
is the germ of the Platonic dialectic. We must remember with regard to Greek logic and reasoning that
philosophy in Greece had its being, to a great extent,
in oral discussion. The Greeks were to an extraordinary
degree a nation of talkers; and therefore not only elo-
quence, rhetoric, and poetry, but the other arts of words,
logic in the true sense and in the sense of mere dispu-
tation, were highly developed among them. Socrates
himself spent his life in talking, and that fact never lost
its effect on Greek philosophy. In Plato we get what
was the habit of Socrates' life formulated as a method of
enquiry. Plato took up the word 'dialectic,' as one
might the word 'logic,' and gave it a meaning which it
has never since entirely lost. It came to mean with
him, first and most commonly, true logical method in
contrast to false or assumed methods; and, secondly, not
the method of knowledge at all, but completed knowledge, or what we may imagine would be the result if the

---

[1] *Mem.* IV. v. 11 and 12. The etymology is of course strained. In
the same passage this intellectual capacity of distinguishing has a moral
side as well: 'only men who control their passions can see what is
best in things, and distinguish between things according to their kinds
in thought or in action; and only they can choose what is good and
refrain from what is bad.'

true method had been carried out completely through all branches of knowledge.

In the first of these senses the word has passed from meaning simply discourse to meaning discourse with the object of attaining the truth, and this discourse may either be carried on by words between two persons or be a 'dialogue silently carried on by the soul with itself[1].' We may ask why a word meaning discourse should be used to signify the true method of gaining knowledge. The fact points to Plato's conviction that the only way to attain truth is to advance step by step, each step being made our own before we go on to the next, and that for this purpose the process of questioning and answering is the natural method. Moreover, his conception of questioning and answering as the natural way of eliciting truth from, and putting truth into, the mind, is closely associated with his idea that education does not mean simply putting something into the mind as if it were a box, but is a turning of the eye of the soul to the light[2], or a process of eliciting from the soul what in a sense it already knows,—a process in which the soul which learns must itself be active. Hence the constant contrast in Plato between the continuous speeches of some distinguished teachers of his time and the conversations of Socrates ; he has a strong feeling that the only true way of communicating knowledge is to bring two minds into contact. Thus in the *Phaedrus*[3] Plato tells us how inferior written truth is to spoken truth, because a book cannot answer the questions which arise in the reader's mind. The same principle applies to the thinking of the individual mind ; if we are to learn we

[1] *Sophist*, 263 E.                    [2] 518 C.

[3] 275 C sqq.

must not simply put the facts of a book into our minds, we must question and answer ourselves.

Again, dialectic, the true logician's reasoning, is reasoning which is in conformity with facts. It is often contrasted with reasoning used merely for the purpose of gaining a victory in argument (ἐριστική or ἀντιλογική [1]). The characteristic of such reasoning is that it reasons according to the names of things. Plato has already described it, in a passage in Book V, as 'pursuing merely verbal oppositions [2],' and as thus opposed to dialectic, which follows the forms of the things in question (that is, distinguishes the precise facts which the name is meant to indicate in each case where it is used). Thus in the passage referred to, where Socrates is talking of community of pursuits between men and women, the objector is made to argue that on Socrates' own principle different pursuits must be assigned to different natures. To reason thus, Socrates says, is only to wrangle; the person who argues so only takes the *words* 'different nature,' 'different pursuits,' and argues from the one to the other, without enquiring what specific forms of difference there are; that is, in this case, what is the specific form of difference between the natures of men and women, and to what specific form of difference in occupation it ought to lead. In what he says of reasoning Plato, we observe, starts with the conception of certain objective differences of kind, differences which are there whether we recognize them or not; it is the function of true reasoning to discover and follow them.

---

[1] Σοφιστική again is reasoning known to be illegitimate and used designedly with the object of blinding another person for one's own advantage.

[2] 454 A " Κατ' αὐτὸ τὸ ὄνομα διώκειν τοῦ λεχθέντος τὴν ἐναντίωσιν."

The differences embodied in ordinary language, the terms of which form a sort of classification of things which is in use amongst ordinary men, are often not real, or at least not the most real differences; they only go a little way in. True logic is therefore a perpetual antagonism to, and criticism of, the ordinary use of words and the ordinary manner of discussion ; it is the knowing how to use words rightly, that is how to use them so that they shall conform not to the fancies of the speaker, but to the real distinctions of things, the real system of the world.

Plato's account of dialectic as a method depends then upon a certain view of the constitution of the world. Anybody's conception of the method of knowledge must ultimately be determined by his conception of the form in which truth exists ; men have always distinguished between reasoning which touches facts and reasoning which does not.  And so Plato's conception of method is the reflex of his metaphysical conception of the nature of things.  How did he conceive the world would look to us if we understood it perfectly ? It is obvious from many of the dialogues that he conceived it would present the form of an articulated whole, what we should probably call an organism or whole of parts in which each part is only understood by reference to other parts and to the whole, and every branch of which exhibits on a small scale the fundamental characteristics of the whole.  Such being the order of the world, we must, as the *Philebus*[1] tells us, in any enquiry, approach things with the expectancy of finding such an order.  The nature of reasoning, as Plato conceives it, is determined by this characteristic of the material it deals with ; it

[1] 16 c to D.

must conform itself to that material. So in the *Phae-drus* [1] he illustrates the nature of discourse (λόγος) by the metaphor of a body, and again in the same dialogue he compares the bad reasoner to the bad cook who cuts across the joints instead of following the natural articulation of the body. Thus the idea of the world as an organic whole gives his theory of knowledge its most prominent characteristic [2].

He himself expresses his leading idea by saying that all knowledge has to do with 'the one in many' and 'the many in one.' This is a technical expression of the idea of organism; for every organism is one in many; each part can only be conceived with reference to the whole; the whole is present in the parts; to understand it we must give attention not to the one alone, nor to the many alone. In the *Philebus* [3], where this idea is most worked out, Plato remarks that the fundamental fact from which dialectic springs is the co-existence of unity and multiplicity in all things. Wherever we take the world it is a one in many; wherever there is something of which we predicate being, we always find that more than one thing may be predicated of it; and everything either is a particularized form of some generic form, principle, or law, or, if it is itself an abstract principle or property of things, exists in a great many different instances, though maintaining its unity throughout them. (We have already met with this conception in Book V.) The method of learning about things must therefore be one which recognizes this fundamental fact. Accordingly dialectic, in the sense of the method of knowledge,

[1] 264 C.
[2] Cf. *Phaedrus*, 265 C sqq., 273 D sq., 276 E to 277 C.
[3] 14 C to 18 E.

will be a double process consisting of combination and
division (συναγωγή and διαίρεσις)[1]. This means that, as
any truth will always be found to be a one in many, the
way to realize it will be either, starting from many
instances of it, to arrive gradually at the unity which
pervades them all (this is συναγωγή), or, if you start with
the one principle or law, to see how it can be divided up
into its many instances (this is διαίρεσις).

Under this simple form we recognize what, from
Plato's time onward, have been held to be the two
sides of all scientific method. In 'inductive' reasoning
you start with a number of different instances and en-
deavour to find one constant principle, the 'law' of them ;
this answers in principle to 'combination.' In 'deductive'
reasoning you start with a given conception or fact and
follow it out in its particular applications or occurrences,
seeing how the general principle applies to a new case,
or, in Plato's phrase, how 'the one' particularizes itself
in 'the many'; this answers in principle to 'division.'
In 'combination' we have the exercise of the same gift
that we have already seen referred to as 'seeing together'
(σύνοψις)[2]. Διαίρεσις, though the word itself is not used
in the *Republic*, is the method that the true reasoner was
said to follow in Book V in the passage already referred
to, where the failure of the contentious reasoner is said
to be failure to distinguish properly the different kinds
of the same thing. 'Combination' is shown primarily
in collecting the 'form' out of the many objects of
sense, and 'division' in seeing how the 'form' appears
in a number of different objects of sense. For the many

[1] *Phaedrus*, 266 B.
[2] In the *Phaedrus* (265 D) Plato uses συνορᾶν, to see together, as an
equivalent to συνάγειν, to bring together.

(πολλὰ ἕκαστα), the multitude of particular instances of the one, mean in the first instance the objects which the senses present to us. And forms are primarily spoken of as elements of unity in a multiplicity of sensible things. But it is important not to overlook the further application of the same principle which is implied in the *Republic*; each form is itself related to other forms, and ultimately all the forms of things are connected together and make one system.

 Thus when Plato describes the perfect reasoner as one who, starting from any single form, could pass up along the ladder of forms to the ultimate unconditional principle on which all depends, and could descend in like manner, the ideal of science which he describes is simply the result of his conception of logical method. True reasoning, in all cases, consists in the union of combination and division; and to do both completely, to see the many in their unity and the one in its multiplicity completely, would be to have a perfect knowledge about the world. All wrong reasoning is the failure to do either the one or the other. Plato tells us in the *Philebus* that most people either pass too hastily from unity to variety, that is from a general principle to a particular case, or generalize too hastily from a number of instances to one principle.

This logical method may be variously applied to the discovery, the communication, or the definition of truth (εὑρίσκειν, διδάσκειν, ὁρίζειν); and these are the three main applications of it that we find considered in Plato [1]. In the attempt to discover truth, the expectation as to the truth with which the enquirer starts makes a great difference, and the main point for him to bear in mind as

---

[1] For its application to teaching cf. *Phaedrus*, 276 B sq.

to the method of discovery is that he must never be
satisfied with what he thinks he has discovered until he
has shown all the differentiations of the single form or
principle which he thinks he sees exemplified in the case
before him, nor until he has brought all the particular
instances of it into unity [1]. The power of defining things
(λόγον ἑκάστου λαμβάνειν τῆς οὐσίας) is made a prominent
characteristic of the dialectician in the *Republic*. Definition plays an enormous part in Greek philosophy; to
be able to define things was its ideal. How then does
definition connect with this conception of method?
Anything we wish to define will necessarily be found
to be a certain specific form of one or more generic forms
or principles. To be able to define it, that is to have
an accurate conception of it, is to be able to see exactly
what modification it is of what form or forms. Merely
to know that a certain act, for example, is a good act,
is not to have a definite conception of it; to have an
adequate conception of a good act we must see exactly
in what sense it is good, or how, in the particular circumstances of the act. good is best realized. We might say
that definition consists in assigning to the particular
its position in reference to the principle of which it is
an instance. Dialectic, Plato tells us in the *Republic* [2],
is the method, and the only method, which attempts
systematically to arrive at the definition of any given
thing. The process of defining a given thing is there
(implicitly) represented as consisting in taking it away
from, and holding it apart from, every other thing with
which it is combined or to which it is akin [3]. But this
process of abstraction is only the other side of the process
of concretion, which sees in what ways a given form or

[1] *Philebus*, 16 D.    [2] 533 B.    [3] 534 B sq.

principle is in fact combined with others. We are sometimes told that modern science aims at the classification,
or again at the explanation, of things, whereas the Greeks
aimed only at defining them. But to explain anything,
or to classify anything, is to assign it its place in the
scheme of knowledge, and to define it is the same.

In the latter part of Book VII, in a passage already
referred to, Plato dwells on the dangers of dialectic. He
describes in a graphic way the effect produced on the
mind in youth by the first taste of logic, which is that
the young man goes about proving that every thing
is something else. Plato connects these first beginnings
of thinking, which are the beginnings of dialectic, with
the first perception of the curious fact of the co-existence
of one and many. This is to him the natural way to
describe the awakening of speculative thought. We have
already seen that he describes thought [1] as beginning with
the perception that the same thing is not the same, or
that one is also many. All through Plato we find that
this old logical problem is that around which all his
conceptions of method hang. It was the first form in
which any metaphysical question forced itself on the
human mind [2].

We may now pass to dialectic as completed science.
This is a sense of the word which is more prominent in
the *Republic* than in other dialogues. The conception
has already been discussed in reference to the passage
at the end of Book VI, where Plato defines νόησις [3], or
thought in the fullest sense, as distinguished from διάνοια.
Dialectic, as completed science, is the result which would
be obtained by the method we have been speaking

---

[1] νόησις in the wider sense as opposed to διάνοια.
[2] Cf. *Philebus*, 15 D sq.          [3] νόησις as opposed to διάνοια.

of, if it could be fully carried out. We often hear
method and result spoken of as if they were two
mutually exclusive conceptions. Is philosophy, we
are asked, a method or a result? It is a result, for
as we advance in philosophy we are conscious of
attaining something. But at the same time we are
compelled to say that no result in knowledge is final,
and therefore knowledge is a perpetual method; and
we may add that the methods of knowledge change
and are modified by every fresh step in knowledge.
Between Plato's conception of perfect knowledge and
his conception of the method of attaining to knowledge there is a very obvious correspondence. Perfect
knowledge would be a state of mind to which all things
presented themselves as a perfectly connected order—
an order in which every part down to the smallest
detail had its proper place, and was seen by the mind
to be eventually connected with every other part and
with the principle which makes them all one. Now
dialectical method applied to the discovery of truth
means coming more and more to see not only that
things are one in many, but *how* they are so; the
dialectical view of things is that which studies them
with a constant regard to their mutual relations[1].
Let us suppose a method like this worked out to its
completion, and we get dialectic in its sense of completed knowledge. This of course would not be brought
about merely by what we call a logical process in the
ordinary sense; it would only be possible if the whole
world of facts lay open to our observation. Dialectic

---

[1] *Sophist*, 253 B sq., may be referred to, together with the passages
already referred to in the *Philebus* and the *Phaedrus*, as throwing
light on Plato's practical conception of dialectic.

therefore is not a branch of science existing alongside other sciences. The word may be used either of a universal method to be applied, differently in different cases, to all the questions with which human thought is concerned, or of an ideal science which is the system of all the sciences, an ideal which can only be realized to a slight extent, but which nevertheless describes the end towards which the progress of human knowledge works [1].

### 4. PLAN OF THE WHOLE COURSE OF EDUCATION.

We have described the studies which the Guardians must go through, and it remains to say what place they are to take in the course of the Guardians' lives, and who are to be chosen to enter upon each successive stage of study. Plato begins by enforcing again the necessity of choosing, to be rulers, men who combine the two complementary qualities of constancy and of intellectual quickness (βεβαιότης and δριμύτης), telling us that hard intellectual work, such as they will have to undergo, will require of them more courage even than hard physical exertion. He dwells upon the evils which result from choosing what he calls 'cripples' to be leaders in the state. By a ' cripple' he means a person who is one-sided, or not developed on all

535 A to
end of VII.

---

[1] [The concluding sentences of the discussion of dialectic may here be noticed. Having hitherto spoken of it in language which suggests that he is occupied only with a remote ideal, Plato suddenly changes his tone and makes Socrates appeal to Glaucon to educate his sons as dialecticians. They are to be educated in dialectic because they may be called upon to deal with important public affairs; and dialectic is described simply as the art of 'asking and answering questions most intelligently or scientifically.'—ED.]

sides of his nature. One form of this one-sidedness is to like athletic exertion but hate intellectual toil; another is the reverse of this. Yet another such defect of nature is insufficient care for truth; it is not enough— to put what Plato says in modern language—to have what is ordinarily called a truthful nature, a man must have that love of truth which makes him not only hate to tell a lie, but hate to be the victim of false ideas[1]. These and other requirements Plato sums up by saying that the Guardians must at the outset be sound in limb and sound in mind. He concludes with a characteristic apology for the earnestness with which he is speaking.

Those who are to go through the advanced course of study that has now been proposed must begin their training young, and even their first studies are to be as little compulsory as possible. Up to the age of about seventeen or eighteen the education of μουσική described in the earlier books will go on; and in addition the elements of the sciences will be learnt, but without system (χύδην). After this will come a course of exclusively 'gymnastic' training, lasting till the age of twenty. This means a systematic bodily training, including military exercises, and directed towards preparing the young men for the service of the state in keeping order at home and in fighting against foreign enemies. It serves the further purpose of giving them a good foundation of bodily health for their future work, and of training them in courage and self-control. It will be so hard that they cannot at this period do any intellectual work; but, says Plato, what a man shows himself to be at his gymnastics will be a very good test of his general character. At the age of twenty, a further

---

[1] Cf. 382 A sq. and 412 E sq.

selection will be made of those who have distinguished themselves most, and these will be advanced to the next stage of education.   This will consist of two parts. There will be a systematic scientific course continuing to the age of thirty ; and, while they are occupied in this, the great point to be attended to will be whether they show the faculty for dialectic, the power of 'seeing things together' (σύνοψις).   But alongside of this a training in the public service, chiefly military, will be going on ; and here the chief test to be applied to a man is whether he is steadfast (μόνιμος) and shows constancy to the principles he has been taught.   At the age of thirty, a further selection will be made.   Those who are now approved will enter upon the study of dialectic proper, which will continue for five years, unaccompanied by any other work.   (Probably this is meant to include a study of the principles of morality and human life ; for it is in this connexion that Plato describes the dangers of dialectic for those who are not fitted for it by the tenacity with which they hold fast to the principles of right that they have been taught [1].)   At thirty-five begins the really serious work of the public service, and it lasts for fifteen years.   During these years the Guardians will be acquiring the experience (ἐμπειρία) necessary for rulers by actual contact with the various forms of good and evil about which they have been taught ; and all the while they will be continually tested to see if they stand being 'pulled about in all directions' by the circumstances with which they have to contend.   From fifty onwards, those who are still approved are, alternately, to study the good itself, and in the light of it to govern and organize the state.   They will be the supreme

---

[1] Cf. *Phaedo*, 90 B and C.

council in the state, dividing their time between theoretical study of the good, and practical government.
Finally, when they die, they will be buried with public
honours, and worshipped, if the Delphic oracle allows,
as divine beings (δαίμονες), or at any rate as blessed and
favoured by the gods (εὐδαίμονες).

The actual machinery of this scheme is the least
important part of it, nor is it of any use to enquire
whether it is practicable, for Plato himself only professes
to be describing an ideal state. The question is, What
substantial truth is there in it for mankind, and in what
sort of way could we appropriate Plato's principles?
There are three important ideas in his system of education. First, there is the idea that education must
meet all the demands that human nature brings with it.
Secondly, there is the conception that as long as the human
soul is capable of growth the work of education ought to
go on. Education should be co-extensive with life, for
education simply means keeping the soul alive; it is
only by a concession to human nature's weakness that it
is supposed to be restricted to the first twenty-five years
of one's life. Thirdly, the great organs of education are
all those things which human nature in the course of its
growth has produced; religion, art, science, philosophy,
and the institutions of government and society are all to
be enlisted in the service of education. Here we see how
utterly remote from Plato is the idea that there can be
any contest between art and science, between study and
practical life, or between any of the great products of the
human mind; he uses all as links in one chain.

Though Plato spends so much time in the *Republic*
upon the higher branches of education, he is really contemplating them as intended only for a very few men; he

thinks that the bulk of those who are educated would stop their education about the same time as we do now. It is only the small number who ultimately rule the state who go through the complete course.   No one can doubt that, if it were possible to do something in his spirit for the training of the most influential people in the state, modern government would be considerably better than it is, for, if the function of government is the hardest and highest of all, it clearly requires the best training and the best instruments.

# XIII.
# SUCCESSIVE STAGES OF DECLINE
# OF SOCIETY AND OF THE SOUL

[*Republic*, VIII and IX to 576 B.]

WE may say that Books II to VII of the *Republic*
put before us a logical picture of the rise of the human
soul to what Plato conceived to be its highest capabilities, while Books VIII and IX give a similar picture
of the fall of the human soul to what seemed to him the
lowest point consistent with its remaining human at all.
The first of these pictures shows us how man may
rise to a level where he is very closely akin to the divine
nature, the second shows us how he may fall to a point
where he is almost on a level with the brute. We called
the first a logical picture because Plato, in describing
a perfect state, or certain stages in the process of forming a perfect state, writes throughout as if one stage of
that process succeeded another in a historical order[1];

[1] [The first stage is the ἀναγκαιοτάτη πόλις, i. e. the state containing the
barest essentials of a healthy state, described in II. 369 B to 372 E. The
second is that described from 372 E to the end of IV. The third, that of
V to VII, which he speaks of (in 543 D) as a state distinct from and
better than that of II to IV.—ED.]

whereas we know all the time that the process is absolutely unhistorical, and that he does not mean that any
state has grown up in this way. The real order of the
development he describes is a purely logical order, based
on his psychological analysis of the main elements in
a perfectly developed society. The appearance of historical order is still more striking in Books VIII and IX,
in which the picturesque element is so much more prominent that some commentators have taken Plato to be
describing the actual evolution of Greek political society,
and have criticized him seriously upon that ground,
pointing out that the various forms of government he
speaks of did not occur in the order he describes [1].
Nothing is easier than to show this, but it is quite
inconceivable that Plato should have been ignorant of
such elementary facts. If we look closer we see that
here too the order of arrangement is logical and psychological. The question he puts before himself is this :
The human soul being as we have described it, and
having in it a certain capacity for evil as well as for
good, what would it come to, and through what stages
would it pass, if its capacity for evil were realized
gradually but without any abatement? In actual
human experience there is always some abatement;
there are always counteracting circumstances which
prevent any one tendency working itself out in isolation
and unhindered ; but the philosopher may, as Plato here
does, work out the result of a single tendency logically.
These books therefore put before us an ideal history of
evil, as the previous books put before us an ideal history
of good.

Plato has undertaken in the *Republic* to explain human

[1] Aristotle (*Politics*, 1316 A and B) criticizes Plato on this ground.

life psychologically (that word being taken in the widest sense). He has here to interpret in this manner Greek history and Greek life. He has asked himself, How can we show that the various forms of Greek life are traceable to the working of certain forces in human nature? To do this he has ransacked Greek life to find material, and has concentrated in these books a most extraordinary knowledge of human nature in general and of Greek nature in particular. Each of the constitutions of society which he describes is really an expression of the domination of a certain psychological tendency which, if unchecked, will inevitably produce certain results in society and individual life. In modern times an enquirer with a similar object might ask what in its essence is the democratic spirit; having defined it, he might then go on to ask how in the various so-called democracies of the world this spirit has manifested itself; and he would not confine himself to democracies alone, he would find democratic elements in countries in which the government is not strictly democratic. If he then put together into a picture all the material he had collected, it would answer to no actual form of democracy, but it would give in a concentrated shape what he conceived to be the general effects of the democratic spirit. This is the method which Plato has followed here.

What are the tendencies of which Plato traces the working? His conception of the soul is the same that has been unfolded in Books II to IV. The soul is one thing, but it is also triple; its normal, natural, and ideal condition is that in which each one of its three elements contributes its proper work to the economy of the whole. Further, this condition of the soul involves society, for the soul reaches out to other souls at every point. An ideal community of souls would be one in which the capacities of every individual soul were fully developed and its wants fully satisfied. This would be the case if the philosophic element in man ruled, because this is the element in him which is capable of understanding his true interests, and of living for those interests—that is, living a common life. Any other organization than that in which the philosophic element rules is necessarily, in its degree, imperfect, and is one in which the relative position of the elements of human nature is not normal. The progress of evil is therefore a progress in disorganization; that is to say, as it goes on, different organs or elements of society or of the individual soul come more and more to perform their wrong functions. What Plato calls timocracy, the first stage in the downward progress, is that state of life in which the 'spirited' element dominates; the philosophic element is not thereby eliminated, it simply sinks to a lower level and performs functions not its own, becoming the servant of 'spirit.' The next logical step is taken when 'appetite' becomes dominant, and 'spirit' and reason fall into the position of its servants and instruments; this is 'oligarchy,' which makes the satisfaction of material wants the end of life, but preserves a certain external order by subjecting the crowd of appetites under the rule of one. The next step downward is within the region of appetite; freed from the domination of the desire for wealth, the appetites struggle promiscuously for the mastery, till a sort of temporary equilibrium without any principle is effected between them; this is 'democracy.' The last step is taken when this equilibrium of appetites passes into the absolute despotism of the lowest or of several of the lowest—that is to say, the least compatible with the common life of society, the most selfish ; this is 'tyranny.'

In the picture given of each of these stages we must understand the relation between the individual man described and the community described.  Plato describes the man and the state as they are, and also the process by which they came to be what they are.  In each of these accounts the individual represents the inner psychological condition which, if sufficiently dominant in a state, will give it a certain character or bring about in it a certain change ; but he does not intend to imply that such an individual can exist only in a corresponding state.  Take oligarchy, for example.  The individual oligarchic man is one who is dominated by the principle of seeking material wealth; he is oligarchic so far as he consistently lives for the accumulation of wealth.  Suppose a large number of such men get together in any society and are backed by a certain amount of force, you will inevitably get a political oligarchy based on wealth.  Such men will naturally try to rule the rest, and the ruling principle in themselves will direct them to form a constitution in accordance with itself.  An oligarchic state is thus the oligarchic principle in men 'writ large.'  But there may of course be many oligarchic men in society without the government being an oligarchy.  In the same way we must interpret Plato's descriptions of the transitions from one of these types to another.  As has been said, he does not give them as historical accounts of how any particular Greek constitutions arose.  He has taken certain salient features in the history of a number of individuals and a number of societies, and compounded them together into typical cases made to illustrate a certain principle in the clearest way. His account, for instance, of the transition from oligarchy to democracy means that, if you get a state of society in which the pursuit of wealth is the absorbing object of life to the leading people, then it is only a question of time for that tendency to sap the strength of the community and substitute for it a lower form, and that a similar degradation is inevitable in the case of individual men or of families when once they have come to regard wealth as the chief aim in life. In each picture all the traits described are symptoms of a psychological change going on within ; and all the details are worth studying. These Books have been called the first attempt to construct a philosophy of history. A philosophy of history implies that the historian can see certain laws or principles of which human history exhibits the working. Plato has taken certain inherent tendencies of human nature, and interprets Greek history in the light of them ; not that the tendencies he describes were actually working alone, so that historically events could exactly correspond to his description, but that wherever he looks in Greek society he sees symptoms of them working underneath.

Plato arrives finally at the exact reverse of what he has pictured as the ideal good state of man and society. The best man would be one whose self was as nearly as possible identified with the life of the society of which he was a member, and ultimately with the laws or order of the world of which he, and the society also, were parts. Men never completely accomplish this ideal, but they are actually good in proportion as they accomplish it ; the test of a man's goodness and of his greatness is the extent to which he can lead a common

life (not necessarily in the most obvious way of doing
so [1]), or can identify himself with, and throw himself into,
something not himself; and this applies to men of the
meanest station as well as to the philosophic statesman.
Accordingly the worst man in the world is the man who
is most limited and selfish.    Plato's typical tyrant,
who embodies the tyrannical principle, satisfies at all
costs one of the poorest of his appetites.    Supposing
such a person in circumstances which are not favourable,
he remains the ' tyrannical man,' the slave of a despotic
passion.    But supposing him to find a favourable environment, and supposing him to have this passion strongly
enough, he becomes a full-blown ' tyrant,' just as the
philosopher, if he finds a state that is fit for him,
becomes a king, a constitutional ruler.    The tyrant is the
exact counterpart of the philosopher.    The philosophic
king is at one with everybody and everything about him.
The tyrant—his personality concentrated in a single
dominant passion—is absolutely alone; he is the enemy
of his own better self, of the human kind, and of God.
Theoretically the owner of the state, in reality he is
absolutely poor.

Throughout the downward course by which this
lowest condition is reached, the end which men set
before themselves in life becomes gradually less and less
worthy of human nature ; and, as it is with the end in
life, so it is with the various parts of life which work for
this end.    At each step the true principles of education
are more and more neglected, and the soul fails more
and more to find its proper nurture.

545 C to    The account of these various stages of decline begins
547 A.    with the fall of the ideal state.    How does decay first set

---

[1] Cf. Section X. p. 227 of the Lectures.

in in the perfect state? In asking this Plato really has before him the general problem of the origin of evil— the question, how does it come about that the world is not so perfect as it might be? But the transition from the ideal society to timocracy is related as if it were an historical event. It is impossible to say whether Plato thought there actually had been forms of human life much more perfect than existed in Greece in the times of which he knew. He certainly saw in what he believed to be the best forms of society in Greece some imperfect approximations to what human society might be, but we need not suppose that he thought any more perfect approximation to it had gone before these. Having formed his own ideal conception as a standard of criticism, he naturally represents the types of existing society which he is going to judge as so many removes from it ; but this does not imply a serious belief in the existence of his ideal. He is however quite serious with the idea, which he here expresses, that no human institutions, even the most perfect, can be permanent. 'Can our present European civilization permanently progress, or permanently exist ?' 'Can any national life go on without decay?'—these are analogous questions to that which was in Plato's mind.

The cause of decline in any society must, he asserts, be division and faction (στάσις) among its rulers. As long as they are of like mind, it is impossible for the society to break up. So much is clear, but we must call on the Muses to tell us the beginning of divisions in our ideal state. This is an example of a way of speaking, half serious, half humorous, which Plato uses when he comes across a question that cannot be scientifically dealt with ; in the same way he adopts the lan-

# 302    LECTURES ON PLATO'S 'REPUBLIC'

guage of mythology or poetry when he is speaking of the ultimate destiny of the soul. 'Let us suppose,' he says here, 'that the Muses are speaking to us jestingly, as if we were children, and in language of mock solemnity.'

The principle at the foundation of the answer given by the Muses is that everything which has come into being is liable to cease to be. Therefore human society, which has come into being, however well it may be knit together, is subject to dissolution. And what form will the dissolution of this society take? Here another general law is enunciated, applying to all organic life, or, as he says, to everything in which soul and body are united. All organic things have predestined periods, longer or shorter according to their nature, upon which their inherent vitality and power of reproducing themselves depend[1]. At certain intervals the vitality of souls that are in human bodies becomes feeble and the soul is comparatively unproductive. If a number of children are produced at such times they will form an inferior race, and society must decline. The number which Plato now gives in an enigmatic way expresses the periods at which these critical moments occur. We need not attach any importance to the particular number; the passage expresses Plato's belief that there are fixed laws governing this matter, which are capable of being definitely stated. But, he says, however wise the best minds of a society may be, their intelligence is necessarily alloyed with sense; hence they will not perfectly understand the

---

[1] The notion of fixed recurring periods of fatal importance to the soul is found in various forms in *Politicus*, 269 C sqq. (especially 272 D and E); *Phaedrus*, 248 A to 249 D; *Laws*, X. 903 B sqq.; *Timaeus*, 42 B–E; and *Republic*, X. 617 D.

laws of human generation, and owing to their mistakes children will inevitably be born who are inferior to their parents ; and, when the decline has once set in, it will inevitably increase. Thus the decline of human society is brought about by its failure to understand the laws of its own life.

Plato has anticipated the notion that a human society is in some sense an organic thing, having its own laws of growth and decay. He offers no evidence for what he says, but his fundamental idea, that there are unknown conditions favourable and unfavourable to the maintenance of the vigour of a race, has remained to the present day. It still seems to many natural to suppose that every decay of a nation is caused by some loss of vital power, and that there are laws, however undiscoverable they may be, upon which the loss or maintenance of that vital power depends.

Society then will inevitably fall away from the ideal 547 A to state ; at any rate the best forms of existing society are 550 C. a compromise between that which is highest and that which is lowest in human nature. What are the particular symptoms of imperfection which even the best, timocracy[1], exhibits? Its inherent imperfection shows itself, when judged by the standard of the ideal state, in two main points. The first is the institution of private property in the possession of the ruling class ; the second is the fact that those who are ruled are regarded as the subjects and slaves of the rulers. The first of these defects does away with the perfect identity of interests between the rulers and the state. The second destroys

[1] Timocracy means here the state in which honour is made the dominant motive of action. It is used in quite another sense in Aristotle, *Eth. Nic.* VIII. x. 1.

the relation of perfect co-operation and give and take,
which ought to exist between the different classes of
the community.  Those who are ruled should regard the
ruling class as their protectors and saviours, and the
rulers should regard them as the friends who supply
all their material needs[1].  As soon as you get society
divided into subjects and kings, slaves and masters,
this relation of common interests and reciprocal services
is at an end.

Plato traces these facts to their psychological origin.
They are concessions to the selfish principle in man, and
they express the fact that the highest element in human
nature, reason, has been dethroned from its place.  In
its stead 'spirit,' the honour-loving element, the element
that seeks for personal distinction, rules.  Personal distinction is the guiding principle of the timocratic man;
that is to say, it is the thing which such a man at his best
moments lives for.  From the rule of 'spirit' result several
features of Spartan life, which Plato mentions with
approval : the prevailing respect for authority, the attention paid to gymnastic and military training, the common
meals of the governing class (ξυσσιτία), and the law that
they should not engage in trade.  On the other hand
reason has been degraded and made merely the servant
of military organization and strategy.  Therefore reason
itself becomes degenerate, and the general suspicion in
which exceptional abilities are held shows that reason,
not being exercised on the highest object, the good of
the community, loses its simplicity and integrity.  And,
as the highest element suffers, so the whole life of the
society suffers.  The appetites for the commodities which
give the command of enjoyment, instead of being kept in

[1] Cf. V. 463 B.

their place and being absorbed in providing the necessaries of life, begin to assert themselves on their own
account; the great symptom of this which Plato notices
is that avarice, which is professedly tabooed in this society,
is nevertheless growing up in the dark. You cannot
eradicate appetite, and the more you fail to educate the
best things in human nature the more the worst things
will assert themselves; and so beneath the fair exterior
of honour one of the lowest qualities is developing
itself. The secret growth of avarice in spite of the laws
is alluded to by Aristotle[1] also as a feature of Spartan
society in his time[2]. Here, in the description of the
typical timocratic state, the love of money is represented
as growing till it becomes the dominant force in social
life, and the institutions of the state are transformed in
accordance with it, political power being made to depend
on wealth.

In the life of the individual timocratic man a similar
process is at work. The typical timocratic man is
represented as the son of a 'good man,' a philosopher,
in a state where the best men are divorced from public
life, and where public affairs are in the hands of the
selfish and unprincipled. Ambition makes him despise
his father's ways, and he plunges into a public career.
At first honour keeps him straight; but as he gets
older this impulse, unsupported in his case by reason,
degenerates into mere self-assertion, and, the appetitive element breaking loose, he ends by becoming a
lover of money. This takes place because he has
neglected the 'one thing that can preserve a man's

[1] *Politics*, 1270 A, 11 sqq., and 1307 A, 34 sq.
[2] For the explicit connexion of timocracy with Sparta and with Crete
see 544 C.

goodness through his life, reason blended with music
(λόγος μουσικῇ κεκραμένος).'

Plato's view of Sparta is well illustrated by a
passage in the *Laws*[1]. He there tells us that the self-
control of which the Spartans are so proud fails under
circumstances to which they are not used, namely when
they are exposed to the temptations of pleasure instead
of those of danger and pain. His admiration of Sparta,
like Aristotle's, was confined to one point. The Spartans
were the only people in Greece who had deliberately
adopted a certain principle of life and had carried it
through; and both writers admired the care given to
education of a certain kind, the respect for order and
discipline, and the absorption of the individual in the
social organization, which resulted from this; but both
saw well enough that the Spartan life and the objects
at which this organization aimed were very narrow[2].

550 C to
555 A.

The rule of 'spirit' (unsupported by reason, which was
made to lead and not to serve) having allowed appetite,
the third element in human nature, to grow, this in turn
becomes the ruling power, and first in its most respectable form, desire for wealth. Oligarchy means to Plato
the supremacy of those appetites for the necessaries
of life, which, when kept in their proper subordination,
are the most serviceable appetites. It is that form of
constitution in which wealth is openly acknowledged as
the end of life, the thing most worth living for, and the
thing the possession of which makes one man better than
another. The political constitution by which political
power is given to the wealthy is only the expression and

[1] I. 633 B sqq.
[2] Cf. Aristotle, *Eth. Nic.* X. 9, § 13; also *Politics*, 1333 B, 12 sqq.;
1337 A, 31; 1338 B, 9 sqq.; and 1294 B, 18 sq.

public recognition of what the leading men in the state believe to be the true end of life. The most important typical consequences of the adoption of this constitution are now described. First, it still further breaks up the unity of the state [1], which depends upon every class doing its own proper work for the community; there are now two cities, one of rich, and one of poor, no longer bound together by community of interest, but separated by diversity of interests. Secondly, the strength of the state diminishes as its unity diminishes; for the rich are afraid to arm the poor, and they themselves are getting less and less capable of military service; there is growing physical degeneracy. Thirdly, the growth of money-getting involves the growth, alongside of it, of money-wasting; and the laws, which are made of course in the interest of the rich nobility, allow and encourage unlimited alienation of property. Outside the ranks of the rich, there is poverty sinking into pauperism and generating a dangerous class, which is swelled by numbers of ruined spendthrifts from the ranks above. The existence of this dangerous class involves forcible repression, but the government does not continue long to be backed by force.

In the account of the genesis of the oligarchic man we have a typical picture of Greek life. Aspirants to political distinction are constantly being ruined by malicious accusations ($\sigma\upsilon\kappa o\phi\alpha\nu\tau\iota a$), and therefore a revulsion from public life takes place in the better class, and they narrow their minds to trade and commerce. Reason is now still further degraded into a mere instrument of money-making; and spirit is schooled into a worship of rich men and riches. Continued neglect of education

---

[1] In the 'timocracy' there was still unity for purposes of military defence.

(ἀπαιδευσία, 552 E, 554 B) continues to produce lowering of character. Externally there is decency, order, and respectability in the life of the oligarchic man, but the 'drone appetites' are beginning to make themselves felt, though as yet kept in check by the absorbing appetite for wealth. As in the state the rich restrain but do not direct the poor, so in the individual this dominant passion chains the others but does not employ them, and they develop into a dangerous element within him. The man, like the state, is becoming weak because he cannot employ the whole of himself.

555 B to 562 A. Plato's picture of the rise of 'democracy' makes clearer than before the principles which underlie his description of the gradual decline of human life. In the first place, this decline is determined throughout by a gradual change in that which is made the good or end of life. In the second place, the course it takes follows logically from the principle that, when men have an appetite for a certain thing, that appetite must grow stronger and stronger unless there is something else in them competent to check it ; at each stage of the decline mere appetite absorbs more and more of man's life into itself[1]. The psychological explanation of the origin of democracy is found in the object which is recognized as the good in oligarchy, and the insatiable appetite for it which oligarchy encourages. In the oligarchic state everything is done with a view to wealth, and the character of the legislation, the most important means by which the life of society is regulated, expresses openly the recognition of greed as the true principle of life by the dominant people in the state. This principle ultimately overthrows the state. Oligarchic legislation fails

---

[1] Cf. IV. 424 A, where the opposite process to this decline is referred to.

to check that accumulation of wealth in a few hands which leads to the overthrow of oligarchy. Plato mentions two possible legislative checks upon this accumu: lation, restrictions upon the alienation of private property, which would hinder its accumulation in a few hands, and the abolition of legal means for the recovery of debts[1], which would check the gradual ruin of the spendthrift class. Neither of these steps is taken in the oligarchic state, because it is the interest of the leading people to sell up as many of their own class as possible. Ultimately oligarchy is overthrown because the rulers, being set upon wealth only, become degenerate, and the people discover their weakness; having overthrown them, either with foreign help or through factions among the oligarchs themselves, the people come into power.

Democracy in Plato means that form of it which Aristotle distinguishes as unmitigated or pure democracy, in which liberty and equality, in the sense of the liberty of everybody to do whatever he pleases, and the equality of everybody with everybody else in every respect, are the strongest principles in the constitution. It violates, and in all but the most intense way, the first principle of society. That principle is that everybody differs from others, and should do that which he is fit to do and nothing else. In defiance of this, democracy 'assigns equality alike to the equal and the unequal.' This sums up Plato's charge against what he understands by democracy. The most vital point in which this comes out is government; democracy asserts that there is no need at all for anybody to be or to make himself peculiarly fitted in order to be able to govern[2].

[1] Cf. Arist. *Eth. Nic.* IX. i. 9.          [2] Cf. VI. 488 B.

The democratic man exhibits in his individual life the character which, when it becomes dominant and commands public approval, produces democracy in the sense that has been described. The psychological foundation of democracy is a new form of the rule of appetite in the individuals who give the state its character. In the oligarchic man the desires which are most necessary, and are also most orderly, concentrated, and respectable, dominate ; in the democratic man no particular appetite, but appetite generally, governs. This absence of principle he, like the democratic state, makes into a principle. To distinguish him from the oligarchic man Plato here gives us a division of the appetitive element in the soul ; there are two great classes of appetites, the necessary and the unnecessary. ' Necessary appetites ' are those which cannot be got rid of, and to this class belong all those the satisfaction of which does good—good, that is to say, to the whole man. ' Unnecessary appetites' are those which can be got rid of by education and practice, and these are appetites the satisfaction of which does no good. The necessary appetites are also called the ' wealth-getting' appetites ($\chi\rho\eta\mu\alpha\tau\iota\sigma\tau\iota\kappa\alpha\acute{\iota}$), because they are productive of something which is of use ; and the unnecessary appetites, which are unproductive, are called the 'spending' appetites. Thus the appetite for food up to the point to which it is good for the bodily organism is necessary and productive ; desire for food beyond that point is unnecessary and unproductive. The typical democratic man, then, is the son of an oligarchic man in whom the productive desires are predominant. He is brought up without education, and he comes into fashionable and fast society. He has nothing to feed his reason upon ; therefore there is nothing to give unity to his appetites, and so they become 'motley and many-headed.' They fall, however, into two main divisions; one of these consists of appetites which are still partly rational, and at first these have the mastery over those which are wholly irrational, being supported by the traditions of the man's family. But, as the more rational appetites are unsupported in their control by anything in the man himself, that is by his reason, the unproductive appetites, however much they have been cut down, sprout again whenever the external influences which have helped to repress them are removed. The empty place of reason in such a man is occupied by a counterfeit reason ; quack theories (ψευδεῖς καὶ ἀλαζόνες λόγοι), which ally themselves with his unproductive appetites, develop into a brilliant cynicism which ex-poses the fallacies of so-called morality. This is the stage of 'initiation,' in which the soul gets rid of illusions, and comes to see through many things and to call them by their right names, calling, for example, all sense of shame cowardice. Through this stage the soul passes into freedom, or living as one pleases, in other words anarchy. Such a life tends to bring about the ultimate mastery of one ruling passion, which is 'tyranny'; but, with luck, as the man grows older, he will settle down into a state of compromise or balance of appetites, in which his principle is to be the creature of the moment. He denies any distinction of better or worse, and gives himself in turn to every desire upon which the lot falls. Asceticism and debauchery, philosophy, sport, idleness, politics, war, successively engage him[1]; and this is what he calls the free development of his nature. Such a

---

[1] Cf. Dryden's Zimri in *Absalom and Achitophel*, 544 sqq.

man will be the object of general admiration and envy in the democratic state.

As democracy developed out of oligarchy, so the tyrannic principle develops logically out of the democratic. Tyranny arises from the inevitable excessive pursuit of that which democracy recognizes as the good, namely absolute liberty. All appetite is essentially insatiate [1], and it is the inherent tendency of the democratic desire for liberty to grow, unless it is checked. All the peculiar institutions ascribed to extreme democracy proceed from this, and the tendency increases until at last it makes people so 'delicate' that they can stand no restraint whatever. There is, Plato observes, a law of reaction, to be seen in the changes of the weather and in the varying states of physical organisms, and in the history of political communities no less, according to which excess in one direction is generally followed by excess in the opposite direction. And so, in the case of the democratic state, out of absolute liberty absolute servitude proceeds. In the typical case of such a revolution, which he goes on to describe, democratic society has fallen into three main divisions. There is a class of ruined spendthrifts and adventurers, which already existed under oligarchy, but which under democracy has become the most prominent and the loudest-voiced element in the state. There is a class of orderly and quiet money-makers whose wealth forms the 'pasture of the drones' of society. There is lastly the mass of citizens who work with their hands. Theoretically they are the ruling class, for they have the majority of votes, but they only can or only will take a constant part in public affairs if they are paid for so doing, and accordingly the

[1] Cf. Arist. *Eth. Nic.* III. xii. 7.

adventurers, who are the political leaders of the state, are always paying them out of the money of the rich[1]. In time the rich come to an end of their endurance, and resist this system of plunder. Thereupon an outcry is raised against them, they are denounced as cursed oligarchs, and accusations of seditious conspiracy are brought against them. In this time of excitement the boldest and most unscrupulous of the political adventurers steps forward as the friend of the people and the champion of democracy. The critical point, when his destiny is decided, and the champion of the people becomes a tyrant, is reached when he first sheds the blood of the rich who oppose him. He is then no longer his own master, but is inevitably driven on to shed more blood. Under the pretext that the enemies of the state are plotting against his life, he persuades the people to grant him a body-guard. When armed force is once at his disposal he has obtained the power of a tyrant, and the necessities and fears of the position in which he is now placed lead him to further and further acts of tyranny, to establish his power.

In describing how the 'tyrannic' type of individual character arises, Plato brings in a further division of the appetitive elements in the soul. Among the unnecessary appetites there are some that are altogether lawless, 'wild-beast' appetites[2]. These, Plato says, exist even in men of the best regulated life, but they are kept in check, or come out only in dreams, when reason has least

---

[1] Cf. Aristophanes, *Knights*, 791 sqq. and 1218 sqq. (in attack on Cleon); also Demosthenes, *Olynth.* III. 31.

[2] Τὸ θηριῶδές τε καὶ ἄγριον. In somewhat the same way Aristotle (*Eth.* VII. i. and v.) describes the θηριώδεις ἕξεις as the extreme of human badness, corresponding to 'heroic and divine virtues' which are the extreme of human goodness.

control over the soul[1]. They cannot be tamed; most desires can be made to fill a serviceable part in the economy of life, but these cannot. The tyrannic man, of whom the actual tyrant is the most extreme type, is one who is himself tyrannized over by a single dominant appetite of this sort. He thus differs from the democratic man. The soul of the democratic man has gradually lost its unity, but a sort of equilibrium exists between the varied desires which sway it. He can only remain democratic, and live upon the principle of having no principle, so long as this equilibrium lasts. But it cannot be expected to last long; the tendency must be for a few of his appetites, and ultimately for a single appetite, to become dominant over the others; and, when once a single appetite has got the lead, it goes on, like the tyrant in the state, extending its sway, till at last it swallows up the whole man. A man so mastered by a single bestial passion will for the sake of it commit any crime. When there are only a few such men in a state, they will be criminals on a small scale, but when this lawless character becomes common, the end will be that the most tyrannic man, the man most dominated by his one passion, will make himself tyrant of the state.

[1] On dreams and visions in this connexion cf. *Tim.* 70 D–72 B.

# XIV. COMPARISON OF THE JUST
# AND THE UNJUST LIFE

[*Republic*, IX. 576 B to end.]

THE leading types of imperfect states and of imperfect individual lives have now been described, ending with a state which is in the utmost conceivable degree opposite to the ideal state[1], and with a life which is in the utmost conceivable degree opposite to the just life. Plato proceeds to deal with the question of the happiness of these lives, matching the just man against the unjust in three comparisons drawn from three different points of view, three Olympic contests as he calls them, in which Glaucon, who began by stating the claims of injustice, is made to declare which is victor.

[1] [This state is no longer called ἀριστοκρατία, as in VIII. 544 E, 545 D, but (by implication) βασιλεία (legitimate monarchy), i. e. the state in which the one best man of all has most power, the extreme opposite to τύραννις. See *Politicus*, 302 B sq., and cf. Aristotle, *Politics*, 1279 A, 33 sq. In the connecting section at the end of IV. (445 D) the ideal state, we are told, may be called indifferently ἀριστοκρατία or βασιλεία. There is probably no political significance in the change of phrase here; the βασιλεύς is brought in for the sake of comparison with the τύραννος, being the good man placed in the position where his goodness can develop itself on the largest scale.—ED.]

This is therefore the formal answer to the original question with which the argument began in Book II.

The discussion that follows is unsatisfactory, as any discussion of the relative values of different states of consciousness always must be. Nobody can prove that his own life or his own form of happiness is better worth having than another, for everybody is ultimately his own judge. But, if there is to be a discussion in which, as in this case, the arguer has practically prejudged the question before he begins his argument, its interest for us lies in observing the principle upon which he has formed his judgment, and the canons of criticism which he applies. Here Plato begins by laying down the principle upon which the comparison between these different lives is to be made. It must be made not upon an external view but on a view which penetrates to the inner life of the man, and which sees him, not as he shows himself to the world, but stripped and bare ; or, as we may say, interpreting the method which Plato actually applies, it must be made upon a complete view which takes in the whole man.

577 B to 580 C.    (1) First of all Plato takes three of the principal forms of well-being: freedom, wealth, and security from fear, which answer in some degree to the ends which the democratic, the oligarchic, and the timocratic characters respectively set themselves to obtain. He asks, from the point of view of an intelligent and impartial outsider who has observed the different lives as they have been described, Which man is really free, which is really rich, which is really without fears—the most just or the most unjust? The most important point in this passage is the conception of freedom which it involves. It may be said, no doubt, that the tyrannic man, being one who

does exactly what he pleases, is the freest man, and especially if circumstances let him develop to the full and he becomes a tyrant, for he is then *ex hypothesi* autocratic and omnipotent.  Plato asserts on the contrary that he is an absolute slave, because if you look at his whole soul you will see that he least of all men does what he wishes.  This is a simple expression of Plato's conception of freedom of will.  Freedom is doing what one wills, the freest man is he who most does what he wills, and that means the man whose whole self does what it wills.  Now in the tyrannic man nearly the whole self is in abeyance; it is enslaved to one shred or fragment of human nature.  Similarly in the *Gorgias* [1] Plato declares that tyrants do nothing that they desire (ἃ βούλονται).  Here 'what one desires' means the really desirable (in Aristotle's phrase, ἁπλῶς βουλητόν).  The really desirable is that which is desirable to the real or true self, and the real self means the whole self. Throughout the moral philosophy of Plato and Aristotle there runs the conception of an order not only of the physical but of the moral world, to which we must conform if we would be at our best, or, in other words, ·if we would satisfy our nature: and along with this goes the kindred idea that the higher nature is, so to speak, the truth of the lower, that is that the lower nature finds what it aims at in the satisfaction of the higher.  Freedom, accordingly, or doing what one wills, is not the power to satisfy any and every desire, but the power to satisfy those desires in which the whole self finds satisfaction.

The idea of true wealth, which is next introduced in this passage, and which is like that of the New Tes-

[1] 466 D sqq.

tament, has already appeared in Book III, where Plato refused to let the Guardians be rich in money and land on the ground that, if they lived up to their position, they would always have the true wealth [1]. Unlike them the tyrannic soul is emphatically poor, for it is always wanting and never satisfied; it is incapable of being filled (ἄπληστος) [2]. Similarly, it is the nature of such a soul always to have something to fear and never to feel secure.

The tyrannic soul, then, is all unsatisfied desire. But, completely to realize this ideal of misery, the tyrannic man must have scope given to his nature by becoming a full-blown tyrant. As the philosopher is not all that he can be unless he finds a state meet for him, where his activity has full scope [3], so it is with the tyrannic man. It is only when he becomes the ruler of a community that he reaches the full measure of his destructiveness, and then he attains the complete misery of absolute isolation. The ideal of well-being is that a man should realize to the full his communion with his fellow men ; the tyrant is absolutely cut off from his fellows. · Moreover, seeming to be free and powerful, he, beyond all other men, is under the compulsion of constant fear.

580 D to 583 A.    (2) In the second part of the comparison between the just and the unjust, the question put is how these different lives compare in respect of pleasantness (ἡδονή). The point of view from which Plato enquires into this is psychological, and the passage throws a good deal of light on his conception of the soul.

[1] 416 E.
[2] Cf. *Gorgias*, 493 A to D, where the soul of the incontinent man is compared to a sieve.
[3] 497 A.

There are, as we have already learned in Book IV,
three 'parts' or 'forms' of the soul, the rational, the
spirited, and the appetitive (ἐπιθυμητικόν). To each of
these forms, as we are now told, there corresponds
a typical object of desire (ἐπιθυμία), and a pleasure
which attends the satisfaction of that desire. Plato
thus attributes a desire to the two higher forms of
this soul as well as to the part called *par excellence*
ἐπιθυμητικόν. Ἐπιθυμία, that is, is used, as in this passage,
in the general sense of desire (desire for food, or for
truth, or for anything else), and also (like the English
'appetite') in the narrower and more usual sense of
physical desires. It is in the latter sense that the
name ἐπιθυμητικόν has been given to the third element in
the soul. It is given because certain bodily appetites,
owing to their intensity (σφοδρότης), have acquired
such a prominence among the different desires of
this part of our nature that they may be allowed
to give the name to it (580 E). But the dominant
object among all the various objects which the 'appetitive' element seeks is material wealth, because that
is the general instrument for satisfying appetites.
Accordingly Plato here calls this element the 'wealth-
seeking' or 'gain-seeking' part of the soul (φιλοχρήματον[1]
καὶ φιλοκερδές); and in speaking of those in whom the
appetitive side of the soul predominates as lovers of
gain he does not distinguish the oligarchic, the democratic, and the tyrannic characters[2]. By the appetitive

---

[1] Also in IV. 435 E.

[2] Some of those who are here classed together may of course be
prodigal of money, but they all the same set their hearts upon the
things which money can buy. In the description of the tyrannic man
573 sq. the development of lust is represented as bringing with it at first
prodigality, then avarice and extortion.

man he does not at all necessarily mean a sensual man,
but merely one whose dominant wish is to be physically
comfortable and satisfied [1]; and he represents the great
majority of men in every state as appetitive, not because
he thinks the majority of men are sensualists and volup-
tuaries, but because the desire for physical comfort plays
a very large part in most men's lives.  In the present
passage, then, for the sake of simplicity the pleasure of
material gain is taken as the characteristic pleasure of
this form of soul.  Next, to the spirited element the
typical object of desire is to win, and to get distinction,
the reward of winning (νικᾶν καὶ εὐδοκιμεῖν); so it may
be described as that which loves strife and loves honour
(φιλόνεικον and φιλότιμον).  Lastly, the desire of the
rational element is to see things as they are, and it
may therefore be described as that which loves knowledge and wisdom (φιλομαθὲς καὶ φιλόσοφον).

Mankind, then, falls into three great classes, according
as one or another of these three elements in the soul
prevails in them.  Each class judges its own pleasure
to be the most pleasant, and regards the pleasures of
the other two as not worth having.  How can we decide
which judges best?  The question must be decided by
intelligent experience and by reasoning (ἐμπειρίᾳ καὶ
φρονήσει καὶ λόγῳ).  Which then of these three types
of men has the widest experience to enable him to

[1] [Nor are all the tastes in which a man shows himself ἐπιθυμητικός
necessarily tastes for bodily pleasures and comforts, τὸ ἐπιθυμητικόν
covers besides bodily appetites the desire for anything that we should
call mere amusement.  The democratic man, for instance, amuses himself
with philosophy and even with occasional ascetic practices, without Plato
thinking him any the less ἐπιθυμητικός for that.   Art and literature also,
not only when they are specially sensuous, but so far as they are simply
the gratification of fancy, emphatically minister to the pleasure of τὸ
ἐπιθυμητικόν.—ED.]

judge? The philosopher has necessarily from his earliest years had experience of the pleasures which men derive from gain ; and the pleasure of winning, and of the honour which rewards winning, has been experienced by everybody who has ever attained what he has striven for, since success and its rewards are not the prerogative of any one kind of man. Therefore, so far as personal experience goes, the philosopher has the experience of the others ; but they have not his ; nor has their experience been intelligent ($\mu\epsilon\tau\grave{a}$ $\phi\rho\sigma\nu\acute{\eta}\sigma\epsilon\omega s$) ; and, so far as reasoning on the matter goes, he is of course the best reasoner. He then is the best judge.

The argument is unsatisfactory, because the question at issue could only be solved for any one by an appeal to his own personal experience ; a man who had no experience of a kind of pleasure which he was asked to believe was better than his own could not be convinced by the experience of another. So that, if such an appeal as this is to be made to a man, he must start with some conception of a higher and a lower personality in himself. But the passage is interesting because it shows that by the philosophic form of soul Plato does not mean one which exists, so to say, alongside of and to the exclusion of the others. He thinks of it as the fullest form of human nature. As you go downwards from this fullest form of personality, experience becomes more limited. We may illustrate this conception from the case of what we call 'genius.' We should all recognize in Shakespeare a personality which was not exclusive, but which might be said to have embraced the experience of all kinds of lives. We cannot understand the works of such a genius

fully, because we have not the experience to follow
it, and so genius is generally incomprehensible to the
majority of mankind; but so far as we can follow the
works of genius we do enter into its experience, and
we should admit that we therein taste of a fuller
experience than our own. We must be careful, again,
not to misunderstand what Plato means by experience.
When he speaks here of the philosophic soul having
of necessity the experience of the other souls, he does
not mean that the philosopher, any more than the
great poet, has gone about the world testing various
kinds of life, but that the higher kind of man learns
more from the experience which he shares with the
lower kind without having to go through nearly the
same amount of it; and, as a matter of fact, this is true.

583 B to
588 A.
(3) In the third place Plato compares the pleasures
of these different kinds of life in another way. The form
in which he puts his question is no longer, Which is
the pleasantest of these pleasures? or, Which is the
best worth having? but, Which is the most real pleasure?
The pleasure of the lower kind of life is, he contends,
comparatively not pleasure at all. First, he endeavours
to show that something which is not really pleasure is
constantly by an illusion taken for pleasure. True or
unmixed (καθαρά) pleasure cannot, he says, consist in
mere relief from pain, nor true pain in mere cessation
of pleasure. Between pleasure and pain there is a neutral
state which is neither. When pain passes away and they
enter into this state, people call it pleasure, and equally
when pleasure ceases and they enter into this state they
call it pain. But it is logically absurd to call a state,
which is neither pleasure nor pain, both pleasure and
pain. This neutral state is one of quiescence (ἡσυχία),

whereas both pleasure and pain are movements (κινήσεις) of the soul. Now, it can be shown by simple instances that there are pleasures which are not preceded by pain, and of which the cessation is painless ; but most of what are ordinarily called bodily pleasures are of the nature of cessation of pain ; and, on the principle just laid down, they cannot be real pleasures. But it is easy to see how the name of pleasure gets appropriated to them by so many people. Just as a man who has risen half-way from a lower to a higher elevation, and who has never seen beyond half-way, may think him-self at the top, so these cessations of pain are regarded as pleasure by those who have no experience of what real pleasure is. Now what is the real pleasure? Pleasure means being satisfied (πλήρωσις) with that which naturally satisfies. The reality of the pleasure is proportionate to the reality of the satisfaction at-tained. If the satisfaction is transient and the want keeps recurring, there is no real satisfaction and no real pleasure. And so the question, What is the real pleasure? brings us back to the question : What is the most real element in the human soul ; or what do we mean by ourselves? For the real satisfaction is that which satisfies our real selves [1].

Plato's question whether certain pleasures are real is difficult to understand. There is a difficulty in all questions about the truth of feelings. In one sense all feelings are real ; what we feel, we feel ; and we cannot suppose that Plato is questioning that. But the same

[1] [In the last few sentences and in parts of the following discussion certain points in Plato's argument acquire a relatively stronger emphasis than they have in the original ; but it has been thought better to leave the passage untouched.—ED.]

remark applies to anything of which the reality is called in question. Everything is in one sense real ; and when we ask, Is this real? we do not mean, Is this what it is? but, Is it what it suggests? or, Is it accompanied by what we suppose it to be accompanied by? or, Is it related as we suppose it to be related? or, Does it occupy the place that we believe it to occupy? In fact, it is absolutely true that, in asking whether a given thing is real, we are always asking about something else besides it. Suppose, to take an instance of a feeling other than pleasure, that some one asked, Am I really hot? would that be a sensible question? It would only be so if he meant, Is this feeling, which I have, connected with certain processes in my body which a physiologist would associate with heat? or, If I applied a thermometer to myself would the mercury rise to a certain height? or something of that sort. The question can only be intelligently asked and answered if there is, in the feeling which it concerns, an implied reference to something else ; for asking the question implies the possibility of testing the feeling, and it cannot be tested by itself, but only by something other than it. To apply this to Plato's question about the reality of pleasure and pain, there can be no discussion as to whether a man does or does not feel pleasure or pain, in what is perhaps the most obvious sense of the words, ('you cannot argue a man out of his feelings,' as we say). If Plato's question is to be asked and answered intelligently, there must be in pleasure or pain an implied reference to something else.

Now Plato takes pleasure in the sense of being satisfied[1]

---

[1] [The only difficulty of the most important part of the argument arises from the fact that neither ' pleasure ' in English nor ' ἡδονή ' in Greek is

(τὸ πληροῦσθαι), which is a natural enough way of defining
it. In this sense any particular part of the self receives
pleasure when it is satisfied with its own appropriate
object, and it can be satisfied with none but its own appropriate object; you cannot satisfy hunger with drink or
thirst with solid food. This gives us a point of view from
which it can be asked which is the most real pleasure.
If we answer that the self or soul, though it is a manifold
thing, is still one thing, it is intelligible to ask, In which
of the various kinds of satisfaction is the self most really
satisfied? and that is what Plato means when he asks
which is the most real pleasure. He puts the question
in a naïve and simple form. Is the self, he asks, equally
satisfied in the satisfaction of hunger and in the satisfaction which attends the attainment of truth? Satisfaction
is real in proportion as it is permanent (βέβαιος). Now
when we satisfy hunger the satisfaction attained has
very little permanence indeed; we are always getting
hungry, and we cannot say that our hunger becomes
more satisfied as we grow older. To put this in another
way: the self which is satisfied by eating is neither

necessarily or indeed commonly equivalent to this. The word 'pleasure'
applies to a temporary state of feeling, and we use it sometimes with
more, sometimes with less reference to the belief on which that feeling
depends, and to the feelings which will succeed it, and to the other
feelings, pleasant or painful, with which the specific feeling we are speaking of is inextricably bound up ; sometimes we use it with no such
reference at all. In the narrow sense, which is very common, a pleasure
is just as truly and as really a pleasure, even if it depends on an entire
mistake, or if none but a fool would feel it. Aristotle, in the tenth Book
of the *Ethics*, expressly limits the use of the word ἡδονή to this narrow
sense, and opposes it to what Plato here calls pleasure. This latter is
what a man would deliberately and with full understanding choose, and
be permanently content to have had, and which is therefore of course
a more real pleasure the more a man can choose it deliberately and with
his whole mind.—ED.]

a large part of the self, nor a part which is constantly and permanently present in the self. We might try to imagine a self which had nothing to satisfy but physical hunger, and we might ask how much satisfaction it attains; or we might equally ask how much of a self it is, what is the amount of its reality; for we must remember that the self and the satisfaction of the self are not separable, the self *is* the satisfaction it attains. Such a being would be always going up and down from pain to satisfaction, and from satisfaction to pain; it would be in a state of perpetual fluctuation between these limits; and we should have to say that the satisfaction attained in such a life was very small indeed, that it was very little of a life, and the self very little of a self. Now we may ask another question: Why do we all despise a man who lives to eat? The ultimate reason is that we assume that there are in him other capacities requiring satisfaction, and that the part of the man's self which is satisfied in eating is very small. Adopting Plato's phraseology, we may say that the man who lives to eat sacrifices nearly the whole of self to one small fragment. A very good practical test to apply to the value of different satisfactions is to ask how much of oneself is honestly satisfied by each. All reflexions on the transient nature of certain satisfactions come back to this fact: self does not exist merely in isolated moments of satisfaction; each satisfaction has to be taken as a contribution to the satisfaction of self as a whole, as is seen in the fact that we may feel remorse even in the moments of satisfaction.

Thus Plato's comparison of the pleasures of the higher and lower forms of life resolves itself into this: that in the higher form of life a larger part of what there is in the soul is satisfied; that in it the soul as a whole is more fully what it has the capacity to be. This view he helps out by various arguments and figures. In the first place there is the figure (584 D sq.), derived from space, of the higher and the lower. He compares life with its changing states of pleasure and pain to rising and falling in space (and many other people have described pleasure as the sense of elevation). He applies this figure seriously; and his question may be put in the form: In what kind of satisfaction does the soul rise to its highest elevation, and remain most permanently at a high elevation? Every soul is perpetually, in the language of this figure, rising and sinking; no one lives at a permanent height.

Plato lays stress (584 C and 586 B sq.) upon the observation that in the satisfaction of most bodily appetites [1] the pleasure which results is of a markedly relative character; as he and Aristotle say, these are 'mixed pleasures.' The very intensity of many of these pleasures, Plato and Aristotle notice, is due to the fact that they are in felt contrast with a previous pain. The previous pain is, so to say, carried on into the pleasure and 'colours' it [2]. Thus these pleasures are not pure or unmixed (καθαραί), and in some cases, Plato points out in the *Philebus* [3], it is impossible to say whether a feeling is pleasant or painful, and a phrase like our 'bitter-sweet' has to be invented to describe it.

In the satisfaction of bodily want, the sense of transi-

---

[1] We commonly use the phrase 'bodily pleasures' of pleasures which we have come to localize in different parts of the body, but of course all pleasures are consciousness and in that sense not bodily.

[2] 586 B. Cf. Aristotle, *Eth. Nic.* VII. xiv. 4.

[3] 46 C. The word occurs in a fragment of Sappho (37), ἔρος . . . γλυκύπικρον ἀμάχανον ὄρπετον.

tion from one state to another is often very prominent
and violent, and probably it was mainly this which led
Plato to describe pleasure as a movement (κίνησις)[1]. In
all pleasures whatever we are conscious of transition
to some extent. Every human being, when he is pleased,
is conscious of passing from a state, which was at any
rate negative in regard to pleasure, into a new state. It

---

[1] [This must not be taken to imply that Plato uses the word κίνησις
with special reference to the class of pleasures in which the sense of
transition is most violent. In the passage where it is brought in (583 E)
the bodily pleasures which are said to be so intensely felt because they
are transitions from previous pain are not more of the nature of κινήσεις
than the other and more real pleasures are. The point there made about
them is that they arise merely from the recovery of the soul from the
previous κίνησις of want and pain, its return to the original state in which
it was before the pain came (ἡσυχία). It is implied that the pleasure
the soul gets in obtaining hold of truth is a more real κίνησις, because
it is the accompaniment of an elevation of the soul above its original
level, and not of a mere recovery from previous depression, and because
this elevation is, comparatively at least, permanent. In the more obvious
sense Plato would certainly have said that the lower kind of soul was
more subject to movement and change. But its movement is mere
fluctuation (πλάνη) between two points which it never gets beyond
(586 A). Pleasure was described as a κίνησις of the soul by Democritus
(v. Ritter and Preller, 158), who meant that it was literally a disturbance
of the arrangement of the material atoms of which the soul consisted.
He contrasted pleasure with εὐθυμία (content), which was the real good
thing to aim at in life, and which, according to Seneca, he took to be
'stabilis animi sedes' (perhaps 'stable equilibrium of the soul' would
be the best translation). In contrast with this idea Plato and Aristotle
conceive the good state of the soul not simply as a state in which it is
undisturbed by πάθη (though it is that), but as a state in which it steadily
develops into all that it has in it to become. Possibly the fact that here
Plato describes the higher satisfactions of the soul as κινήσεις (though
κίνησις consisting not in fluctuation but in progress) is a symptom of
this difference in his view. But, though the word κίνησις was probably
derived directly or indirectly from Democritus, there is of course no
reason to assume any allusion to his views. Nor is it necessary in this
confused passage to assume that all the ideas which come in can be
developed consistently with one another.—ED.]

is true, no doubt, as Aristotle remarks[1], that the actual
sense of pleasure is not a sense of change, but still it
implies change. (Can we imagine a being perfectly unchangeable to feel pleasure or pain? Plato's own statement[2] that pleasure cannot be predicated of a divine
life may strike us as a paradox; yet we also, while we
regard the capacity to change for the better as an advantage, on the other hand regard the necessity for
change as a mark of imperfection; and so to us a perfectly changeless being may either mean one so far
above us as not to require change, or one so far below
us that it cannot change for the better[3].) Now, most
people would agree with Plato that in the higher kinds
of satisfaction the sense of transition is much less violent
and marked than in the bodily pleasures: for example,
in the enjoyment of art it is so.

But an objection might be raised. Is it not an equal
necessity, whether the satisfaction be higher or lower,
that it should always be preceded by a want? Why
too, we may ask, does Plato dilate on the insatiable
nature (ἀπληστία) of bodily appetite, insisting that bodily
satisfaction is no satisfaction, as if there was some kind
of satisfaction which left no desire behind? For the
answer to these questions we must go back to Plato's
notion of permanence in satisfaction. The want of
knowledge is a want, and a want which is never completely satisfied; but in the case of the satisfaction,
partial though it may be, which we can obtain for this
want the soul is not always falling back to the same

[1] *Eth. Nic.* X. iii. 4.          [2] *Phil.* 33 B.
[3] Aristotle, in *Eth. Nic.* VII. xiv. 8, after describing the necessity for
change as an imperfection of our mortal nature, declares that 'God enjoys
ever one simple pleasure.'

level as before the satisfaction. There is progress made, the self definitely advances, and each satisfaction remains a permanent element in the self. Plato expresses this in a bold figure. The part of the soul which bodily pleasures satisfy is the part which is not 'water-tight' (στέγον 586 B). In the *Gorgias*[1] the metaphor is developed, and the appetitive part of the soul, at least in those who live for the satisfaction of it alone, is compared to a vessel full of holes. The idea which these passages bring out is that, if there is any self at all, there must be a permanent satisfaction for it. For the fact is that the soul or self is exactly as much as it gets out of the world; and so far as the satisfaction it gets is perishable the self is perishable, and so far no self. The only test we can apply to different forms of satisfaction of ourselves is the question, How far is each, when we have obtained it, a permanent element in ourselves?

Here (585 B sq.) and in the *Gorgias* the idea of the unsatisfactory nature of certain pleasures is associated with the idea of their illusoriness. We should recognize that to take what will not satisfy us for what will is a form of mental illusion, but we should not naturally dwell upon that side of moral failure. In Plato, however, the ideas of intellectual illusion generally, and of moral failure to find satisfaction, are closely associated. As in the sphere of knowledge, according to his idea, the soul is what it gets and retains of truth, so in the sphere of desire the soul is what it gets and retains. On the side of knowledge and on the side of desire, the soul identifies itself with the object which it pursues. On each of these

[1] 493 A to D.

sides, if that with which we identify ourselves is unreal and transient, so too are we.

What has been said of living for the satisfaction of bodily desires applies also, Plato briefly tells us (586 c sq.), to the pursuit of the satisfaction of the 'spirited' element of the soul for its own sake, the 'seeking to attain personal distinction, or victory over others, or the satisfaction of one's anger without reason and sense.' Then follows an important passage. Not only are the lower kinds of satisfaction less true and real than the higher, but, further, the amount of reality which they have is proportionate to the degree in which they are subservient to higher satisfactions. At first this sounds rather a paradox ; there are reasons which might make us say that, the more independent of any ulterior object a desire is, the more likely it is to find full satisfaction. Plato puts the matter in the opposite way ; throughout Books VIII and IX he continually asserts that, the more one element of the soul disengages itself from the whole, the less satisfaction it attains. To take a crude instance, a person who lived merely for eating would get less out of eating, less permanent satisfaction for himself, than a person who ate with the consciousness that eating served some higher pur-pose. A person who could say with St. Paul, ' whether I eat or drink, I do all to the glory of God,' might mean : That in the most trivial satisfactions there may be a sense of serving something wider and higher than animal appetite ; that this gives to the satisfaction of appetite a permanence and a satisfactoriness which by itself it cannot have ; and yet that in this lies the only appropriate satisfaction of appetite, or, as Plato says, its 'own' (οἰκεῖον) satisfaction.

We have now finished the threefold comparison
between the bliss of two lives, that of the tyrannical soul
which lives most completely in its own lowest element,
and that of the kingly soul which lives most completely in
its highest ; and Plato winds up the discussion with
a fantastic mathematical expression of the difference we
have found between them (587 A sq.). Starting with
the original triple division of the soul upon which the
description of these lives was based, and measuring in
one dimension the differences which we have found
between them, we may say that the life of the timocratic
man, in which the highest element of soul is unsatisfied,
reaches two-thirds as far as that of the philosopher or
king, in which all these elements are satisfied, and
that the life of the oligarchic man, in which only the
appetitive element is satisfied, reaches one-third as far.
Then taking the oligarchic life, which is the life of
appetite at its best, and remembering the triple division
of the appetitive soul, we may say that the democratic
life reaches two-thirds as far as the oligarchic and the
tyrannic one-third as far. So the tyrannic life reaches
one-ninth as far as the kingly. But this measurement
does not give us the full extent of the difference[1]. We
must measure the difference in three dimensions, developing the line into the square, and the square into
the cube, which is a complete and perfect thing. The
result is that the bliss of the philosopher king is $9 \times 9 \times 9$
$= 729$ times as full as that of the tyrant.

588 A to
end of IX. Socrates is now made to look back to the beginning
of the whole argument and the contention of Thrasy-

---

[1] [In the triple division of the soul, and again in that of the appetitive
element, the three parts were not each of equal value in the life of the
soul, which is what the calculation if it stopped here would imply.—ED.]

machus that perfect injustice is the true interest of man.
He will express the main facts which he has shown
about the life of man in a figure which will make it
clear how far injustice is from being man's interest.
The general drift of this section is to throw the whole
question of interest back upon the inner life of the soul ;
happiness, interest, gain, must be expressed in terms of
man's most inward life, or seen in their relation to the
essence of his soul. ' What shall a man give in exchange
for his soul ?' is the burden of the section ; ' we have
talked of gain or profit—what is the ultimately precious
thing (τίμιον) ?'

First (588 B to E) Plato repeats his analysis of human
nature. Man, while he is indeed not only one in his
bodily form, but one self or soul, is at the same time
a complex creature [1]. A new light is here thrown on the
elements of which he is composed. The appetitive
element is represented as a many-headed beast, constantly changing and capable of an infinite development
of new heads out of itself; this beast is partly wild and
partly tame ; it is, in bulk, the largest element in human
nature. The 'spirited' element is represented as a lion.
It was no mere figure of speech with Plato to represent
these psychical tendencies in man as animals, for he
clearly believed that there was continuity between the
different forms in which life appears; that somehow or
other souls rose and fell in the scale of being according
as they behaved in each form in which they were
embodied ; and that there was a real identity between
certain elements in man's soul and certain elements in
other organic creatures. Such an idea receives a new

[1] For the idea of man as a strangely composite being, cf. *Phaedrus*,
229 E sq.

light from the modern conception of evolution. The third element in human nature, and in bulk the smallest, is the strictly human element, the man in us. This element is also represented as the divine in man[1]. This again, though not much is here made of it, is a very important idea for consideration in a theory of human nature. Both Plato and Aristotle thought that there was in human nature a certain imperfect presence of God, and that it was this divine presence, however small, which made it specifically *human* nature[2]. It is in this conception that the true anticipations of such Christian ideas as that of the Incarnation—'taking the manhood into God'—are to be found. Plato here literally identifies the truly human nature in us with the divine. But the ideas are not developed in Plato and Aristotle.

Such then is man. The question of his true gain and profit has to be considered on the basis of this analysis. When a man says that injustice secures the real interest of human nature, he cannot realize what he is saying; let us persuade him. To do so, Plato takes the principal recognized forms of moral goodness and badness, and shows what each means in terms of his analysis of human nature (588 E to 590 D). The just and the noble (καλόν) are what brings everything in human nature under the rule of the truly human element in it, which is also the truly divine. The unjust and the base (αἰσχρόν) are what enslaves the man in us to the beast. When a man says that it pays or profits him to do a base action, such as taking a bribe, he is really saying that he gains by enslaving what is more precious to him than wife or child to the most godless thing in him. 'Intemperance' or profligacy, again (τὸ ἀκολασταίνειν, the opposite of σωφρο-

---

[1] 589 D.    [2] Aristotle, *Eth. Nic.* X. vii. 1, and 7 to 9.

σύνη), means the letting loose of the wild creature within us.  Self-will (αὐθάδεια) and discontent or irritability (δυσκολία) arise from the lion-like element being developed in bad adjustment to its place in our nature.  Both 'spirit' and 'appetite' are however involved in them[1]; in the description of the timocratic man in whom 'spirit' is dominant, and who is then said to be 'self-willed,' we were shown how under the dominion of 'spirit' certain excessive appetites were growing up in the dark, because the highest element in man had been dethroned from its place.  Next, the vices of effeminacy, luxury, and the like come from the weakening of the 'spirited' element in us.  Flattery and meanness imply that it is being enslaved to the mob of appetites, and that in consequence the lion in us is being turned into an ape[2].  Lastly come βαναυσία and χειροτεχνία.  These words, which signify a sort of vulgarity which was associated with certain occupations, may be compared with the word 'mechanic' as used in a depreciatory sense in Shakespeare.  The Greeks thought that mechanical occupations had a tendency, not necessarily fulfilled in every case, to develop this fault; as indeed every nation stigmatizes certain occupations, and uses words derived from them, e. g. 'flunkeyism,' to describe certain vices.  The vices

[1] Especially if we read λεοντῶδές τε καὶ ὀχλῶδες (turbulent), the latter being 'appetite.'  The MSS. read λεοντῶδές τε καὶ ὀφεῶδες; the latter (serpent-like) would be a new name for the 'spirited' element. But ὀφεῶδες, which is a strangely formed word and does not occur elsewhere (except in late writers who might have derived it from this passage after it had been corrupted), is very likely a mistake for ὀχλῶδες, which occurs just below as a designation of the appetitive element.  If however we read ὀφεῶδες, the introduction of this new term still implies that the 'lion-like' element is to some degree identifying itself with the πολυειδὲς θρέμμα.

[2] Cf. X. 620 c, where the soul of Thersites is (at his own choice) turned into an ape.

named here really mean that the truly human element is in some degree enslaved to the appetitive.

Thus, in brief, Plato has indicated the nature of various sorts of vice. They are all of them forms of disorganization of the soul, all of them forms of slavery. The question for man (590 D to 591 B) is, What is the right slavery—the slavery which is not to the hurt of the slave? It is that he should be the slave of that in him which is most fit to rule. Everything in man should serve what is divine in him. It is best of all that he should have the ruling principle in himself; but, if he has it not, the next best is that he should obey it as imposed on him from without. This shows us the principle upon which both the law in states and the education of children are based [1]. Law was represented at the outset by Glaucon as a restraint which a reasonable man would overcome or evade wherever he was able to do so. But law is the public reason embodied, the ally of everybody in the community without distinction, because the ally of that which is best in him. On the same principle we do not allow children to be their own masters until, by education, we have set up a 'constitution' in them and enabled them to be to some extent a law to themselves. In moral education, the principle which is at first imposed on the learner from without gradually becomes his own principle. This, which parents and teachers aim at accomplishing for children, the law also aims at accomplishing for every member of the community.

Human nature then being what it is, it is impossible that it can 'profit' a man to be unjust. Nor will his injustice profit him any the more for being undetected

---

[1] Cf. Aristotle, *Eth. Nic.* X. ix.

and unpunished by the law. Thrasymachus has maintained that if a man could do any wrong he pleased and
escape punishment he would be prosperous; here it is
asserted that the greatest ill that can befall a man is
that he should do wrong and escape punishment [1].

In conclusion (591 C to end of IX) Plato sums up the
principles upon which a wise man will regulate his life.
First, as to what he will wish to learn: he will value
every study in proportion as it helps to bring the soul
into that good state which has here been described [2].
Next as regards his body; he will not make the dominant principle in his life the attainment of simply animal
pleasures, neither will he make it the attainment simply
of bodily health and strength, for he will value health
and strength of body according as they promote the
control of reason within him (σωφροσύνη). He will
regulate the harmony of his body for the sake of the
harmony of his soul, if he wishes to be really μουσικός [3];
the phrase is like the saying of Milton, that the true poet
must make his life a poem. Similarly with wealth; he
will regulate his acquisition of wealth by asking whether
it does or does not put the 'constitution' within him out
of gear. So lastly, as to honour and power, he will or
will not seek them according as he conceives that they
will or will not make him better.

Here follows a curious passage: the mention of honour
makes Glaucon say, 'Then he will not take part in public
life,' and Socrates answers, 'Indeed he will in his own
city, but perhaps not in the city where he was born, unless

---

[1] Cf. *Gorgias*, 472 D sqq.

[2] i.e. He will regard the object of all study as intended to give the
philosophic or divine element in the soul the nurture necessary for its
development.

[3] Cf. 410 and 411.

some divine chance befalls.' In Book VI[1] Plato says it
is only by divine grace, that is by some process which,
humanly speaking, cannot be reckoned on, that a great
character can escape demoralization in present society.
In a similar spirit he says here that it will only be as an
exception that a man who has attained harmony of the
soul will find public life congenial to him or compatible
with it; only under exceptional circumstances will the
'goodness of the man' and the 'goodness of the citizen'
coincide[2]. But such a man will carry about the ideal
state with him and live the life of it; whether it exists
anywhere on earth (or even in heaven) makes no difference to that. Plato in the *Republic* oscillates between
two conflicting feelings. His dominant feeling is that
the philosopher does neither the best for himself nor the
best for the world unless he finds a state in which he can
play the part he is fit for (προσήκουσα πολιτεία). The
loss which results in every direction from the highest
minds not being applied to the government of society
forces itself upon him as an appalling loss. But another
feeling runs under this and emerges from time to time
in passages like the present. It is that, as the world
stands, the divorce between the philosopher and political
affairs is, humanly speaking, inevitable, and that the highest
life for man will generally have to be not a public life.
In describing the philosophic life in the *Theaetetus*[3]
Plato almost glories in the fact that, in the ordinary
sense, it is of no use. We find precisely the same two
ideas struggling in many Christian writers. The saving

---

[1] 492 A.   Cf. 493 A, 499 C.
[2] Cf. Aristotle, *Pol.* 1276 B, 16 sqq., 1278 A, 41 sq., and also 1324 A, 4 to
1325 B, 30.
[3] 173 C sqq.

of one's soul has often been represented as inconsistent with 'living in the world.' This mode of thought was fairly well known in Greece even before Plato's time; both before his time and later there were philosophers who lived, in retirement, a sort of monastic and ascetic life. On the other hand we are familiar with the view that the Christian principle is best realized in some kind of public service, or in doing good in some sort of social life. This idea is no doubt that which is most prominent in Greek philosophy, and represents the ultimate outcome of Greek moral thought in its best form.

# XV. DIGRESSION ON POETRY

[*Republic*, X. to 608 B.]

THE first half of Book X is disconnected from the rest
of the *Republic*, and the transition to the subject of art
and poetry, which is here made, is sudden and unnatural.
We may, indeed, gather from the opening sentences
what is the connexion of ideas in Plato's mind. The
latter part of Book IX has brought vividly before us,
by a fresh analysis, what human nature really is ; moral
evil has been described as the surrender of the self to
the inferior elements in it : and this has been constantly
represented as the submission of the mind to living in
a kind of illusory world. This perhaps suggests the real
nature of the danger of imitative art, which has been
pointed out to some extent already. It tends to stimulate the illusoriness of feeling ; above all it panders to
an inferior kind of emotion, whether of pleasure or of
pain ; and Plato's peculiar way of describing the inferiority of an emotion is to show that it is illusory, dependent on something unreal. So much connexion, then,
is traceable. Still this section breaks the continuity
of the *Republic*. It does not bear in any way on the
last section of Book X, in which the immortality of

the soul is treated, and which would naturally follow at the end of Book IX, forming a fitting conclusion to the whole work. Further, within each of these two sections it is easy to see the traces of more than one redaction of the same topic[1].

From the very apologetic opening and the nevertheless polemical tone which pervades the whole discussion, one might infer that Plato had been attacked by critics for what he had previously said about poetry, and that he therefore returned to the subject with greater *animus*, prepared to go a good deal further. In any case he writes throughout with a deep feeling that the influence of the poetry of his time, especially the dramatic poetry, is almost entirely bad, and that the extravagant belief which prevails in the educational value of Homer and other poets is unjustifiable and pernicious. He tells us that it was claimed for Homer and the tragic poets that they knew all arts, all things human, whether bearing on virtue or vice, and even things divine, and again that it was said that Homer was the educator of Greece, and that a man might direct his whole life by what he learnt from him[2]. To us Homer is mere literature; no one regulates his life according to Homer; but we must take these statements as representing facts, or we cannot understand Plato's attitude. He treats the matter as in the utmost degree a serious one. People sometimes say that Homer was the Greek Bible, and this expresses in a crude way what Plato is here referring to. Extravagant and illogical claims made for the Bible have produced similar attacks upon it.

[1] See, for example, the passages referred to in a note on p. 349, and at the beginning of the next section of the Lectures.
[2] 598 D sq. and 606 E.

Plato here treats poetry as a great means of tickling the palate of the Athenian demos; it is a mere caterer of excitement. We must take what he says in connexion with various other passages in his dialogues, where the power of words to produce illusion is dwelt upon. There has never been a greater master of words than Plato himself, and it seems as if this made him all the more conscious that the art of using language is beset with weaknesses and dangers. Thus, as he insists in the *Phaedrus*[1], the written word, whether rhetoric or poetry or what not, is only valuable as a sort of record and suggestion of the 'living word,' which is the truth that the writer has present to his mind; unless a writer can feel that he knows something better than he writes, he is not really a good writer; and as soon as he begins to think that words are the best thing he ceases to understand them[2]. (The antithesis of 'letter' and 'spirit' embodies the same idea.) In his own time, Plato felt, literature was written for the sake of the pleasure that the mere words gave. Thus in the *Gorgias* poetry, especially tragic poetry, is classed with rhetoric as a branch of the art of appealing to and pleasing the crowd; and it is associated with the arts of the confectioner and the perfumer[3]. Various passages in the *Laws* too describe bitterly the change that has come over the Athenian stage; in the old days the audience were swayed by people who knew better than they; at present there is a 'theatrocracy,' the taste of the general public is a law to the dramatist[4].

[1] [Of which dialogue, it is to be noticed, a large part is an exhibition (given for a special purpose) of Plato's mastery of various styles of composition.—ED.]

[2] 275 C to end.  [3] *Gorgias*, 501 and 502.

[4] *Laws*, III, 701 A.

There are two leading ideas in this attack on art and poetry. First, there is the idea that imitative art from its very nature can only represent what things look like, their outsides, which are a very little part of them; and that if any one takes the outsides of things for the whole of them—as, it is implied, a great many people do—then he is living in a world of illusion. Secondly, there is the feeling that the emotions generally appealed to and stimulated by contemporary art, and especially by dramatic poetry, are not those which are worth appealing to and stimulating. The whole treatment of the subject presents us with the reverse side of the picture of art given by Aristotle in the *Poetics*. The two works do not deal with the subject from the same point of view. Plato has set himself to write an indictment of art. He deals with its perversions, and what he says of them is to a great extent true, though no doubt he accounts for the bad effects of art by a theory which makes it look, at any rate, as if they necessarily followed from the nature of imitative art, and not merely from perversions of it. Aristotle's treatise, on the contrary (so far as it refers to the same subject), may be said to aim at a definition of tragedy as it is in its essence and at its best. It is a matter of indifference to him whether there ever was a tragedy answering to his definition, he wants to get at the typical or ideal nature of tragedy. The situations of the two men, according to ordinary conceptions of their characters, are here reversed; Aristotle puts the ideal side of things, while Plato writes like a controversialist concerned only with present facts.

The discussion falls into three parts; in the first, Plato investigates the nature of the 'imitation' which

LECTURES ON PLATO'S 'REPUBLIC'

constitutes art, characterizing objectively the nature of
art (595 C to 602 C); in the second and third he really
puts the same thing from the other side, dealing, in two
separate sections which can hardly be said to differ in
subject, with the subjective effects of imitative art upon
the soul (602 C to 605 C, and 605 C to 608 B).

In the first section of the argument Plato starts with
the implied postulate that art is imitation (μίμησις); he
first explains his theory of the nature of art by taking
the illustration of painting ; he then applies the result to
poetry.

What does he mean by saying that art is imitation ?
A modern writer in calling art imitative would probably
have in mind the question whether the artist copies from
his experience, or creates. It is clear in what Plato says,
and in a great part of what Aristotle says, that this is
not what they had in mind. Plato does not consider
whether the artist originates ; he is thinking of the
extremely obvious fact that the artist does not in any
case put before us the actual objects of real life, but
certain appearances only ; he represents, and only represents. In this, poetry and painting, though very
different in most respects, stand on the same footing. It
is obvious that the painter represents things to us in
colours merely as they appear from a certain point of
view. The poet uses words, as Plato says, ' like paint ';
his words are no more what they describe than painted
colours are what they represent ; the poet, no less than
the painter, presents to us what things look like from
a partial point of view.

Imitation, which both the painter and the poet
exercise, is a certain kind of production or making
(ποίησις) ; but what kind ? According to Plato there

are three grades of making and three corresponding makers to be distinguished. There is, first, the making of that which is in the order of nature (τὸ ἐν τῇ φύσει, ὃ ἔστι, τὸ ὄν, τὸ εἶδος, ἡ ἰδέα), of which the only maker is God, who is therefore called the maker of the original or natural (φυτουργός). Secondly, there are the ordinary artificial things used in life, which are made by the craftsman or artisan; he makes, Plato tells us, something like that which God makes (τοιοῦτον οἷον τὸ ὄν), a particular form[1] of the thing God is maker of. Thirdly, there is a product which consists in the appearance of such things (particular concrete objects) as the artisan makes, and the maker of this product is the artist, who makes the appearance as a man might make it by holding up a mirror before a thing. We see at once that this is not a true account of artistic production; yet the artist's production and the reflexion in a mirror are so far alike that they both represent only partial aspects of things. The artist, according to Plato, merely holds up the mirror to nature, and does nothing more.

What does Plato mean by 'that which is in the order of nature,' and the various phrases he uses as equivalent to this? He takes an instance which it is very difficult to make sense of. What meaning is there in speaking of the 'idea' of a table or of a bed; of a table as it is in nature; of a table in a sense in which there is one table and no more; of a table which is really a table, while the things we call tables are not? To get at the meaning of Plato's language, we may start by asking what we imply when we say that of two or more quite different

---

[1] [Not, of course, 'form' in the sense of εἶδος or ἰδέα as above.—ED.]

tables each is a form or example of table. We clearly
imply that there is something in them which is the same
and therefore one. In the fact that they are many and
different forms of the one thing after which they are
called, Plato sees this consequence involved : each is
meant to be what it is called, but no one of them is really
quite what it is called or what it is meant to be. And
it is true that they are not quite what they are meant
to be, nor (it may be said) what they are called. Every
table has limitations; to begin with, it perishes; but,
besides that, it never absolulely answers its purpose,
we can always find some defect in it, and at any rate it
only serves its purpose under certain conditions. This
then is the import of the particularity of tables ; they all
purport to be the same thing, namely, that which they
are really meant to be, but none of them is that thing.

The meaning of the conception is much more obvious
in the case of things to which we apply the notions of an
ideal, or of perfection. For instance, there are many
just acts, many forms of justice, each of which is only
partially what we call it; and we easily understand such
a conception as 'justice itself,' the one principle which
all just acts imperfectly embody. Plato applies the
same conception to tables and beds in a way that sounds
harsh and ludicrous. .In the ordinary sense, as we should
at once say, there is no such thing as this one table that
he talks about. Nevertheless there is a truth about the
construction of tables, and the truth of everything must
be supposed to exist eternally. We may think of this
truth, or of the 'true table' in this sense, as existing in
what we might call an ideal order of the world (what
Plato here calls φύσις), which we imperfectly apprehend
and reproduce, or as existing in the mind of the Creator ;

Plato would probably say that these were only different
ways of putting the same thing [1].
This distinction of three things—the nature of tables,
which is made not by the craftsman but by the Creator,
the actual table which the craftsman makes, and the
copy of a table which the artist makes—leads up to
a comparison (601 C sqq.) of the knowledge that the
artist must possess of a thing to copy it successfully,
and the knowledge that other men may possess of the
same thing. The man for whom the craftsman makes
any instrument, and who knows how to use it, knows
most about its nature and what it should be like; the
horseman, for instance, knows what harness should be;
this is not the kind of knowledge the artist has of harness,
or tables, or beds, or any object that he may imitate.
The craftsman who is not himself the user of what he
makes has not this knowledge either; but he has
a certain right opinion (ὀρθὴ δόξα) about the thing he
makes, he can carry out the directions of the man for
whom he makes it. The knowledge of the artist who
can only produce the superficial resemblance of the
thing is clearly much less than this. It corresponds,
though the word is not used here, to the 'conjecture'
(εἰκασία) of Book VI, and this passage throws a light
on the four-fold division of knowledge in that Book.
The conclusion drawn from this comparison is that what
the artist does is not earnest but play; and this conclusion is applied to all artistic or poetic imitation; if we

---

[1] Nothing is said here about the manifold particular objects, not made
by human craftsmen, which make up the sensible world; but, as here the
craftsman makes artificial objects after a pattern which is represented
as existing eternally, so in the *Timaeus* the whole sensible world is
represented as being the expression to sense of an eternal intelligible
παράδειγμα. Cf. *Timaeus*, 28 C sq.

take such imitation seriously we are making ourselves the victims of illusion.

How far such a description of the work of artists and poets is justified depends first on the particular artist or poet in question, on his own conception of his functions, and on the way in which he carries it out; it depends, secondly, on the attitude of those who see or read his works. Plato here has in the main great poets and artists in view. Even in the case of the greatest poet he is prepared to maintain that his work is not the highest kind of work; if he had done the things he relates he would have been a greater man. The comparative value of poetic or artistic work and of other kinds of work is an unprofitable question to discuss. It is certain that poets and artists perform a great function, and that the great poets and artists have done a great service to mankind. But it is also true that they are constantly misunderstood by their admirers, that poetry and art are often taken as if they were something which they are not, and that claims are made for them which fairly provoke the sort of reaction that we find here, where Plato describes them as mere play. He clearly has in mind people who fancy that merely to read literature and gather impressions of life from it is enough to give one an understanding of life. Such persons are as much under an illusion as if they were taken in by clever scene-painting. Doubtless only a childish or untrained mind can be so taken in[1]; but language is a far subtler thing than colour and form, and, in reading things which strongly affect us, we are liable to suppose that the fact of being strongly affected

[1] And we are not to suppose that any great painter or other artist makes illusion his object.

by the representation gives us a grasp of the thing represented. The question whether a poet adds something to your understanding of the world, or gives you nothing but the mere pleasure of representation and expression, really depends on your understanding of the poet. Having in mind people who imagine that the mere enjoyment of poetry is something more than it is, Plato contends that the presentation of life in literature gets hold of a very small part of it. The condemnation he passes on imaginative literature is valid as against a certain misunderstanding of its true function. But the point of view from which imaginative literature could be looked upon as containing the whole reality of life, and from which Plato answers that it gives one merely the most superficial appearance, is not one which comes very naturally to us.

The two sections which follow are slightly different treatments of one question[1]: Imaginative art being, as it has just been described, the production of mere superficial appearance, what is its effect on the soul; what is it that it appeals to in the soul, and what is the result upon the soul of its so appealing?

In the former of these sections Plato again begins 602 c to with painting, imitation which appeals to the eye, and 605 c. applies the analogy of it to poetry. The success of painting, he points out, depends upon its exercising a certain illusion, making us, by means of ingenious devices, think of a certain object as being in three dimensions when it is really in two[2]. It follows from

---

[1] The opening words of the section beginning 605 c do not naturally follow on the words which precede (there is nothing for αὐτῆς to refer to), but they would naturally follow on the concluding words of the section which ends at 602 B.

[2] He illustrates this by referring to reflexions in water and the like, which were his examples of 'εἰκασία' in Book VI.

this that, for painting to exercise its influence, reason (by which he means the scientific impulse, which leads us to set right all the illusions of sense by measuring and weighing things, and the like) must be in abeyance. As painting takes advantage of certain illusions of sight, so poetry takes advantage of certain illusions of feeling and emotion ; and as, in the case of painting, reason is for the time being kept in abeyance by mere appearance, so, for poetry to have its effect, the feeling of the moment must blind us to some facts. Take, for example, the case when poetry makes us feel keenly about what we should call a great misfortune. When we think about it we see that we do not know whether what gives us pain is really an evil or not, we see again that grieving over it does no good, and (Plato says) that nothing human is worthy of grave consideration. These facts are analogous to those which reason tells us when we test the data of sight by measurement and calculation ; and as in enjoying a painting we are made to occupy ourselves with the simple appearance of things from a single point of view, to the exclusion of the facts of which reason would inform us, so it is when we enter into the feeling of poetry. Poetry makes the emotion of the moment exercise a sort of illusion over us. Further, Plato dwells upon the fact that under the influence of a tragedy, and similar influences, a man allows himself to enter into emotions which he would be ashamed to give way to in real life. Moreover, he points out that the subject-matter which best lends itself to effective representation in poetry is indiscriminate variety of feeling and emotion, not feeling and emotion restrained by a principle. The conclusion to be drawn from all this is that imitative poetry nourishes and strengthens, not the rational part of the soul, but that which is the source of illusion.

The main subject of the latter section of the discussion 605 c to is one which Plato has glanced at immediately before, 608 B. namely, the encouragement given to unworthy emotions by hearing or reading emotional poetry. This effect, he shows, is produced not only by tragedy but by comedy, and by artistic representation generally. It appeals to the appetitive side of our nature, letting loose the emotional element in us, while keeping in abeyance reason, which should restrain appetite. If then we allow the Muse of sweetness to prevail in our city, we shall be governed by pleasure and pain, and not by principles and by regard for the common good. Poetry, then, in the ideal community must be bound within very narrow limits. Religion and patriotism are its two great legitimate themes. Hymns to the gods, and panegyrics on heroes, are the two forms of poetry which this criticism has left uncondemned.

While Plato writes chiefly with the influence of the drama in view, we should not look to the stage, in England at any rate, for an analogous influence now. In considering the new question about imaginative literature which these sections raise we should most naturally have in mind the effect of novels. No doubt the effect of imaginative literature is due to the fact that we are emotionally susceptible ; it appeals in the first instance to one side of our nature ; and further it is true, as Plato says, that when we are strongly acted upon by imaginative literature a certain part of us is in abeyance for the time being ; it takes us, as we say, out of ourselves. But the question is *what* self it is that it takes us out of. Does it take us out of our common, every-day, mean self? Are the emotions which it appeals to, not emotions which we should be ashamed to feel in ordinary life, but emotions which we are not able to feel in ordinary life? Does it, to put the question in the form which Aristotle suggests, give to pity and fear something worth pitying and something worth fearing for? Or does it, as Plato thinks, give us feelings which in the ordinary business of life, or at any time if we thought people could see into us, we should be ashamed to feel? and does it take us, not out of our prosaic self, but out of the self that is practically useful in life? These questions represent a real issue; we could easily find examples of each of these effects of imaginative literature; and most people have had some experience of the worse as well as of the better effects of such literature upon themselves. Most of us, for instance, would have to admit that a great deal of the excitement which we get out of novels does not develop the particular things in us of which we are proud, though we cannot deny the great effectiveness and charm of many of those works. Plato here writes with nothing in view but the lower kind of effects that imaginative literature can produce. There can be no doubt that there are times in the history of the world when only the lower sorts of art become popular, when imaginative art does aim at mere popularity, and when its only interest is to appeal to those susceptibilities of human nature which are commonest or strongest, because it has to cater for excitement. Further, it is true in a certain sense, as Plato says, that, the more indiscriminate you are in what you appeal to, the easier artistic work becomes; it is much easier to excite if you do not care what you excite, or how. In Book III, where also Plato discusses the effects of imitation, taking the word in a narrower sense than here, he objects to the drama (the literature which is in that sense most imitative) on the ground that the merely imitative instinct is probably a symptom of, and certainly stimulates, weakness of character, want of personality. Here, again, we can hardly doubt that the readiness, which he speaks of, to throw oneself into different characters *can* have the effect which he attributes to it; but on the other hand one of the greatest helps to the development of character lies in being encouraged to put oneself into characters above one's ordinary level; and this help is what great art gives. But, rightly or wrongly, Plato has here come to the conclusion that nearly all the imitative art of his time has degenerated into indiscriminate catering for common excitement. He treats art as being this and only this, and in consequence the whole passage remains rather an attack upon certain developments of art than an adequate theoretical treatment of it.

Plato characteristically represents the dispute in which he here engages, not as one between the moral and the immoral in literature, but as one between poetry generally and philosophy generally (607 B sq.). He quotes sentences to express the feeling which certain poets on their side have about philosophy and science; they regard them as the spinning of cobwebs, or as audacious and blasphemous talk about things above us. The same feeling of antagonism between poetry and philosophy is often expressed now by saying that philosophy and science take the interest and the mystery out of life. To Plato, on the contrary, the real ground of quarrel seems to be that poetry gets hold only of the outside of things, appealing always to the most superficial susceptibilities of man, while philosophy gets hold of the real laws and facts of the world. Now there is no reason why a poet should not really in his own way be animated by the same spirit as a philosopher. There is a point, as Wordsworth indicated, where philosophy and poetry, imagination and science, meet. It is generally in their lower phases that poetry and philosophy strike one another as antagonistic. The greatest philosophers and the greatest poets have not as a rule felt themselves to be at enmity. Plato himself is something very like a great poet.

# XVI. THE FUTURE LIFE OF THE
# SOUL

[*Republic*, X. 608 c to end.]

THE second part of Book X, like the first, shows symptoms of having been left in an unfinished state. In the opening words which introduce the subject of immortality, 'And yet nothing has been said of the greatest prizes and rewards of virtue' (608 C), there is no transition from what has gone before. Plato has not, as they imply, been talking of the rewards of justice on earth. He first begins to speak of them in 612 A; and after that there occurs in 614 A another opening similar to that in 608 C, and this time in its proper connexion. Thus the argument about immortality (608 C to 612 A) does not seem to be in any organic connexion either with what actually precedes or with what actually follows it. It would seem that Plato had two plans in his mind as to how to finish the *Republic* [1].

[1] Notice too the fragmentary character of 611 A, where the doctrine that the number of souls existing must remain constant is introduced abruptly, and dismissed in a single sentence.

Taking the section, however, as it stands, we find that in the first part of it Plato asserts that the soul is immortal, and gives a brief argument in support of this belief, asserting that the true nature and capacities of the soul cannot be seen in its earthly state (608 C to 612 A). He then passes to the question whether justice, which has been shown to be good in itself apart from consequences, is not also attended by external rewards; and, having pointed out that on the whole it is so in this life (612 A to 614 A), he winds up the whole work by discoursing, by means of the Myth of Er, on the destiny of the soul after death (614 A to end).

608 C to
611 A.

Plato makes no attempt here to deal completely with the question of the immortality of the soul. In the *Phaedo* he treats the whole question, but here it is only its bearing on morality that concerns him, and the question is touched upon just far enough to give completion to his picture of the destiny of the soul on earth. The point of view from which he argues that the soul is immortal is one which is in keeping with the whole subject of the *Republic*. Throughout the *Republic* the question has been, What is the real good and the real evil of the soul? In accordance with all that has gone before, Plato here insists that the only form of evil or of good that affects the soul is moral or spiritual. Now moral or spiritual evil does not make the soul die, in the ordinary sense. Hence, he argues, the soul is not subject to death in the ordinary sense; death is a form of evil which affects the body only.

611 B to
612 A.

Having said that the soul in its essence does not die with bodily death, Plato modifies this statement. When we assert the immortality of the soul we must remember that this immortality only belongs to it in its true nature, and that on earth we never see it in its true nature. The soul as it exists in union with the human body is emphatically a composite thing, and the composition is by no means perfect; so that the soul as it appears in its earthly life is liable to all kinds of internal distraction and inconsistency. The ideal condition of the soul is one of harmony and perfect synthesis, and this is unattainable under the conditions of human life; so that, as we see the soul here, its original nature is almost entirely obscured, like the human form of the sea-god Glaucus in the myth, by overgrowths which come upon it when it enters the body. If we want to see the immortal part of it we must look at the element of philosophy which is in it; we must imagine what the soul would be if it could entirely follow the impulse of philosophy, which would lift it out of this sea in which it is now sunk and show us its real nature[1]. Aristotle[2], in the same way, tells us that the immortality of the soul lies in νοῦς, and is to be seen in the speculative capacity of the mind. With Aristotle and Plato the impulse of the soul, or of reason, the truly human element in it, is, literally, to be at one with the eternal being in the world. The imagery in which the present condition of the soul is described as one of being sunk in the sea, and there much beaten about and grown over with various extraneous growths, is not mere figure of speech. In the *Phaedo*[3] we find the idea that our position on the earth

---

[1] Cf. 490 B. See also 519 B, where Plato represents the soul as fettered with leaden weights attached to it at birth, which means the affections to which the body makes the soul liable; and 518 E, where reason is the divine thing in the soul, which, however much perverted and rendered useless, still retains its ancient power. Cf. with the whole passage *Phaedo*, 64 A to 68 B.

[2] *Eth. Nic.* X. vii. 8, 9.          [3] 109 A sq.

is really comparable to being at the bottom of a hollow or in some deep marshy place; if we could get up higher we should come to a region where everything was purer, and where we should see much more clearly. Both Plato and Aristotle regarded the earth as imposing all kinds of restrictions and hindrances on the life of the soul; both thought, further, that the fixed stars were made of finer matter, and that the souls connected with them had correspondingly finer perceptions[1]. Their view of the soul is bound up with a physical theory of the universe[2].

The soul then, whatever metamorphosis it may undergo when it enters the body, is in the essential part of it immortal; and the *Republic*, which may be regarded (612 A) as a picture of the affections which the soul undergoes and the forms which it assumes in human life, its highest aspirations, its lowest descents, and the intermediate forms of life between them, will fittingly conclude with the prospect that lies before the soul after death.

612 A to
613 E.
But first Plato returns to the question, which was laid aside at the outset of the argument in Book II, of the rewards of justice. Socrates had been asked to show that justice was the true interest of the soul, without regard to any external results of justice in this world or another; it has now been admitted that he has done so, and he may turn to the further question of the facts about the external results of justice. Plato, having devoted the whole dialogue so far to showing that the good and evil of man are the good and evil

---

[1] Aristotle, *Frag.* 19. 1477 A, 31 ff., from Cicero, *de Nat. Deorum*, II. 15.

[2] Cf. *Timaeus* 90 A-D, where Plato asserts that in coming to understand the laws of nature, e. g. of the motion of the stars, the soul on earth gets some sort of anticipation of its own true life and nature.

of the soul, does not, as has sometimes been said, retract this because he here proceeds to reward the just man with external goods. He points out first that, assuming the moral nature of God, we must believe that the good soul pleases God, and that, whatever appearances there may be to the contrary, the good man is never neglected by God; all things must be well for the good man, except so far as there is some evil made necessary for him by previous sin[1]. Again, if we turn to the relations of other men to those who are just, the case is not as Thrasymachus represented it. Experience shows rather that honesty is good policy. Thrasymachus had appealed to certain common and admitted facts, Socrates appeals to other common and admitted facts. But his conclusion that justice is man's true interest is not drawn from the account he gives of its usual external results, and he does not abandon his position that justice is good apart from all outward consequences, as being nothing else than the healthy life of the soul.

The purport of the mythical account which now follows 613 E to of the soul's fate after death is to insist that whatever is end. done by the soul on earth has a direct effect upon its future. Under all the mythological and poetical forms in which Plato clothes what he says of the past and future of the soul, one thought is present, that the immortality of the soul, involving as it does the continuity of its existence, adds to the moral responsibility which lies upon us. The concluding words of the *Republic* give us the key-note of the whole passage ; the one thing to study on earth is how to make oneself better and wiser, not for this life alone, but for another, and in order that we may choose wisely when the chance comes to us, as it will, of

---

[1] Cf. 379 C to 380 B on the nature of human ill-fortune.

choosing another form of life.    Life on earth is a great
process of learning and gaining experience [1].

According to the tale of what was seen by Er the
Armenian, who twelve days after he had been killed in
battle was sent back to life, the soul immediately after
death proceeds to a spot where it is judged.    The just
souls are there seen ascending, through an opening in the
sky on the right hand, to a thousand years of happiness,
and the unjust descending, through an opening in the
ground on the left, to a thousand years of punishment [2].
At the same spot, also, perpetual streams of souls are
seen arriving, some coming down by another opening in
the sky from their sojourn in heaven, others coming up
by another opening in the earth from their sojourn below.
As each soul returns, whether from bliss or from pain, it
goes into a meadow, where it rests for seven days before
it chooses a new life upon earth.    The ordinary punishment allotted to the unjust soul at death is the requital
ten times over of the evil done in life ; and so too the
recompense to the just of the good done in life is tenfold.
But there are other measures of punishment also.    Those
whose lives have been very short are differently dealt with.
Some again whose guilt has been extreme are held not
to have been sufficiently punished when they return after
a thousand years, and are sent back again ; and there are
some incurable sinners who are cast for ever into Tar-
tarus [3].    In the *Gorgias* we are told that such souls serve
as examples.    The punishment of all who are not incurable
is of the nature of purgatory, and souls generally return
the wiser for what they have undergone.    Conversely, the

[1] Cf. VI. 498 D.
[2] Cf. *Gorgias*, 524 A sqq., and *Phaedrus*, 248 E to 249 D.
[3] Cf. *Gorgias*, 525 B sq., and *Phaedo*, 113 D sq.

THE FUTURE LIFE OF THE SOUL    361

enjoyment of bliss sometimes leads a soul to make a worse
choice than it would otherwise make of the life to which
it will return.    If, however, the soul after being rewarded
makes a wise choice, and goes on living better and better
in each successive life, and getting better and better in
each sojourn in heaven, it at last escapes the necessity of
taking a mortal body again (this we gather from a
passage in the *Phaedrus*[1], if we may put it together
with this passage).

At the end of their seven days' rest the souls which
have returned from bliss or punishment are brought
a long journey into the presence of the three Fates,
the daughters of Necessity, before whom their choice of
a new life has to be made.    The choosing of new lives
takes place at a spot from which the mechanism of the
universe is visible, and of this the myth gives a detailed
description (616 B sqq.)[2].    Plato conceives of the heavens
(οὐρανός) as a hollow sphere which revolves with a motion
of its own, and of which the outermost portion is that in
which the fixed stars are.    Within it are seven other
hollow spheres containing the orbits of the sun, the moon,
and the five planets which were then known.    These
have various revolutions of their own, in the opposite
direction to the uniform motion of the οὐρανός as a whole.
All these eight spheres revolve round the earth, which is
the centre of the whole.    The whole οὐρανός is bound
round with a band of bright light, which is supposed to
mean the Milky Way[3].    This astronomical conception

[1] 249 A.
[2] For the astronomical part of this description see Böckh, *Kleine
Schriften*, III. p. 297 foll.
[3] The souls on their journey are said to see this band of light first as
an upright column in front of them.    This looks at first as if it was a pole
passing from top to bottom of the sphere, but the word ὑπόζωμα suggests

is combined by Plato with the old notions of Necessity
moving the world, and of destiny being spun by the
Fates; and the image which results from this combination is, of course, not clear or consistent in all its
details. The whole hollow sphere, with the seven
separate spheres with separate motions of their own
fitted in it, forms the whorl (σφόνδυλος) of the spindle
(ἄτρακτος) of Necessity. It is fastened by the Milky
Way and other bands to the hook (ἄγκιστρον) of the
spindle. The shaft (ἠλακάτη) of the spindle passes
right through the whole of the eight spheres; and,
around the point where it enters them, the lips of the
spheres are seen as a continuous surface of eight con-
centric rings, of which the colours and the relative widths
are described in accordance with the colours and the
relative distances from the earth ascribed to the heavenly
bodies which move with them. The spindle rests on the
knees of Necessity, and the whole mechanism is turned
by the Fates—Clotho, Lachesis, whose name signifies
chance, and Atropos, whose name signifies the inevitable.
The shaft and the hook of the spindle are of adamant,
that is to say they are imperishable and unchanging;
but the whorl, the system of spheres, that is to say the
whole visible universe, is partly of adamant, partly of
other substances, which means that the universe partly
exhibits uniform and eternal law, and partly irregularity
and change.

a band passing round the sphere, and moreover the shaft of the distaff
passes through the centre of the sphere. The souls must be supposed to
be taken to a point outside the whole sphere ; the word νῶτον, in 616 E (cf.
*Phaedrus*, 247 C), shows this, and further they pass under the throne of
Necessity, upon whose knees the spindle upon which the sphere turns
is resting. From a certain point outside the sphere a band passing
round it would be seen as an upright column.

Plato further introduces into the image the. Pythagorean idea that in some way the motions of the heavenly bodies make up a musical harmony.  It arose from the attempt to find a law regulating the various distances of these bodies from the earth; some Pythagoreans imagined that a relation could be established between these distances and the intervals between the notes of the scale.  This is the origin of the idea of the 'music of the spheres.'  In Plato's picture a Siren sits upon each of the rings formed by the spheres, and is carried round with it.  Each Siren sings a single note, and the eight notes make a scale (ἁρμονία).  The three Fates sing to the music of the spheres, Lachesis of the past, Clotho of the present, Atropos of the future.

The choice which the souls make of life is the all-important crisis in their history.  Plato in his description of their choosing (617 D sqq.) has expressed his opinion upon Free Will and Necessity.  In every human life there is an element of necessity or of what (so far as the man himself is concerned) may be called chance; there is also an element of choice.  This idea is applied here to the causes which determine the conditions under which a man is born.  In the first place, the order in which the souls choose is determined for them by lot.  In the second place, however late in the order a soul gets its choice, it still gets a choice, and, as is proclaimed to them in the name of the Fates, even the soul that chooses last will have a life worth living, if it chooses wisely, and thereafter lives intently (συντόνως).  In the third place, when the soul has made its choice of life it has chosen its destiny (δαίμων) [1]; that is to say, practically, a man's

---

[1] For the δαίμων cf. *Phaedo*, 107 D–108 C, where the δαίμων takes the soul back to the other world when it has finished its life on earth.   Here, in

own will is his destiny, in the sense that he can never reverse what he has once willed to do, nor its con- sequences [1]. Circumstances, the fact of choice, and the irrevocableness of choice are the three great elements in life.

At this choosing of lives, many souls of animals become men, and vice versa (620 A sq.). As has been seen already, Plato was quite serious in the idea of continuity between animal and human life. There is no doubt, too, that he was perfectly serious in the belief—which is expressed in the whole myth of Er, and particularly where the soul's choice of a new life is represented as the outcome of the way in which it has previously lived—that man's conduct in one phase of existence has a determining effect on his destiny in some future phase.

620 E, the Fates send with each soul a δαίμων to attend it through life and fulfil for it the destiny it has chosen. This is a sort of mythological expression of the idea that the man's character or personality determines his own particular destiny. Cf. *Timaeus*, 90 A, where Plato speaks of the highest element of the soul as a man's δαίμων. It is easy to pass from this to the notion of attendant spirits watching over men's lives, and that is the connexion between the sense of δαίμων here and the sense in which great men are said to be worshipped as δαίμονες (540 C).

[1] In the βίων παραδείγματα (samples of lives) which are thrown before the souls to choose from, all kinds of circumstances in various combinations are present in a determinate character, but the one vital element of the de- terminate character of the soul itself, ψυχῆς τάξις, is said not to be present, ' because it is fated that the soul in choosing a given life should become like what it chooses.' Here we have the old distinction of the externals of life and the actual vital principle itself; the soul is to choose the external conditions of its life, but by its choice of life it becomes what it is to be (618 B).

THE END.

www.ingramcontent.com/pod-product-compliance
Lightning Source LLC
Chambersburg PA
CBHW030910270326
41929CB00008B/644